PRINCETON STUDIES IN

INTERNATIONAL HISTORY AND POLITICS

Series Editors
John Lewis Gaddis
Jack L. Snyder
Richard H. Ullman

MERCENARIES, PIRATES, AND SOVEREIGNS

Acknowledgments

THIS BOOK is the result of nearly six years' work. During that time I have incurred many debts.

Financial and administrative resources for my research and writing were provided by Stanford University, the MacArthur Foundation, the University of Washington Political Science Department and Graduate School Research Fund, and the John M. Olin Institute for Strategic Studies at Harvard University. I am grateful to these institutions for their generous support.

Earlier versions of portions of this book were published as "Global Transactions and the Consolidation of Sovereignty" (with Stephen D. Krasner) in Ernst-Otto Czempiel and James N. Rosenau, eds., *Global Changes and Theoretical Challenges: Approaches to World Politics for the 1990s* (Lexington, Mass.: Lexington Books), copyright © 1989 by Lexington Books, adapted with permission from Macmillan Publishing Company; "Sovereignty in Historical Perspective," in James A. Caporaso, ed., *The Elusive State* (Newbury Park, Calif.: Sage), copyright © 1989 by Sage Publications, adapted with permission from Sage Publications; and "State Practices, International Norms, and the Decline of Mercenarism," *International Studies Quarterly* 34 (March 1990), adapted with permission from Blackwell Publishers. The painting on the book's cover, entitled *Signing of the HBC Charter By Charles II on May 2nd, 1670* (HBCA P-379), is used with the permission of the Hudson's Bay Company (reproduction courtesy of Hudson's Bay Company Archives, Provincial Archives of Manitoba).

My intellectual debts are much more numerous, and I hope the following list excludes no one who has provided me with important criticisms and suggestions. First, I would like to acknowledge the helpful commentary offered by the faculty and graduate students of the political science departments to which I presented my research. These include the University of Washington, Stanford University, Northwestern University, Yale University, Duke University, the University of Minnesota, Arizona State University, and the University of Victoria. The individuals who have carefully read and commented on the book or the various chapters which comprise it include Alexander George, Jim Caporaso, George Modelski, Margaret Levi, Charles Tilly, Rob Walker, Cynthia Weber, Ellis Goldberg, Michael Taylor, Jonathan Pool, Peter Rohn, Robert Keohane, Nina Halperin, Michael Webb, Alison Brysk, Julie Strickland, Gero Lenhardt, Pat McGowen, David Lake, and David Campbell. I also received able research assistance from Veronique Bazelle, Young Choi, and Aurora Almeda, at the University of Washington.

My greatest debts are to Steve Krasner, Rick Ashley, and John Meyer, who provided me with intellectual inspiration and support in pursuing a rather unconventional study of some unconventional international actors.

MERCENARIES, PIRATES, AND SOVEREIGNS

STATE–BUILDING AND EXTRATERRITORIAL VIOLENCE IN EARLY MODERN EUROPE

Janice E. Thomson

PRINCETON UNIVERSITY PRESS   PRINCETON, NEW JERSEY

Library of Congress Cataloging-in-Publication Data
Thompson, Janice E., 1949–
Mercenaries, pirates and sovereigns : state-building and
extraterritorial violence in early modern Europe / Janice E. Thompson
p. cm. — (Princeton studies in international history and politics)
Includes bibliographical references and index.
ISBN 0-691-08658-3 (cloth : alk. paper)
1. Europe—Politics and government. 2. Violence—Europe—
History. 3. Sovereignty. 4. Mercantile system—Europe—History.
5. Mercenary troops—Europe—History. 6. Pirates—
Europe—History. I. Title. II. Series.
D210.T53 1994
355.3′5—dc20 93-23880 CIP

This book has been composed in Laser Sabon

Printed in the United States of America

1   3   5   7   9   10   8   6   4   2

For Nomy and Jim

Contents

Tables

MERCENARIES, PIRATES, AND SOVEREIGNS

Introduction

WHY are global coercive capabilities organized the way they are? Why do we have centralized bureaucracies—states—that claim a monopoly on violence? Why is this monopoly based on territorial boundaries? Why is coercion not an international market commodity?

The contemporary organization of global violence is neither timeless nor natural. It is distinctively modern. In the six centuries leading up to 1900, global violence was democratized, marketized, and internationalized. Nonstate violence dominated the international system. Individuals and groups used their own means of violence in pursuit of their particular aims, whether honor and glory, wealth, or political power. People bought and sold military manpower like a commodity on the global market. The identity of suppliers or purchasers meant almost nothing.

The puzzle that inspired the research reported in this book is: How did we get from there to here? What made this transition possible?

Charles Tilly's work provides one essential part of the story. He documents the long and bloody struggle by state-builders to extract coercive capabilities from other individuals, groups, and organizations within their territory. States did not monopolize violence even within their territorial borders. Urban militias, private armies, fiscal agents, armies of regional lords and rival claimants to royal power, police forces, and state armies all claimed the right to exercise violence.[1] Authority and control over domestic violence was dispersed, overlapping, and democratized.

The process by which control over violence was centralized, monopolized, and made hierarchical entailed not the state's establishment and defense of a new legal order but the state's imposing itself as the defender of that order. Societal groups vigorously resisted state-builders' drive to monopolize political authority and the coercion on which it ultimately rested. In the process state rulers struck bargains with various societal groups in which the latter provided war-making resources in exchange for property, political, and other rights. These bargains constitute subplots in the central drama in which the state achieved ultimate authority, especially on the use of coercion, within its territory.

There is, however, another aspect of the story that concerns the state's monopolization of extraterritorial violence. How did the state achieve a monopoly on violence beyond its borders that emanates from its territory? What explains the elimination of nonstate violence from global politics? That is the subject of this book.

The organization of violence is an (if not the) essential feature of any political order. Politics is about governance, about the exercise of authority. And authority is ultimately grounded in the actual or threatened use of violence. Organized violence in the contemporary world is both statist and territorial. It is a stunningly unique feature of the twentieth-century state system, distinguishing it from prior world political orders and their institutions of governance.

This book attempts to understand this crucial, distinctive aspect of the modern state system. In so doing, it joins with students of the world system and *longue durée*, such as Braudel, Giddens, Wallerstein, and Mann, who have embraced the task of delineating and explaining that system's unique features in nonteleological, nonfunctionalist, nondeterministic terms.

I argue that the "disarming" of nonstate transnational activities marked the transition from heteronomy to sovereignty and the transformation of states into the national state system. The essential feature of this transformation was a new way of organizing global coercive resources. In the heteronomous system of the medieval period, violence was democratized, marketized, and internationalized. In the system characterized by sovereignty, the state could not claim a monopoly on violence within its territory and disclaim responsibility for violence emanating from that space. Thus, the transformation entailed the state's monopolization of the authority to deploy violence beyond its borders *and* the state's acceptance of responsibility for violence emanating from its territory. Violence was shifted from the nonstate, economic, and international realms of authority into the state, political, and domestic realms of authority. It was dedemocratized, demarketized, and territorialized.

I demonstrate that the impetus for state monopolization of extraterritorial violence was systemic; it came from the collectivity of European state rulers. The delegitimation and abolition of nonstate violence was the result of interactions between state rulers. The demand for disarming nonstate actors came not from society but from other state rulers. While domestic politics did present a powerful set of constraints on state action, the state's role as an international actor provided it with an external source of power to extract authority over coercion from society.

In chapter 1, I discuss and critique Weberian conceptions of the state, emphasizing the analytical confusion presented by the predominant definitions of the state. I argue that while control over violence is the key distinguishing characteristic of the state, theorists have generally not recognized the distinction between internal, or domestic, violence and external, or international, violence. I argue that the national state is qualitatively different from the traditional state precisely because the national state has made good its claim to monopolize violence beyond its borders. It is, by nature, a systemic actor.

What is at issue here is how boundaries—between the domestic and international, between the economic and political, and between the state and nonstate realms of authority—are drawn, delegitimated, and redrawn. These boundaries are neither self-evident nor eternal. My analysis demonstrates that international violence before 1900 was a creature of the international, economic, and nonstate realms of authority. During the nineteenth century, the boundaries were redrawn such that authority over the use of violence was placed in the domestic, political, and state realms of authority.

I argue that it is useful to understand these processes in terms of the international institution of sovereignty. After discussing different conceptions of sovereignty, I present my own view, which is that sovereignty is the international institution that organizes global politics. In it are embedded the norms that specify where the lines in each of the three aforementioned authority realms should be drawn. I argue that this study provides empirical support for the argument that this institution of sovereignty is produced and reproduced by the collectivity of state rulers; it is the outcome of ongoing interactions between states in which the practically derived norms of sovereignty emerge. As such, sovereignty should be treated not as an attribute, nor as a set of normative constraints, but as an institution that empowers states vis-à-vis people.

The method used in this book is historical narrative.[2] Application of a truly comparative methodology is precluded in this instance. The "dependent variable," the elimination of nonstate violence, constitutes a single case. And while I have identified a number of forms that nonstate violence took, these cannot be treated as wholly independent cases. Within these limitations, however, I do attempt to identify the conditions under which each form was delegitimated and compare them to see how they were similar or varied. The basic method, then, is to chart change in state authority over nonstate, extraterritorial violence (the dependent variable), identify the proximate causes for those changes, and develop a theoretical explanation for the linkages between the causes and the outcome.

I range widely over the literature on international relations theory, international law, sociology, and history. No new data are presented; rather, what is known is articulated in a new light. To the best of my knowledge, no one has treated the myriad of early state-system practices of international violence as instances of a single theoretical concept, namely, nonstate violence. There are large literatures on mercenaries and mercantile companies, for example, but they have not been grouped and analyzed as instances of a single phenomenon: the exercise of violence by nonstate actors beyond state borders.

Chapter 2 describes the origin and evolution of the principal forms of

6 INTRODUCTION

nonstate violence in the early state system. It examines the rise of the mercantile company, privateering, and mercenarism in Europe and describes their accomplishments. Here I argue that violence was marketized, democratized, and internationalized through the actions of state rulers seeking to escape feudalism's constraints on the exercise of violence and intent on amassing wealth and military power autonomous from their subjects and other rulers.

The focus in chapter 3 is on the unintended consequences of the move to authorize nonstate violence. Not only was the state unable to control those it authorized, but the authorized forms gave rise to unauthorized forms. Most importantly, nonstate violence was often turned against the state itself.

I then turn, in chapter 4, to the context in which the legitimate practices were delegitimated, banned, and eliminated. This chapter focuses on the crucial transition of the nineteenth century in which state-authorized nonstate practices were abolished. Here my analysis of the various cases is guided by a common set of questions about the delegitimation process and the implementation of proscriptive, or control, norms. The historical evidence indicates that the demise of each practice resulted from a unique set of circumstances. More importantly, the demise of nonstate violence per se was the unintended consequence of a series of ad hoc, largely unrelated instances of interstate interaction.

In chapter 5, I examine efforts to eliminate traditional forms of unauthorized nonstate violence and trace the rise and decline of a new practice, filibustering. Eliminating this practice firmly established the principle that even under a democratic regime, the state and not individual citizens would decide on the use of force beyond a country's borders. This consolidated the territorial basis of state authority and the boundary between domestic and international politics. The national state, then, is defined as a polity consisting of people who live within geographical borders and whose exercise of violence is subject to exclusive state authority.

Chapter 6 summarizes the empirical results of this study, develops some of their theoretical implications, and suggests some avenues for further research. I conclude with some speculations on the status of sovereignty, the state, and violence in the post–World War II period.

CHAPTER ONE

The State, Violence, and Sovereignty

THE STATE AND VIOLENCE IN THEORY

Weberians conventionally define the state, in part, in terms of its control over coercion. According to Weber, one of the essential characteristics of the state is that it "successfully upholds a claim to the monopoly of the legitimate use of physical force in the enforcement of its order."[1] Similarly, Tilly includes "controlling the principal means of coercion within a given territory" in his definition of the state.[2] More recently, Giddens defines the nation-state, in part, as having "direct control of the means of internal and external violence" within "a territory demarcated by boundaries (borders)."[3]

The differences in the wording of these definitions are subtle but important. First, Tilly and Giddens do not include legitimacy, as Weber does. Second, Weber speaks of a *monopolization* of the *use* of force, Tilly of *controlling* the *principal means*, and Giddens of *direct control* of the *means* of *internal and external* violence. These definitional differences raise a number of questions:

    1. Is legitimacy a useful concept in describing state coercion?

    2. Must the state control the use or the means of violence (coercion) or both?

    3. What is the difference between control, direct control, and monopolization?

    4. If it is the means that matter, does the state control the principal means or all the means?

    5. Must the state control the use or means of violence only internally or both internally and externally?

I will consider each of these issues in turn.

Legitimacy does not appear in Tilly's or Giddens's definition, presumably because of its normative implications. The obvious question is: Legitimate for whom? Early state-builders' use of violence was not viewed as legitimate by the majority of the people who for centuries resisted their drive for control. And the exercise of coercion in the vast majority of states in the twentieth century has certainly not been viewed as legitimate by much of their own and other populations. Tilly, following Stinchcombe, argues that "legitimacy is the probability that other

TABLE 1.1
Analytical Framework

Decision-Making Authority	Allocation		Ownership	
	Authoritative	*Market*	*State*	*Nonstate*
State	1	2	5	6
	Loan troops to ally	Lease troops to ally	Modern standing army	Privateers
Nonstate	3	4	7	8
	International brigades	Soldier of fortune	Filibusters	Pirates

authorities will act to confirm the decisions of a given authority." It is not clear whether Tilly's "other authorities" are domestic actors or other states.[4] However, if we take states themselves as the assessors of legitimacy, it is clear that the state is the legitimate deployer of coercion. Rebel groups, separatist movements, and transnational groups are not viewed as legitimate deployers of coercion by the states or statesmen as a group.[5]

The next three questions concern how much control the state exerts over what aspects of violence. The confusion over whether the state controls the use or the means of violence stems from a blurring of three analytically distinct dimensions of control: decision-making authority, allocation, and ownership. State control over the use of violence implies decision-making authority over the deployment of violence—the authority to decide the ends to which violence is deployed. As table 1.1 indicates, the alternative to state authority is nonstate authority. However, as the table also suggests, whether the decision-making authority chooses to allocate its coercive capabilities authoritatively or through the market is a separate issue.

Authority to decide on the use of coercion may be claimed by the state or be left to nonstate actors. Where the state claims the authority, the allocation of coercive resources may be made authoritatively or left to the market. Authoritative allocations are generally based on noneconomic considerations. An example of an authoritative allocation (box 1) is a state that supplies troops to an ally for political or ideological reasons. This practice predominates in the twentieth-century state system. Market allocations, while never purely apolitical, are based more on economic incentives. The pre-nineteenth-century practice of poor states leasing or selling armies to rich states is an apt example of this type of state-authorized, market-based allocation (box 2).

Nonstate deployers of violence may also allocate violence authoritatively or through the market. The international brigades of the Spanish Civil War are one example of nonstate actors that authoritatively allocate violence (box 3). These volunteers supplied coercive resources to the Republican side not for profit but for ideological reasons. The classic soldier of fortune who kills for money is probably the purest case of a market allocation of violence (box 4).

Control over the means of violence is a separate issue, and suggests a third dimension, as indicated in table 1.1. Exercising coercion requires two basic resources: labor and property. Labor includes mental labor, such as leadership and technical skills, as well as the physical labor of the soldier. Property includes the armaments and money required to sustain a coercive project. Ownership of and decision-making authority over these resources may reside with the state or nonstate actors.

The modern standing armed forces are an example of case 5. States both own their military forces and assert decision-making authority over them.[6] The sixth set of cases, where the state asserts decision-making authority over resources owned by nonstate actors, is nicely illustrated by the practice of privateering. Here the state authorized nonstate actors to deploy their individually owned armed naval vessels against foreign shipping. Individuals who engaged in this activity without state authority were labeled pirates (box 8).

Examples of nonstate actors exerting decision-making authority over state-owned resources (box 7) are more difficult to find. One possibility is certain nineteenth-century military expeditions that were mounted by private individuals and groups in the United States but that employed U.S. Army officers, soldiers, and equipment. The current arrangement between Pakistan and Saudi Arabia is perhaps another example. Pakistan provides troops to Saudi Arabia in exchange for economic aid, a practice that is not unusual. What is unusual, however, is that many of the Pakistani troops are fully integrated into the Saudi forces, even wearing Saudi uniforms. Thus, Saudi Arabia exercises decision-making authority over labor resources that are owned by the Pakistani state.

This brief analysis suggests that state control over violence is not only multidimensional but highly variable. Whether the state exerts control, direct control, or monopolistic control over the use, means, or principal means of violence is an empirical question. This book describes the process by which violence was removed from the realm of nonstate decision making (boxes 3, 4, 7, and 8), nonstate ownership of armies but not armaments (box 6),[7] and market allocation (box 2). By 1900, states monopolized decision-making authority and ownership of the means of violence, and allocated violence authoritatively rather than through the market (boxes 1 and 5).

The final question that is raised in comparing the three definitions of the state—Must the state control the use or means of violence only internally or both internally and externally?—points to yet another dimension of the state-control problem. Only Giddens's definition includes control over the means of external as well as internal violence, because it is a definition of the *nation-state*, which he argues differs in fundamental respects from pre-nineteenth-century state forms.

While these three definitions are all Weberian, their differences do not simply reflect the distinctiveness of their authors. What appear to be synchronic differences are indicative of diachronic changes in the very nature of the state. Thus, legitimacy drops out, territoriality creeps in, and external violence suddenly appears. In short, these definitional differences reflect fundamental change in the organization of violence.

THE STATE AND VIOLENCE IN HISTORY

State control over the use of violence in the international system today is substantially greater than it was as recently as the midnineteenth century. In the eighteenth century, all the major European armies relied heavily on foreign mercenaries for troops. Half the Prussian army was comprised of mercenaries.[8] Foreigners constituted one-third of the French army.[9] Britain used 18,000 mercenaries in the American War for Independence and 33,000 mercenaries in its 1793 war with France.[10] The presence of large numbers of mercenaries in eighteenth-century armies suggests that military labor was internationalized. Mercenarism was a legitimate practice in the state system for about three centuries. Today, the vast majority of armies are composed of citizen soldiers. What accounts for this change?

Privateers played an important role in eighteenth-century naval warfare. British and American privateers captured more than 2,000 prizes during the War of the Spanish Succession.[11] French privateers nearly put an end to slave trade between Africa and British colonies in the Americas. In its War for Independence, the United States commissioned more than 2,500 privateers, who captured 2,300 prizes from the British. French privateers seized 2,100 English vessels between 1793 and 1796. In the War of 1812, one U.S. privateer captured or destroyed $5 million worth of English property.[12] Privateering was a legitimate practice in the state system for nearly six centuries. How do we explain its demise?

The transition from private to state naval warfare was marked by the rise and demise of a new and unique force—the naval fleets of the mercantile companies.[13] Mercantile companies were based on a state-granted monopoly on trade between the home country and regions outside of Europe. Though they were financed largely with "private" capital, they were not private organizations in the modern sense. They possessed military, judicial, and diplomatic power. For example, the charter of United East India Company of the Netherlands granted it the power "to make war, conclude treaties, acquire territories and build fortresses."[14] These companies made treaties with each other and with foreign governments, governed subjects of their home states, raised armies,[15] and even coined their own money.[16] Initially, their "trading" activities were nothing more than acts of piracy.[17] The mercantile company as an institution was obsolescent by the early nineteenth century and defunct by 1870.[18] The mercantile companies thrived for nearly three centuries; what accounts for their demise?

These practices suggest that little more than a century ago, the state did not monopolize the exercise of coercion beyond its borders.[19] This means that the state, portrayed in theory as monopolizing coercion, is distinctively modern. It emerged only after some three hundred years of state-building. This new state form, which I will call the national state,[20] reflected a redrawing of authority claims such that authority over the use of violence was moved from the nonstate, economic, and international domains and placed in the state, political, and domestic realms of authority. What requires explanation, then, is this fundamental restructuring of authority over coercion. These changes in authority claims, as I argue below, are indicative of changes in the institution of sovereignty.

SOVEREIGNTY IN THEORY

Authority, violence, territory, the state, sovereignty: these are the stuff of global politics. As such, one might well expect them to be central to international relations theory. Yet, until recently, international relations specialists have treated them as uncontested concepts, relegating them to the realm of assumption.[21]

Realism, the dominant theory of international relations, treats sovereignty as an attribute of the state qua state. States are, by definition, externally sovereign because there is no higher authority in the international system. States are internally sovereign because they monopolize violence and, therefore, political decision-making authority. In short, sovereignty is an assumption of neorealist theory. It presupposes sovereign states and then theorizes relations between them.[22]

In the 1970s, liberals launched an attack on this theoretical edifice, arguing that such a state-centric theory was ill-equipped to explain global politics in a world increasingly characterized by economic interdependence, democratic government, and weapons of mass destruction. They amassed an impressive body of empirical evidence indicating that the state and sovereignty are not parameters of but variables in world politics. These data suggested that the unitary, sovereign state of theory was increasingly obsolescent in the real, twentieth-century world.[23]

This liberal assault on realist assumptions about the state and sovereignty was easily beaten back. Some realists denied that interdependence had really increased.[24] Others claimed that if economic interdependence were indeed on the rise, it merely reflected states' interest in allowing or sponsoring it.[25] Either way, state sovereignty was not under attack from economic or technological developments, as liberals suggested.

A more powerful challenge to the assumptions of realist theory came in the 1980s from (what I shall call) critical theorists. According to Robert Cox, critical theory

> stands apart from the prevailing order of the world and asks how that order came about. Critical theory, unlike problem-solving theory, does not take institutions and social and power relations for granted but calls them into question by concerning itself with their origins and how and whether they might be in the process of changing.[26]

In the 1980s these theorists produced a powerful and persuasive critique of neorealism's ontology, epistemology, logic, intellectual heritage, and politics. This generated a wide-ranging and often heated, but highly productive, debate in the field of international relations.

Ruggie fired the opening shot in this battle, with his claim that neorealism and its assumptions about sovereignty made it incapable of explaining change.[27] In his incisive 1983 *World Politics* article, Ruggie charged that Waltz's neorealist theory has one major flaw, namely, that "it provides no means by which to account for, or even describe, the most important contextual change in international politics in this *millennium*: the shift from the medieval to the modern international system."[28] Ruggie argues that this shift reflected the transformation of the basic organizing principle of global politics—from heteronomy to sovereignty. Sovereignty is not a timeless attribute of world politics; it is unique to the modern state system. This outlook implies that significant change in global politics would entail a new organizing principle or a return to heteronomy.[29]

There is now a vast literature based on this debate, and to review it here in detail would take us too far afield.[30] Instead, I simply want to highlight what I take to be critical theorists' most valuable contribution to the debate on sovereignty—to point to the variable, contingent, and practical nature of sovereignty. Critical theorists restate the question of sovereignty as: How is it possible that states are sovereign?

Ashley suggests that sovereignty should be treated as an institution or regime:

> The modern concept of sovereignty designates the collectively recognized competence of entities subject to international law and superior to municipal law. It thus involves not only the possession of self and the exclusion of

others but also the limitation of self in the respect of others, for its authority presupposes the recognition of others who, per force of their recognition, agree to be so excluded. In effect, sovereignty is a practical category whose empirical contents are not fixed but evolve in a way reflecting the active practical consensus among coreflective statesmen.[31]

Sovereignty is a variable, social, and practically constituted regime. Walker echoes this view when he writes that "sovereignty is not a permanent principle of international order. On the contrary, it has been constituted and reconstituted historically."[32] In short, critical theorists bring people back in by pointing to the social and practical nature of sovereignty. But they also bring the international system back in by demonstrating the role of the collectivity of state rulers in constituting sovereignty. As Giddens argues, "the development of the sovereignty of the modern state from its beginnings depends upon a reflexively monitored set of relations between states."[33]

This perspective on sovereignty directs our efforts to an analysis of boundaries. In the modern world, there is a marked tendency to accept boundaries as given, permanent, and even natural. We take for granted such distinctions as those between domestic and international politics, economics and politics, and public and private. Yet, as critical theorists argue, these boundaries are not fixed, and there is nothing natural about them. On the contrary, they are arbitrary, contested, and ever-changing. They are artifacts of human practice. From the standpoint of critical theory, the puzzle is: How are these boundaries produced, reproduced, legitimated, contested, changed, and naturalized?

In theorizing about global politics, the most important boundary, as critical theorists suggest, is that which delineates the domestic from the international.[34] Linklater argues that "sovereignty denotes the institutionalization of the distinction between insiders and outsiders, and reflects the fact that the former have granted each other a special status which is not possessed by outsiders."[35] Walker seems to agree when he writes that

> I have come to believe that it is less important to insist on the possibility of a critical social theory of international relations as such than to refuse the Cartesian demarcations between inside and outside, "Us" and "Other," which permitted the theory of international relations to occur as a discourse of community and anarchy in the first place.[36]

So the critical theorists suggest the following approach to the concept of sovereignty: Sovereignty is new and is unique to the modern state system. It is socially constituted and reproduced through the practices of state rulers. Sovereignty organizes global political space into territorially bound, "juridically mutually exclusive and morally self-entailed domains."[37] It is based on "an ethics of absolute exclusion."[38]

Discourse among critical theorists generally has been conducted at a highly abstract level. While their critique of neorealism is very persuasive, they do not suggest a clear empirical research agenda.[39] As Pauline Rosenau notes, many scholars respond to this literature by asking, "How do I handle this in my own work?"[40]

Some critical theorists have turned to postmodernism or poststructuralism and pursued the method of deconstructionism.[41] This work is in its very early stages, so it is too soon to make a final judgment on its merits. Rosenau is undoubtedly correct in her conclusion that "the international relations of tomorrow, already manifest today, may not be post-modernist, but it will surely bear traces of the post-modernist perspective."[42] This book, for example, clearly bears the traces of that perspective in that postmodernist critiques of mainstream theory provided the inspiration for the research reported here.

However, the postmodernist deconstruction project is not the only empirical research program to emerge from the critical theorists' critique of neorealism.[43] Another group of scholars has attempted to bring empirical content to the critical theorists' arguments using more conventional methods.[44] It is not the case that "interpretivists" have produced no research program; indeed, they have inspired a highly productive and increasingly cumulative research program that appears to be developing into an alternative paradigm.[45] We might term this paradigm *institutionalist*.[46] In this protoparadigm, the focus is on the historical development and evolution of sovereignty as an institution that defines and empowers the state.

THE INSTITUTION OF SOVEREIGNTY

Analytically, sovereignty is best seen as a set of institutionalized authority claims.[47] It has two dimensions. On the one hand, it is the claim to ultimate or final authority in a particular political space. This is the aspect on which state-building theorists focus. In the modern system, political space is divided on the basis of territorial segmentation. But as Ruggie reminds us, authoritative units may be differentiated (separated) according to consanguinity or territoriality, nomadic or fixed territoriality, multiple-titled fixed territoriality, or exclusive fixed territoriality.[48] Ruggie argues that the transformation of the medieval into the modern international system reflected a change in the basis upon which political space was organized. "The medieval system of rule reflected 'a patchwork of overlapping and incomplete rights of government,' which were 'inextricably superimposed and tangled,' and in which different juridical instances were geographically interwoven and stratified, and plural allegiances, asymmetrical suzerainties and anomalous enclaves abounded." This "heteronomous organization of territorial rights and claims" was replaced by sovereignty, which "differentiates units in terms of juridically mutually exclusive and morally self-entailed domains" based on single-titled or exclusive, fixed territoriality.[49]

So the monopolization of violence within a particular territorial space is not a defining characteristic of the state qua state. As Giddens notes, "all traditional states have laid claim to the formalized monopoly over the means of violence within their territories." But this claim was not effectively defended until the advent of the modern nation-state system.[50] Territorial segmentation reflects a unique way of organizing political space—as coterminous with clear geographical boundaries—and the monopolization of violence within that space is derivative of the differentiation principle of sovereignty.

The second dimension of sovereignty is the specific set of authority claims made by a state over a range of activities within its political space. It specifies the particular things over which the state claims to be the ultimate authority. This can vary enormously across issue areas and states, and over time. For example, post–World War II industrialized states exert a much more extensive set of authority claims than did either medieval states or nineteenth-century liberal states.

We can view these two dimensions of sovereignty as the basis on which global politics are structured. As we have seen, international relations theory views global politics from the bottom up. That is, we begin with the story, as told by social contractarians, of how domestic "society" was created out of the state of nature, and then theorize about what happens when these separate, self-contained "societies" interact with each other.[51]

From a top-down perspective, we start with the notion that political space is global, and that its segmentation entails the division of that space into a domestic and an international realm. Ruggie's description of the medieval state system emphasizes this point:

> This system of rule was inherently "international." To begin with, the distinction between "internal" and "external" political realms, separated by clearly demarcated "boundaries," made little sense until late in the day. . . . And the feudal ruling class was mobile in a manner not dreamed of since— able to travel and assume governance from one end of the continent to the other without hesitation or difficulty because "public territories formed a continuum with private estates."[52]

Conceptually, then, it is the first dimension of sovereignty that establishes a boundary between the domestic and international realms of politics.

This dimension constitutes the state as *the actor* in international politics by designating the state, rather than a religious or economic organization, as the repository of ultimate authority within a political space that is defined territorially. Thus, I will refer to it as the *constitutive dimension of sovereignty.*

The second dimension of sovereignty is the specific authority claims made by the state. These claims establish the boundary between the political and economic and the state and nonstate realms of authority. They delineate the range of activities over which the state deploys coercion to enforce compliance with a particular normative order. This dimension of sovereignty reflects the state's penetration of the political space contained within its territorial boundaries. Because it delineates the specific functions over which the state as legitimate authority can legitimately claim authority, I term this the *functional dimension of sovereignty.*[53]

The key to a theory of global politics is an understanding of the relationship between these two dimensions of sovereignty.[54] The constitutive dimension of sovereignty sets up the state as the entity through which systemic forces are to be channeled. At the same time, the functional dimension allows for variations in domestic political structures that, again channeled through the state, enter into the international system. The first dimension establishes the realm in which the state can claim and is acknowledged to be final authority. It establishes a political space or jurisdiction from which an individual state excludes external, including state, authority claimants. According to neorealist theory, how effectively the state defends that claim is a matter of its power vis-à-vis internal and external actors.[55] But, as a number of scholars have noted,[56] there is no way to explain in strict power terms the creation, perpetuation, and growth of small, weak states. To use an economic analogy, these states are noncompetitive and should have vanished from the international power market long ago.

Legitimacy is an appropriate, even indispensable, element in the definition of the state. However, it is not that the ends to which the state deploys violence are legitimate in the eyes of those within its jurisdiction. Rather, it is that from the point of view of statesmen, the legitimate deployer of violence is the state. In Meyer's words, "Once a population is incorporated into complete citizenship, a nation-state is given almost complete authority to subordinate the population. It can expropriate, kill, and starve with relatively little fear of external intervention."[57] It is not that killing and starvation are legitimate ends, but that state rulers agree that the state is the legitimate actor to engage in such practices.

According to Meyer, "the nation-state system is given world-wide support and legitimacy, and is importantly exogenous to individual societies." This exogenous force is the world polity, elites of the world who share a common set of values ("especially, science, technology and the universal professions") that constitutes a world culture.[58] Ashley argues that it is the autonomous community of statesmen which designates who is to "be a power," and the entity that this community empowers is the state.[59] Giddens claims that, following World War I, states clearly recognized the nation-state as the legitimate form of political organization in global politics.[60] The point these scholars make is that there is external authorization for the state to be the ultimate authority claimant. Sovereignty as final authority is not an attribute of the state but is attributed to the state by the world polity or other state rulers.

Meyer argues that "states are given legitimated controls over" territory, population, and the means of violence, and that their control is assured through the delegitimation and "weakening of alternative organizational forms."[61] However, states are not merely *authorized* to do these things; they are *expected* to do them. "To be recognized as a power, that is, as a sovereign state, a state must satisfy certain minimal requisites (e.g., effectively patrolled territory)."[62] Thus, what we commonly take to be a defining characteristic of the state—control over violence within its territory—is actually an expectation of the world polity or of statesmen, an expectation whose realization may vary across time and states.[63] In the theoretical perspective developed here, then, variations in state control over violence emanating from its territory reflect changes in state rulers' appraisal of what the state is expected to control and how much control it is expected to exert.

So one linkage between the two dimensions of sovereignty runs from the external, or international, realm to the internal, or domestic, realm. The constitutive dimension divides global political space on the basis of single-titled, exclusive territoriality. With this dimension, statesmen authorize the state as the legitimate deployer of violence within a geographically bounded political space with the expectation that the state will control violence within that space.

The two dimensions of sovereignty are related through an internal to external linkage as well. While the constitutive dimension sets the boundary between domestic and international political space, the functional dimension establishes the boundaries between the economic and political spheres and between state and nonstate realms of decision-making authority. These functional boundaries are not, however, established unilaterally in a geopolitical vacuum. Their positions are a matter of concern for other states or the world polity because they will have external effects. When a state claims authority over a specific range of activities, it at the same time disclaims authority over another set of activities. These specific claims made by a state are conducive to a particular pattern of domestic flows and transactions. But since these flows do not stop at the territorial border, the individual state's authority claims have implications for the international system. For example, all states claim authority over the flow of people across their borders. "Illegal" immigration and political defection are terms that are meaningful only in a system where states claim authority over the movement of people across their borders. So if the U.S. central state claims authority to exclude Central American refugees on the basis that they are not refugees but economic migrants, the international effect is to channel such people into Mexico and Canada.

As critical theory suggests, the boundaries between the domestic and international, the economic and political, and the state and nonstate realms of authority are not fixed but are always subject to contestation, struggle, and change. Military intervention, for example, calls into question the position of the domestic-international boundary.[64] An intervention is clearly an internationalization of the target state's domestic political space, and thus problematizes the constitutive dimension of sovereignty. International political economy theorists have argued that the boundary between the economic and political realms shifted rather dramatically as nineteenth-century laissez-faire liberalism gave way to twentieth-century embedded liberalism.[65] Krasner's study of North-South relations demonstrates the centrality of the contest over where the line between state and private authority should be drawn in a wide range of issue areas.[66] States in the South, he argues, generally push for an expansion of the state authority realm, while the liberal industrialized countries defend an enlarged realm of private authority. Finally, in a study of mother-child relations, Meyer and others demonstrate that issues such as child care, abuse, and rearing, which were traditionally left to the family, have increasingly become subject to public decision making.[67] In other words, the boundary between the realms of state and nonstate decision making has shifted to enlarge the state's realm.

If all of these boundaries are contested and contingent, the question is, How are they produced and reproduced such that they appear permanent, fixed, and natural? Why do we think we know what sovereignty is? Put differently, how are Ruggie's "hegemonic form of state/society relations" or Ashley's "hegemonic exemplar" of "a normalized sovereignty" constructed?[68] A preliminary answer to this question, provided by the analysis presented in this book, is sketched out in the next section.

THE ARGUMENT

The puzzle is how and why the boundaries between the domestic and international, the economic and political, and the state and nonstate realms of authority were redrawn such that nonstate violence in the international system was eliminated. What accounts for this fundamental change in the institution of sovereignty that occurred in the nineteenth century?

Boundaries before the nineteenth century were unclear. So long as nonstate violence persisted, the boundaries between the state and nonstate realms of authority, between the political and economic, and between the domestic and international realms were blurred or did not exist. Because states authorized nonstate violence, it was difficult to determine which acts of nonstate violence were state sanctioned and which were private, independent, or free-lance. Because individual rulers personally profited from nonstate enterprises, it is difficult to say whether such enterprises were driven by economic or political motives. Because military forces were multinational, the distinction between the domestic and the international was unclear. What the institutional change in sovereignty produced was a clarification of the boundaries—both authoritative and territorial—that characterize the modern national-state system.

This transformation of sovereignty reflected the solidification of external claims as territorially based and the inclusion of an internal or domestic set of authority claims. State authority was made coterminous with territorial boundaries, and states were held accountable for the transborder coercive activities of individuals residing within their borders. Violence, which for three or four centuries was an international market commodity, was by 1900 taken off the market. States could no longer buy an army or navy from the international system. Individuals could no longer join the armed forces of the state offering the highest wage, nor could they use violence to pursue their own interests in the international system.

With these changes in the organization of violence, I argue, traditional states were transformed into a system of national states that held one another accountable for any individual violence emanating from their respective territories. Sovereignty was redefined such that the state not only claimed ultimate authority within its jurisdiction, defined in geographic terms, but accepted responsibility for transborder violence emanating from its territory.

My explanation for these changes in the institution of sovereignty entails three related arguments. First, I argue that this transformation of sovereignty was the result of the practices of the collectivity of state rulers. Interstate relations and not domestic politics were the crucial determinants in this transformative process. European state rulers first encouraged nonstate violence, then delegitimated it, and finally eliminated it. Efforts to abolish nonstate violent practices were generally met with strong resistance on the part of citizens and subjects. Other statesmen empowered the state to exert these new controls. They decided the form state control would take and the limits to the responsibility they would accept for their subjects' or citizens' behavior. European statesmen made the rules, which they then spread to or imposed on non-European areas.

Domestic politics were not irrelevant. Peculiarities in the domestic political structures of various states gave rise to the proliferation of nonstate violence in the first place. Domestic institutions produced the practices that other states came to define as a problem statesmen needed to address. Moreover, the ways in which nonstate violence was dealt with depended on domestic political institutions as well. Whether a state chose to seal its borders, use force against individuals, or impose legal restrictions depended on the domestic institutional structure already in place. So different domestic political systems both produced different forms of nonstate violence and shaped the way in which states implemented new controls on those practices.

The second part of my argument is that the changes in sovereignty, which accompanied the elimination of nonstate violence, were unintended. State rulers did not set out to abolish nonstate violence, though that was the ultimate outcome. Rather, each practice was politicized in a very specific set of geopolitical circumstances when a particular state saw its interests threatened by another state's citizens' or subjects' engaging in that practice. The removal of violence from the international market was the unintended consequence of a number of unrelated instances of strategic interaction.

Third, I argue that physical power capabilities are not the deciding factor in this process, though the Great Powers as a group dominate it. Both weak and strong states produced nonstate violence. Both weak and strong states defined nonstate violence as a threat. Both weak and strong states set the standard for how a particular practice would be eliminated. There was no hegemon or world leader making the rules.

State rulers want power and wealth. To achieve those ends, they chose to exploit nonstate violence—a choice that produced the desired results. It also generated unintended consequences in the form of nonstate violent practices that states did not authorize, could not control, and themselves fell victim to. State preferences did not change; rulers' knowledge of the unintended consequences of their early attempts to realize those preferences did. Moreover, state efforts to eliminate specific forms of nonstate violence produced their own unintended consequence: the elimination of nonstate violence in the national state system.

These arguments will be further developed in chapter 6, but their persuasiveness can be assessed only against empirical evidence drawn from the historical record. Articulating and analyzing that history is the task of the next four chapters.

CHAPTER TWO

Nonstate Violence Unleashed

RULERS began authorizing nonstate violence as early as the thirteenth century, when privateering was invented.[1] Large-scale private armies dominated Europe during the fourteenth and fifteenth centuries. Mercenary armies were the norm for eighteenth-century European states; naval mercenaries were common through the eighteenth century. Mercantile companies flourished from the sixteenth to the nineteenth century. All of these practices reflected the marketization and internationalization of violence that began with the Hundred Years' War.

One reason for this turn to nonstate violence was the ruler's lack of revenue. By authorizing individuals and groups to exercise political power and violence, rulers avoided the expense associated with some foreign ventures.

> If the leaders of the propertied classes were not always entirely responsive to orders of the central government, at the same time they saved the government trouble and expense by assuming certain political burdens. The founding of colonies was a conspicuous example of well-to-do men performing a function that seemed desirable to, but beyond the resources of, early modern states."[2]

These practices were legitimated with the concept of plausible deniability, which state rulers invented at the turn of the seventeenth century. If a "private" undertaking that a ruler authorized met with success, s/he could claim a share in the profits. If the enterprise caused conflict with another state, the ruler could claim it was a private operation for which s/he could not be held responsible. These practices, as we will see, effectively blurred practical and theoretical distinctions between state and nonstate authority and between economics and politics.

This method of power building was highly successful. In this chapter, I explore the years in which these practices flourished. The aim is to provide the reader with some sense of how the practices originated and what they achieved in their heyday. As the following stories make clear, these nonstate practices were not a trivial feature of global politics in the years between 1600 and 1800. All of the practices of nonstate violence described here were authorized by states. They were officially sanctioned. Each reflected an effort by state rulers to overcome economic, political, or military constraints on achieving their goals.

PRIVATEERING

In international law, privateers are defined as "vessels belonging to private owners, and sailing under a commission of war empowering the person to whom it is granted to carry on all forms of hostility which are permissible at sea by the usages of war." Privateers are usually required to post a bond to ensure their compliance with the government's instructions, and their commissions are subject to inspection by public warships.[3] In contrast, "piracy may be said to consist in acts of violence done upon the ocean or unappropriated lands, or within the territory of a state through descent from the sea, by a body of men acting independently of any politically organized society."[4]

Acts of piracy are distinguished from other acts of violence on or emanating from the high seas by the fact that the former "are done under conditions which render it impossible or unfair to hold any state responsible for their commission." Though "the absence of competent authority is the test of piracy, its essence consists in the pursuit of private, as contrasted with public, ends." Thus, the distinction between a privateer and a pirate is that the former acts under the authority of a state that accepts or is charged with responsibility for his acts, while the latter acts in his own interests and on his own authority. "Most acts of war which become piratical through being done without due authority are acts of war when done under the authority of a state."[5]

English privateering apparently began in the 1200s, when the king ordered vessels of the Cinque Ports (Hastings, Hythe, Dover, Sandwich, and Romney)[6] to attack France. In 1243, Henry III issued the first privateer commissions, which provided that the king would receive half the proceeds. The English monarchy was also the first to issue a letter of marque,[7] which was directed against Portugal, in 1295.

Initially there was a strong distinction between private reprisals and privateering.[8] Letters of marque, which were issued in peacetime, allowed individuals to seek redress for depredations they suffered at the hands of foreigners on the high seas.[9] For example, if an Englishman's vessel were attacked by a Frenchman, a letter of marque would authorize the Englishman to seize something of equal value from any French vessel he encountered. This practice was an old one, dating back to well before the thirteenth century, and was based upon "the early theory that the group was responsible for the wrongs of each of its members."[10] It also reflected the absence of permanent embassies as a mechanism for resolving private international disputes on a regular basis.[11]

Privateering, on the other hand, was a strictly wartime practice in which states authorized individuals to attack enemy commerce and to keep some portion of what they captured as their pay. Early on, however, the two practices became confused, apparently because "whenever a war broke out each party always claimed to be the party aggrieved, and when it justified its acts of hostility at all, it did so by connecting them in some way with the notion of reprisals."[12] Already boundaries between the legitimate and illegitimate were under practical challenge.

Adding a further complication to these practices was piracy. In 1413 England defined piracy as high treason. For over a century, the English king had turned a blind eye to the piracy of the Cinque Ports, probably because their piratical activities honed the skills sailors needed when serving as the king's wartime privateers. As the Cinque Ports' depredations escalated, however, the English passed an antipiracy statute. Nevertheless, because the ports were accustomed to engaging in piracy and because the well-born earned a good income by investing in piracy, English piracy was not suppressed.[13]

In 1544 Henry VIII, in his war with France, gave blanket authorization for privateering and allowed the privateers to keep all the loot they seized. With the gradual crackdown on piracy and the requirement that privateers share their prizes with a host of public officials, the privateers' contribution to British naval capacity had declined. Henry VIII's action was designed to increase the incentives for privateering.[14]

England gained naval superiority over Spain largely through the action of the Elizabethan Sea Dogs.[15] These private adventurers, in collusion with the English Crown, engaged in all kinds of violent activities directed against Spain in the New World. Besides plundering Spanish ships and settlements, such Sea Dogs as Drake, Cavendish, Clifford (the third earl of Cumberland), and Raleigh engaged in what might be termed state-sponsored terrorism. For example, Drake extorted large ransoms from two Spanish colonial cities by threatening to burn them to the ground. He actually destroyed three other cities. His sack of Peru netted him and his backers £2.5 million and repaid his backers, including Elizabeth, "47 for 1."[16] Cumberland, leading a purely private expedition, captured Puerto Rico in 1598.[17] Other Sea Dogs behaved similarly, plundering, destroying, and extorting their way to fame and fortune in England and sharing their loot with the English Crown. Drake and Raleigh, of course, were knighted for their achievements.[18]

The execution of Raleigh in 1618 marked the beginning of a temporary decline in English privateering. Though the Stuarts had made peace with Spain, Raleigh continued his depredations in Spanish America, assuming that the English monarchs "would secretly connive at violations of the treaty with Spain."[19] He was wrong.

A new English prize act, passed in 1708, produced the highest level of privateering activity to date. With this act, the privateer was allowed to retain all his prizes and was paid a bounty based on the number of prisoners he took. Moreover, in 1744 the king granted pardons to all criminals who would serve as privateers.[20] By 1757, privateering had become something of a craze in England. During the eighteenth century, "political lobbies formed which defended and promoted the concerns of the 'privateering interest.'"[21] The year 1803 was the most violent and lawless period of maritime warfare in modern history, in part because England and France "were unable, even if willing, to control the hordes of desperate privateers and quasi-privateers who were nominally subject to them."[22]

French privateering differed from its British counterpart in two respects. First, while England allowed privateers to attack neutral commerce, France did not. Second, for England, privateers were auxiliaries to the navy; for France, they were the navy. France in 1400 required privateers to obtain prior consent and in 1398 and 1498 required them to post bond.[23] Sixteenth-century French "privateers" were largely individuals acting on their own initiative. One French merchant, for example, sent seventeen ships to blockade a Portuguese port when one of his ships was seized by a Portuguese vessel. When Spaniards killed the leader of a French colonizing expedition in 1562, a French "gentleman" sent three vessels that made bloody reprisals against Spain.[24]

Like their British counterparts, French privateers committed great depredations in the New World during the seventeenth century and were rewarded with letters of nobility.[25] French *filibustiers*, under the direction of Santo Domingo's governor, ransomed and pillaged Spanish towns. They also drove the English out of Hudson Bay.[26]

The golden age of French privateering occurred after Colbert became secretary of state, despite France's imposition in 1681 of onerous regulations on privateering. These included the requirement that a privateer post a fifteen-thousand livre bond and carry at least six guns, as well as a prohibition on ransoming prizes above a certain value. Apparently it was Colbert's enthusiasm for expanding France's commerce and building its navy that stimulated a heightened interest in maritime activities in general.[27] At any rate, "the principal threat to British trade in the wars between 1689 and 1815 came from a large number of French privateers that put to sea from St. Malo, Dunkirk, and other ports along the French coast." French privateering was greatly stimulated by the wars between 1689 and 1713, which disrupted the ports' normally lucrative trade in the Atlantic and Mediterranean, leaving merchants with little other than privateering in which to invest.[28]

The peak of French privateering occurred during the years 1689 to 1697. Both the number of French privateers and their success declined in subsequent wars. In the American War for Independence (1778–82), French privateers took about four prizes per vessel, while in the French Revolutionary and Napoleonic Wars, they took only about one prize per vessel.[29]

Privateers played a significant role in the War of the Spanish Succession

(1701–13). British and American privateers seized more than 2,000 prizes,[30] with one New York group alone destroying fifty-four French and Spanish vessels.[31] French privateers attacked Dutch, Venetian, and Portuguese ships and towns. In 1711, "a colossal [French] private expedition . . . defeated an entire Portuguese fleet and captured Rio de Janeiro."[32] In the mideighteenth century, French privateers nearly put an end to the slave trade between Africa and the British colonies in the Americas.[33]

The War of the Austrian Succession (1739–48) saw another surge in privateering. Wishing to keep France out of the war, Britain initially discouraged privateering, which was always a potential threat to neutral commerce.[34] Between 1739 and 1741 only 30 prizes were taken by privateers.[35] Once France entered the war, however, English privateering increased in importance. Between 1739 and 1748, New York privateers captured more than 240 prizes worth nearly £620,000. By the final years of the war, "French shipping had been largely driven from the sea lanes."[36] French and Spanish vulnerability to privateering attacks led them to ship their goods in Dutch vessels. The English Crown then turned privateers loose on the Dutch, who lost nearly £1.3 million in the course of the war.[37] Besides attacking enemy shipping, English privateers "acted as auxiliary vessels, carrying troops, scouting, and on occasion even blockading enemy ports." They also convoyed British merchant ships and served as a coast guard for the North American colonies.[38] It is estimated that privateers took about 3,500 prizes during the war.[39]

Privateering reached new heights in the Seven Years' War (1756–63), particularly after England announced its Rule of 1756. With this rule "neutrals were prohibited from carrying on any trade, directly or indirectly, with the French colonies, which trade was not guaranteed to them in time of peace." This struck a "death-blow to the Dutch commerce, which had been growing rich on the French colonial trade for many years."[40] Though the rule brought French trade to a standstill, reprisals against England by other neutrals produced an alarming increase in insurance rates for English merchants, whose complaints led the Crown to tighten control over its privateers. Nevertheless, during the first four years of the war, it is estimated that English vessels took 1,000 French prizes. New York privateers were responsible for more than 300 of these, enjoying a profit of £1.5 million.[41] Despite the English privateers' success, French privateers took more than 300 English prizes.[42] Nevertheless, the "Peace of Paris demonstrated forcibly how little influence privateering usually exercises on the result of a war; the losses of the English shipping were more than double those of the French, yet the treaty of peace was the most disgraceful, perhaps, that France ever signed."[43]

American privateers served both sides in the U.S. War for Independence.[44] In the rebel cause, some 792 privateers captured or destroyed 600 British vessels worth an estimated $18 million. They took a total of

16,000 British prisoners. According to one report, insurance rates for convoyed vessels reached 30 percent and for unconvoyed, 50 percent.[45] Losses to the West Indian trade are estimated at 66 percent.[46] American privateers even operated in British waters so that Britain had to provide naval escort for shipping between Ireland and England.[47] The Armed Neutrality of 1780 prevented any significant privateering activity against anyone but the belligerents.[48] Evaluations of the effects of American privateering on the outcome of the war vary enormously. At one extreme is Maclay, who concludes that "it was this attack on England's commerce that struck the mortal blows to British supremacy in America—not Saratoga nor Yorktown."[49] At the other is Sherry, who writes that

> Yet as effective as the privateers may have been against commerce, they were all but useless against the Royal Navy. As a consequence, the British had no trouble controlling major colonial ports such as New York, Boston, and Charleston. Control of the ports by the Royal Navy meant that the British could move troops as they chose, could resupply easily, and could bring military pressure to bear where and when they chose. It was only when a French fleet blocked the British from relieving Cornwallis's army at Yorktown that the Americans won their war for independence.[50]

During the French Revolutionary wars, French privateers took 2,100 British vessels.[51] In the War of 1812, 517 American privateers captured 1,300 prizes worth an estimated $39 million. They also took many of the 30,000 prisoners captured by American naval forces during the war.[52] One American privateer ship, the *Yankee*, in six cruises captured 40 British vessels and captured or destroyed $5 million of British property.[53]

Up through the first decade of the nineteenth century, privateering was a prominent feature of interstate conflict and war. It was effective as both a substitute and a foundation for state naval power. Privateering evolved into a weapon of the weak against the strong, as in the case of the United States and Britain during the War of 1812. However, it was invented and encouraged by the "strong" states of Europe, whose naval power was largely an outgrowth of privateering.

MERCENARIES

Unlike the case of privateering, there is no consensus on how a mercenary should be defined.[54] We generally think of a mercenary as one who fights for an employer other than his home state and whose motivation is economic. The soldier of fortune is the ideal type of a mercenary.

However, there are mixed forms of military service that meet one but not both of the aforementioned criteria. For example, British officers who are "seconded" to Middle East armed forces serve a foreign army but do so at the behest of their home state. And the volunteers of the International Brigades in the Spanish Civil War fought for a foreign military force and were paid but, it is generally agreed, were motivated by political ideals rather than monetary gain. On the other hand, members of an all-volunteer citizen army are paid to fight but hardly warrant the label of mercenaries. Here it is interesting to note that "etymologically . . . 'soldier' carries the meaning 'he who fights for pay.' "[55] Mockler may be correct in saying that "the real mark of the mercenary [is] a devotion to war for its own sake,"[56] but since individual motivations are impossible to determine, this is not helpful for analysis. For purposes of this study, I will use the term *mercenarism* to refer to the practices of enlisting in and recruiting for a foreign army.

Scholars agree that feudalism's constraints on military service were a major inducement for monarchs to turn to mercenaries.[57] Whatever its other drawbacks, the feudal military system was based on the principle of defense. Knights were duty-bound to serve only a very limited amount of time—something like forty days a year—but, more importantly, were not obligated to serve abroad.[58] Thus, feudal military rights and obligations presented a barrier to launching offensive military campaigns.

In the twelfth century, the English king introduced the system of scutage, which allowed individuals to buy their way out of their military obligations, thus providing the sovereign with the cash to purchase manpower wherever s/he could.[59] By the time of the Hundred Years' War, landholding in France was based on rent, and "knight's service had fallen into disuse."[60] Thus, it appears that the European market for mercenaries was largely the creation of war-makers seeking to escape the constraints of feudal military obligations.[61] War-makers increasingly relied on private or royal subcontractors to raise and supply armies for a profit.

Large-scale mercenarism in the form of the Free Companies flourished in Europe between 1300 and 1450. "Long before absolute monarchy arose, soldiers offering themselves for hire had constituted a major export trade of the Middle Ages, and one of the first to establish a European market."[62] The foreign mercenaries of pre-Renaissance Italy, so maligned by Machiavelli,[63] gave way after the 1379 Battle of Marino to the condottieri (military contractors). These were "Italians" and, increasingly, nobles. "By the end of the fifteenth century . . . condottieri had become dukes, and dukes had become condottieri."[64]

The economic scale of mercenarism reached unprecedented proportions in the seventeenth century, when Wallenstein's private army "was the biggest and best organized private enterprise seen in Europe before the twentieth century."[65] Unfortunately, few rulers could afford to hire such an impressive force.

These private armies also presented a threat to European rulers. For example, the Grand Catalan Company, a force of some sixty-five hundred men, took service with the duke of Athens only to turn on him in 1311 and establish its own "duchy of mercenaries," which survived for sixty-three years.[66] Later, Wallenstein, with two thousand square miles of territory as a base for his army,[67] raised suspicions that he was attempting to form his own state.[68] The solution for European monarchs, imposed first by Charles VII of France in 1445, was to integrate foreign mercenaries into their standing armies or to buy army units from other rulers.[69]

These policies had, by the eighteenth century, turned the typical European standing army into a truly multinational force. Table 2.1 presents data on the composition of four major European armies in the eighteenth century. Foreigners constituted at least one-quarter and as much as 60 percent of these regular standing armies.

German states were the premier suppliers. A German prince was the first to lease a regiment to another state (Venice) in the 1660s.[70] For almost forty years Hesse-Cassel's army was subsidized by the Netherlands, England, and Venice. In 1727 it was completely taken over by the British.[71] William III, landgrave of Hesse-Cassel from 1751 to 1760, said "these troops are our Peru. In losing them we would forfeit all our resources."[72] From 1690 to 1716 the Julich Berg army was paid for by the Netherlands. Wurttemberg's army served the Dutch and the Dutch East India Company in 1707.[73] Hesse, Hanover, Baden, Brunswick, and Waldeck were the main suppliers of mercenaries for Britain.[74] Germans also constituted up to one-third of the prerevolutionary French army.[75]

At the same time, however, German states also employed foreigners. In 1705 two-fifths of Bavarian army officers were foreigners—Italians and Frenchmen. The Bavarian army also "was overrun by Irish refugees" and "French adventurers of dubious character."[76] One Bavarian regiment included soldiers from sixteen countries.[77] Frenchmen provided one-third of Brandenburg-Prussia's officer corps, and Walloon, French, Spanish, Italian, and English officers staffed the Palantine army.[78] On the eve of the Seven Years' War a number of Dutch regiments were on "semipermanent hire to German princelings."[79] In 1693, 35 percent of the Saxon army was foreign, though by 1730 this figure had been reduced to 11 percent.[80]

Frederick the Great recruited all over the Holy Roman Empire, especially in the free towns and the ecclesiastical principalities. At the onset of the Seven Years' War he attempted to incorporate the entire Saxon army into his own. After the war he recruited as far away as Italy and Switzer-

TABLE 2.1
Foreigners in Eighteenth-Century Armies

Country	Year	Foreign Component (Percentage)
Prussia	1713–40	34
	1743	66
	1768	56
	1786	50
Britain	1695	24
	1701	54
	1760s	38
	1778	32
France	1756–63	25
	1789	22
	Pre-Revolution	33
Spain	1751	25
	1799	14

Sources: Herbert Rosinski, *The German Army* (Washington, D.C. : Infantry Journal, 1944), 20; Fritz Redlich, *The German Military Enterpriser and His Work Force: A Study in European Economic and Social History* (Wiesbaden: Franz Steiner Verlag GMBH, 1965), 2:179, 200, and 201; John Childs, *Armies and Warfare in Europe, 1648–1789* (Manchester: Manchester University Press, 1982), 42, 47, and 48; C. C. Bayley, *Mercenaries for the Crimea: The German, Swiss, and Italian Legions in British Service, 1854–1856* (Montreal: McGill-Queen's University Press, 1977), 4 and 5; Henry Spenser Wilkinson, *The French Army before Napoleon* (Oxford: Clarendon Press, 1915), 85; Richard A. Preston and Sydney F. Wise, *Men in Arms: A History of Warfare and Its Interrelationships with Western Society*, 2d ed. (New York: Praeger, 1970), 139.

land. Frederick the Great also brought officers from France, Italy, Switzerland, Hungary, and Lithuania into the Prussian army.[81]

The Dutch were also both employers and providers of mercenary troops. Their eighteenth-century army was led almost entirely by officers from France, Germany, Scotland, and Ireland. After 1756, the Dutch recruited in the Austro-Hungarian empire.[82] As previously noted, the Dutch loaned regiments to German princelings during the Seven Years' War, but they also provided troops for the British army. Along with Hanoverian and Hessian mercenaries, the Dutch played an important role in Britain's 1701 war with France and in suppressing the 1745 Jacobite Rebellion within Britain itself.[83] When Catherine the Great refused to rent twenty thousand troops to Britain in its war with the American colonies, Britain attempted to hire the United Provinces' Scots Brigade. This Dutch "foreign legion" consisted of Scottish officers and "mercenaries from all over Europe."[84]

Britain's army drew its foreign contingent primarily from the German states and the Netherlands, but it also employed Swiss, Albanians, Italians, and Frenchmen during the Napoleonic Wars.[85] Great Britain also supplied both officers and troops for foreign armies. Englishmen, Irishmen, and Scotsmen served as officers and soldiers in the eighteenth-century French, Prussian, Austrian, Russian, German, and Dutch armies.[86]

"As a peacetime minimum, the French generally possessed nine regiments of Swiss infantry, six from various German states, two from Italian principalities, and six from Ireland."[87] French armies were 20 percent foreign throughout the seventeenth and eighteenth centuries.[88] Significant numbers of Scottish and Flemish soldiers also served in the eighteenth-century French army.[89]

Switzerland was the main supplier of mercenary troops in the sixteenth and seventeenth centuries, especially to France.[90] According to the Perpetual Peace, which France imposed on Switzerland in 1516, "the Swiss agreed never to supply mercenaries to France's enemies."[91] During the eighteenth century, Swiss soldiers and officers served in the Prussian, French, British, Austrian, and Dutch armies.[92] According to one scholar, Switzerland is the only European state that has never employed mercenaries.[93]

From 1688 to 1727 Italy subsidized the Hesse-Cassel army and in 1756 recruited in Austria.[94] Italian regiments served in the mid-eighteenth-century French, Austrian, and Prussian armies.[95] Austria-Hungary recruited from the Netherlands, Switzerland, Austria, Croatia, Hungary, and Italy. At the same time, the Dutch, Hungary and Italy were allowed to recruit in the Austro-Hungarian empire.[96]

At the time of Gustavus Adolphus's death in 1632, less than 10 percent of his army was Swedish, the remainder being mostly German.[97] It is estimated that in the War of Smolensk (1632–34) one-half the Russian army was foreigners. In 1681, Russia's army, which included eighty thousand foreign troops,[98] was led by Scottish and German officers.[99] As many as one-third of the eighteenth-century Russian army officer corps was foreign.[100] Polish nobles served in the Prussian, Austrian, Swedish and Russian armies.[101] The Royal Deux Ponts Regiment, a force of Germans in the employ of France, fought on the American side in the American War for Independence.[102]

Foreigners were not confined to service in armies; navies displayed a similar multinational character. In the 1660s, six thousand French sailors were serving abroad. One-third of the Dutch navy was French. About seven hundred Frenchmen served in the Sicilian navy, and more Frenchmen than Italians served in the Genoese fleet.[103] At the same time, Italian volunteers and "slaves—North African 'Turks' . . . Russians, Negroes from West Africa, and a few Iroquois Indians"—worked as rowers in the French navy.[104]

During the war between Spain and the United Provinces, the Dutch Republic employed privateers from Zeeland while Spain used the services of Dunkirk's privateers.[105]

The eighteenth-century British navy employed French prisoners of war and volunteers from Holland, Germany, Sweden, Norway, Denmark, Switzerland, Portugal, Spain, Italy, Sardinia, Malta, Greece, and Turkey.[106] Part of the reason for the presence of foreigners in the navy was that the British Royal Navy depended on the mercantile marine, whose composition, even in the late Victorian period, was 46 percent foreign.[107]

Though foreigners were supposed to be exempt from British impressment, according to an act of 1739, "a great deal of the correspondence of eighteenth-century admirals is occupied with complaints from foreign embassies seeking to free their subjects."[108] This controversy intensified after the United States gained independence but Great Britain continued to impress U.S. citizens based on the "rule of indelible allegiance, under which a person once a British subject might, although he had acquired citizenship of another country, still be 'recognized' as a British seaman and be impressed accordingly."[109] By 1807, more than six thousand U.S. citizens had been impressed into the British navy.[110] This practice was one of the reasons for Madison's request that Congress declare war against England in 1812.[111]

Lesser naval powers also relied on large contingents of foreigners. In the Russians' 1713 Baltic Sea fleet, "only two out of eleven commanders and seven out of seventy other officers were Russians."[112] In the United States of 1878, "60% of the Navy's enlisted personnel were foreign-born." On average, "28% of the crews of American warships" in the second half of the nineteenth century were foreigners. At least twenty different nationalities were represented, including British, Irish, Scandinavian, Canadian, Central European, Japanese, and Chinese—despite the legal requirement that two-thirds of the seamen be native-born U.S. citizens.[113]

This overview of the employment of foreigners in military forces is certainly not exhaustive. It does suggest, however, that the practices of hiring foreigners and allowing individuals to join other states' armed forces were common in the period of 1600 to 1800. Among European states, only Switzerland apparently never employed foreigners. The market for military manpower was as international as it could ever be. Nationality or country of origin was not the primary basis for determining service obligations. The capabilities of officers, the economic or legal desperation of the soldiers, and the economic interests of rulers determined who served and where. State leaders needed military manpower; they were not particularly choosy about where they obtained it.

MERCANTILE COMPANIES

> The East India Company did not seem to be
> merely a Company formed for the extension of
> the British commerce, but in reality a delegation
> of the whole power and sovereignty of this
> kingdom sent into the East.
> (Edmund Burke)

Perhaps the most fascinating case of nonstate violence is that of the mercantile companies.[114] With these curious institutions, all analytical distinctions—between the economic and political, nonstate and state, property rights and sovereignty, the public and private—broke down. And unlike privateers and mercenaries, the mercantile company was a new entity, a creation of sixteenth-century Europe. As we will see, these companies were not only authorized to use violence but were endowed with nearly all the powers of sovereignty.

The Institution's Forms

The onset of the sixteenth century saw a proliferation of companies chartered by states to engage in long-distance trade or establish colonies. Chartered companies are commonly divided into two categories: the trading and the plantation companies.[115] These divisions are hardly clear-cut, as the same company might engage in trade, privateering, and planting on a single voyage.[116] Only in retrospect, with knowledge of what the companies actually came to specialize in, can we classify them according to this scheme. This chapter deals with both types of company though the emphasis is on the most important: the Dutch East India Company and the English East India Company and Hudson's Bay Company.[117]

In the early sixteenth century, in England at least, the regulated company form predominated. Regulated companies were basically merchant guilds whose membership was restricted to professional merchants who paid a membership fee. Membership was not alienable without permission of the guild. Members agreed to comply with the company's rules and regulations, but their ventures were undertaken at their own risk. In short, the company's trading privileges were shared with merchants in exchange for a fee, but the merchants bore unlimited liability for their individual enterprises. Examples of regulated companies were the Russia, Turkey, and Eastland companies, which were defunct by the end of the eighteenth century.

In the seventeenth century, the English Crown began to grant charters for joint-stock companies, such as the East India,[118] Royal Africa, and Hudson's Bay companies. These were forerunners of the modern corporation, as their shares were freely alienable and their shareholders were liable for only their shares of company stock.[119]

The Dutch East India Company was an intermediate form. It had a "federal structure" composed of six *kamers*, or chambers, one from each province. Since "anyone without restriction to race, religion, sex, or national origin could become a shareholder of any *kamer* he [*sic*] chose," the company at the province level resembled a joint-stock company. At the federal level, however, the company looked more like a regulated company. "Each of the six *kamers* 'equipped' ships of its own," and "each kept its own books." All operated under rules made by the Seventeen, as the company's board of directors was known; for example, a kamer could not borrow outside the company if other kamers could provide the funds. "The assets and liabilities of all six were brought together in Amsterdam to make up the statements of the company's financial condition."[120]

The Dutch East India Company was chartered primarily to trade. Thus, "in the seventeenth century 'the Dutch avoided all continental establishments with the greatest care' and for over 150 years this great company only possessed isolated posts." Even at its most powerful it only "exercised direct administration in and around Batavia, in Ceylon, in a small number of posts and at the Cape [of Good Hope]."[121] Other companies were chartered to establish colonies or plantations. For example, both the English Plymouth Company and Virginia Company were licensed to establish colonies in North America. Generally, the trading companies operated in the East, while the plantation/colonial companies concentrated in the New World.

It is important to note at the outset that these companies varied across countries in their degree of private versus state control. The Dutch companies were the closest to being purely private organizations, while the Portuguese and French companies were for all intents and purposes state enterprises.[122] English companies fell somewhere in between the Dutch, on the one hand, and the French and Portuguese on the other. These differences reflected variations in the institutional structures of the various states.

In France and Portugal, with their highly centralized states and weak or divided merchant classes, the state took the lead in organizing mercantile enterprises. The French state virtually forced its merchants, bankers, and financiers to participate in its various East India companies.[123] At the other extreme was the United Provinces, where the merchants took the lead, with the state stepping in only later to unify the pioneer companies into one national company.

England, with both a monarch and a parliament, produced an intermediate form of company. Here the Crown used its power to grant charters and monopolies in order to develop sources of revenue beyond parliamentary control. By their very nature these companies had at least the appearance of exclusivity. For example, during the 1604 parliamentary debate on a bill to abolish all monopolies, one speaker charged that "governors of these companies by their monopolizing orders have so handled the matter as that the mass of the whole trade of the realm is in the hands of some 200 persons at the most, the rest serving for a show and reaping small benefit."[124] Those not granted the same "privileges" worked through Parliament to expand the range of individuals who could participate in the companies or the commerce. This entailed curbing the Crown's power. Thus, the form of the English companies varied with shifts in the balance of power between the Crown and Parliament. Most notably, following the Glorious Revolution, all monopolies were subject to parliamentary confirmation.[125] Throughout Europe, the mercantile mixture of state and public enterprise depended on the predominance of power of the monarch or the parliament.

These differences were reflected in the primary goals of the companies. While these goals were always a fusion of power and profit, the emphasis varied across countries. The French companies, as state enterprises, tended to be more concerned with increasing state power than with making a profit. At the other extreme was the Dutch East India Company, which aimed at increasing private wealth through purely commercial operations. In between was the English East India Company, whose goal was to profit private individuals and at the same time to provide revenue to the Crown in its struggle for independence from the parliament. Thus, while it is possible to distinguish the mercantile company from other institutional forms, there was considerable variation among the individual companies both across countries and over time.

Since the object of this book is to understand the elimination of nonstate violence, this analysis will concentrate on the Dutch and English companies. These companies were largely private concerns that were endowed with what we consider today the sovereign powers of the state. The next section presents a description of the array of powers that was delegated to some of the most important companies. But first it is important to understand why groups of merchants felt it necessary to obtain a state charter in the first place.

In England, a royal charter was considered a prerequisite for undertaking international commercial ventures, for several reasons. First, without royal authorization, association members were liable to being punished for unlawful assembly. Second, it was generally believed that "foreign trade was prohibited to the King's subjects except in so far as it was 'opened' by Act of Parliament or licensed by the King." Third, such associations needed a formal legal status in order to be able to sue, enforce contracts, and hold property. Fourth, "since English legal theory at that time maintained that the Crown had authority over its subjects abroad," the associations needed legal jurisdiction over their employees in foreign lands. Finally, a royal charter indicated to foreign governments that "the company operated under the aegis of the English Crown and that injuries to the members would be resented by the Crown and might provoke retaliation."[126]

In the case of the Dutch East India Company, a government charter was more or less imposed on the independent traders once it became clear that the Portuguese would use military force to keep them out of the East Indies. To be effective, the merchants had to be organized, as were the Portuguese, and equipped with the military forces required to defend themselves against the armed force of the Portuguese state. In practice this meant that a charter from the Dutch state granting the company military power and a "subsidy from the national treasury to carry on the war against Spain and Portugal" was necessary.[127]

Sovereign Powers Delegated to Mercantile Companies

Mercantile companies were, as a rule, granted full sovereign powers. In addition to their economic privileges of a monopoly on trade with a given region or in a particular commodity[128] and the right to export bullion,[129] they could raise an army or a navy, build forts, make treaties, make war, govern their fellow nationals, and coin their own money.[130] The companies' outposts were headed by governors who "remained the appointees of the companies, as did the military officers, even when they were officially invested with their offices by their governments."[131]

According to its 1602 charter, the Dutch East India Company (United Netherlands Chartered East India Company) "was empowered to conclude treaties of peace and alliance, to wage defensive war, and to build 'fortresses and strongholds' in that region. They could also enlist civilian, naval, and military personnel who would take an oath of loyalty to the Company and to the States-General." The Dutch West India Company in

1621 "was likewise authorized to make war and peace with the indigenous powers, to maintain naval and military forces, and to exercise judicial and administrative functions in those regions."[132]

Under its 1670 charter the Hudson's Bay Company (The Governor and Company of Adventurers of England Trading into Hudson's Bay)[133] was granted "the absolute right to administer law and to judge all cases, civil or criminal, on the spot. It was empowered to employ its own armies and navies, erect forts and generally defend its fiefdom in any way it chose."[134] And the most famous of all the mercantile companies, the English East India Company (The Governor and Company of Merchants of London Trading to the East Indies), was in 1661 granted a new charter that "gave the Company criminal and civil jurisdiction 'over all persons belonging to the said Governor and Company or that shall live under them'; it empowered the Company to make war or peace with non-Christian princes or people; and it authorized the Company to erect fortifications and to export munitions from England."[135]

These citations illustrate not only the extraordinary powers that the companies were given but also the extent to which this delegation of sovereign power was typical. What specifically concerns us here, however, is the companies' sovereign power to exercise violence in the international system. Why were the companies given this power?

Rationale for the Delegation of Military Power

It is important to recognize that the rationale for delegating military power to a company varied according to the company's mission. For example, the Dutch West India Company was "established for the purpose of doing Spain as much damage as possible."[136] It was not organized for commerce but "for preying on Spanish shipping, for privateering against the enemy's American empire."[137] Thus, "the offensive role of the Western Company in the war against the Iberian Atlantic empire was emphasized from the start."[138]

In contrast, the Dutch East India Company and most of the other mercantile companies were granted military power for "defensive" purposes. Mention of even defensive military powers in the Dutch company's charter "was sufficient to frighten away a number of leading investors in the pioneer companies." These "sold their shares rather than transfer them to the VOC,"[139] saying that "they as merchants had themselves organized those companies solely for the purpose of honourably engaging in peaceful and friendly trade, and not to indulge in any hostilities or aggressive actions."[140] Nevertheless, the structure of the Dutch East India Company, which did not exclude any important merchants from participating in the monopoly, made it a more national enterprise than were the English companies. Moreover, as we shall see later, the close connection between the political and merchant classes precluded any need to justify the company's military power.

Curiously, opponents of the companies seldom attacked the companies' military powers but focused on their trade monopolies. The companies were perpetually defending their monopoly privileges, and they did so with what amounted to a public-goods argument. According to the apologists for monopolies, the trade infrastructure, especially the forts and garrisons, established and maintained by the companies constituted public goods:

> Since it was not feasible to charge user fees for infrastructure services, the combination of substantial economies of scale and non-excludability created what today would be termed a free-rider problem. The companies and their proponents argued that in the absence of monopoly charters for trading in particular areas, the free-rider problem would cause a suboptimal level of investment in infrastructure, in turn causing a reduced level of trade or in some cases reducing the level of trade to zero.[141]

The reason the companies needed the military element of the infrastructure—armies, navies, forts, and so on—was, according to their defenders, to protect the trade against attacks by "rampaging natives," other Europeans, and pirates. As Anderson and Tollison convincingly argue, however, the forts and garrisons were more nearly "public bads," since they were "designed to operate as coercive entry barriers which reduced the level of trade while protecting the monopoly rents of their owner-operators." Most telling is their observation that

> it would certainly seem odd, then, if the same trading companies which were advertising the supposed necessity for the provision of forts to defend against rampaging natives were simultaneously supplying the natives with the most effective means available of overcoming forts (cannons). But this is exactly what was occurring on a wide scale.[142]

Thus, the original delegation of military power was justified on the grounds that in order to establish permanent trading relations with extra-European areas, the companies needed the capacity to defend their outposts and ships from attacks by hostile states and people. Once the military infrastructure was in place, the companies argued that their trade monopolies were justified by the expense of maintaining the military infrastructure. Even Adam Smith was amenable to a temporary monopoly, arguing that

> When a company of merchants undertake, at their own risk and expence, to establish a new trade with some remote and barbarous nation, it may not be unreasonable to incorporate them into a joint stock company, and to grant

them, in case of their success, a monopoly of the trade for a certain number of years. It is the easiest and most natural way in which the state can recompense them for hazarding a dangerous and expensive experiment, of which the public is afterwards to reap the benefit.[143]

It seems more likely, however, that the companies' military capabilities were used to defend and enforce their trade monopolies.

There were those who recognized this and argued that the state should assume control of the military infrastructure and leave the trade open to all. It was particularly offensive to the companies' opponents that the British Royal Navy was helping to enforce the monopolies by seizing "interlopers." "The Royal Navy captains who seized vessels engaged in illegal trade shared a portion of the auctioned value of the seized ship and its cargo with the chartered company. Indeed, the British Fleet's primary day-to-day business in Indian waters was its patrol to check for 'illegal practices.'"[144] Thus, the "nation" was paying the Royal Navy to enforce the company's monopoly, with the naval officers and the company sharing the prize money.

Whether the companies' military powers were justified or merely rationalized, the companies staved off their critics for more than a century. During that period the companies exercised violence against a variety of international actors, a subject to which we now turn.

The Companies' Military Capabilities

What kinds of military capabilities did the companies actually develop? Before the mideighteenth century, the Dutch and English East India companies recruited mercenaries in the East. In the late 1670s, the English president at Surat was appointed "Captain-General, Admiral and Commander-in-Chief of the Company's forces in all its possessions, and Director-General of all its mercantile affairs." He "established the English company's first regular military force, made up of infantry, cavalry, and artillery." Eurasians and Indians made up these regular forces, with Indian mercenaries recruited as needed to supplement the regulars.[145] Once the English company's conflict with the Dutch company subsided and its principal foe became the French, it began to rely more on Europeans, especially Swiss and German mercenaries.[146] Still, the company employed some 9,000 "sepoys" in its army of 1765, a number that swelled to 100,000 by 1782.[147]

Despite the Dutch merchants' claims to be peaceful traders, their pre–Dutch East India Company association devoted 30 percent of its spending for voyages to military-related items.

After the formation of the United Company in 1602, the annual figure rose to 50, 60 and even 70 per cent. Indeed the total cost of building Dutch forts on the principal islands of the Moluccas between 1605 and 1612 amounted to no less than 1.72 million florins, almost one-third of the Company's initial capital.

The Dutch East India Company used Indonesian mercenaries in taking Macassar, Sumatra, East Java, and Bantam in the second half of the seventeenth century. Between 1715 and 1719 the Dutch company employed 5,000 Europeans and 20,000 local mercenaries to retake its fort at Calcutta.[148]

In contrast with the Eastern companies, the Hudson's Bay Company relied on its own employees to man its forts and defend its property. The company's "army" at the York Factory had not a single professional soldier but was made up of "little more than fur traders desultorily trained in small arms drill."[149] At the Prince of Wales' Fort, the "garrison" consisted of men who "had signed on with the company as tailors, masons, blacksmiths and labourers and not as soldiers," people whose "desire to court death or dismemberment in the defence of their employer's property was probably slight." In fact, the company seemed more concerned with its liability in case any of them should be killed or injured than in training them to fight.[150] Only when it came into conflict with the North West Company in the nineteenth century did the company raise a mercenary force, and that consisted of only a hundred men.

What did the companies actually do with their military powers? For one thing, they waged war against non-European rulers and people in the interests of "trade."

Companies versus Non-Europeans

East India companies frequently used piracy in the early days of the Eastern trade to intimidate local rulers or punish them for refusing company demands for trading privileges. In 1610 the English East India Company's Henry Middleton seized Indian ships, forced the Indians to trade their goods for his, then ransomed the ships back to their owners.[151] Both the Dutch and English companies seized Indian vessels carrying Portuguese passes. The Dutch company also seized Chinese junks in its attempts to force its way into the China trade and stop the China-Manila trade.[152]

In 1621 the Dutch took over the Banda Islands, enslaving the inhabitants and executing their leaders.[153] The Dutch company fought a five-year war in the Moluccas,[154] where the people revolted in 1649 against the

Dutch policy of uprooting trees to control the production of cloves and against Dutch missionary efforts. Twice, in 1653–55 and 1660, the Dutch government at Batavia declared war against the king of Macassar, "the dominant power in the Celebes." In 1666 it sent a fleet composed of twenty-one ships, six hundred European soldiers, and some Indonesian mercenaries against him. This resulted in a treaty granting the Dutch a trade monopoly and making company vassals of all rulers of territories ceded to the company.[155]

The English East India Company took Bengal by force in the 1764 Battle of Buxar. This war was prompted by the actions of the nawab, whom the company itself had installed. He defied the company by abolishing all internal duties. Since the company's employees supplemented their meager salaries by exploiting their privilege of duty-free trade, abolition of the duties effectively put an end to their advantage. Thus, "the company went to war" and having defeated the nawab, "the company was left in effective control of Bengal."[156]

Company military operations against local rulers were not always successful. In 1688, tired of being "harassed" by local rulers, the English East India Company "strengthened the defences of Bombay, stationed armed vessels in the harbour, interfered with Moghul shipping and treated the Moghul Governor of Surat with contumely." In response, the Mogul seized company factories, imprisoned its factors, and attacked Bombay. The company was forced to accept "humiliating" peace terms, including the payment of a substantial fine.[157]

In 1757 the English East India Company found itself unable to reach an agreement with the ruler of Bengal on its trading privileges and reparations for his recent attacks on its factories, so the company decided to overthrow him.[158] Learning of the plot, the nawab assembled a large military force at Plassey. In its endeavor, the company had the complicity of two of the nawab's generals, who in the subsequent battle "stood still with their large armies."[159] The English company defeated the nawab's army and installed a new nawab,[160] who gave the company the exclusive right to trade in "the whole of eastern India."[161]

In southern India the company fought four wars (in 1769, 1780, 1790–92, and 1799) with the rulers of Mysore. Viewing the latter's expanding political and military power as a threat, the English allied with the Maranthas and Deccans to oust them. The allies succeeded in their endeavor in 1799, and "the new state of Mysore became virtually a dependency of the English."[162]

Next the English turned to the suppression of their erstwhile allies, the Maranthas. Conflicts between the leaders of the Marantha Confederacy led the English to lend military support to their favorites among those leaders. After three wars with the Maranthas (1775–1817), the company established its "imperial rule," with local rulers serving as puppets with no political or military power.[163]

Nepal was similarly taken by force in a war fought between 1814 and 1816. In the Anglo-Sikh Wars (1848–52) and the Anglo-Burmese Wars (1824–26), the company took the Punjab and Burma.[164] "By the third decade of the nineteenth century, practically all of India south and west of the Punjab was either under the direct rule of the company, or was politically controlled by what was later called paramountcy."[165]

Among the important mercantile companies, only the Hudson's Bay Company failed to use force against the local inhabitants. This was not due to any benevolence on the company's part. Rather, the structure of the company's trading operations as well as the geography and climate of the Hudson Bay precluded violent conflicts with the Indians. The company simply made a peace treaty with the Indians, bought land from them, and planted its factories on the bay. It then waited for the Indians to bring their furs from inland via the network of rivers. Since in its first seventy-four years the company did not seek to penetrate the Indians' territory, it did not disrupt the traditional intertribal trading network. In the 1740s and 1750s, when it did try to establish forts inland from Hudson Bay, the Indians killed its employees.[166]

Mercantile companies were state-created institutions that used violence in the pursuit of economic gain and political power for both the state and nonstate actors. With these institutions state rulers were able to exploit nonstate coercive capabilities in conquering or colonizing large areas of the globe. With them, today's theoretical and practical distinctions—between the economic and political and between state and nonstate actors—were meaningless.

CONCLUSION

With the breakdown of the feudal system of military mobilization, European state leaders began to exploit the capabilities of nonstate actors. In doing so, they largely marketized, democratized, and internationalized coercion. States did not pay privateers but allowed them to retain some or all of the prizes they seized. An army's or navy's size and strength were a function of the state's ability to buy soldiers and sailors from the international system. Mercantile companies were granted sovereign powers with which to pursue their economic interests. As a result, it is impossible to draw distinctions between the economic and political, the domestic and international, or the nonstate and state realms of authority when analyzing these practices. All lines were blurred.

State-authorized nonstate violence proved to be highly effective. Privateers dominated naval warfare. Mercenary armies and navies became the norm. Mercantile companies were highly successful in establishing a European economic and political presence outside the European system. The question is: If these practices served state leaders' interests so well, why were they eliminated? As we will see in the next chapter, each of these practices produced unexpected or at least unmanageable problems for states. Part of the problem was the state's inability to control nonstate actors. More important, however, was the state's own behavior. State rulers were consistently unable to resist the temptation to allow or even authorize nonstate violence while they denied responsibility and accountability for its consequences.

CHAPTER THREE

Unintended Consequences

AUTHORIZING nonstate violence in the international system served state interests well. Nonstate actors contributed much to state rulers' political, territorial, and economic goals at little cost to the states themselves. Their efforts were indispensable to the state's projects of making war on other states, suppressing societal resistance, and acquiring a foothold in extra-European territories.

Yet this system was not without its problems. Each nonstate practice produced unanticipated and sometimes bizarre outcomes. Privateering generated organized piracy. Mercenaries threatened to drag their home states into other states' wars. Mercantile companies turned their guns on each other and even on their home states. The result was probably the closest the modern state system has come to experiencing real anarchy.

One reason for this resulting chaos was the state's inability to exercise effective control over those it authorized to use violence beyond its borders. At the heart of these practices lay a paradox. To maximize nonstate actors' effectiveness, states needed to minimize the constraints on their activities and profits. Minimal constraints meant little state control and reduced state autonomy. Conversely, regulations designed to enhance state control reduced nonstate actors' incentives to take the risks entailed in military actions.

A more important reason for this control problem, I argue, was the behavior of state rulers themselves. What these rulers sought was the best of two worlds: maximum freedom with minimum responsibility. To that end, they invented the policy of plausible deniability in the early seventeenth century. In discussing the establishment of the Virginia Company, James I's advisers counseled:

> If the Spaniards complained of the occupation of their territory, he could free himself from blame by placing the responsibility upon the London Company. "If it take not success," his advisors told the King, "it is done by their owne heddes. It is but the attempt of private gentlemen, the State suffers noe losse, noe disreputation. If it takes success, they are your subjects, they doe it for your service, they will lay all at your Majesty's feet and interess your Majesty therein."[1]

With this approach, nonstate violence could be given a wink and a nod, thereby allowing the state to claim a share in successful efforts or to deny responsibility for endeavors producing negative consequences. As a result, neither states nor people could be certain of which practices were backed by state authority and which were not. Was an act of nonstate violence an act of war or a crime?

These issues were resolved, as we will see in chapter 4, in the course of the nineteenth century. Before proceeding to that topic, however, it is important to understand the unintended consequences of unleashing nonstate violence. In this chapter I describe how authorized nonstate violence produced undesirable, complex, or even threatening consequences for the state. As both a practical and theoretical matter, the problems explored in this chapter concern fundamental issues of authority, responsibility, and control. With the lines between the domestic and international, the economic and political, and the state and nonstate realms of authority so blurred, what was an act of war and what was a crime? Who was accountable to whom, and for what?

THE MEDITERRANEAN CORSAIRS

One of the most complicated and persistent problems stemming from the practice of privateering emerged in the seventeenth-century Mediterranean. The issue was whether the Mediterranean corsairs were pirates or privateers. The practical difficulty in distinguishing between the privateer and the pirate, understated by the clear-cut, legal definitions presented in chapter 2, is nicely illustrated by the corsairs of Malta and the Barbary Coast. On the one hand, like privateers, these corsairs were duly authorized by public officials to attack commerce in the area. On the other, while privateers were licensed only in time of war to capture or destroy enemy shipping, the situation of the corsairs was more complex.[2]

First, many of the corsairs were "footloose Europeans" who were "often little more than pirates who sought their fortunes under the star-spangled green banner of Algiers rather than the Jolly Roger."[3] The importance of Western Europeans in Barbary corsairing is indicated by the fact that they introduced the "fighting ship-of-war" into the Barbary fleets and that some of them even became leaders of the Barbary states.[4]

Second, Muslims and Christians were in a virtually permanent state of war in the Mediterranean until the nineteenth century. Moreover, the designated "enemies" varied across countries and over time. From the 1620s on, victims of the Barbary corsairs could remove themselves from the enemies list through treaties with the Barbary states in which the latter agreed to prevent attacks on the former's commerce in exchange for the payment of protection money, frequently in the form of naval stores and other armaments.[5] Yet "even after specific treaties had been signed in the 1620s, the question of whether Turkish and Algerine ships should be treated as pirates or public ships of a sovereign power was still undecided. Such attitudes lingered on until the early eighteenth century." Equally confused was the status of the Maltese corsairs, who, as Christians, were to confine their attacks to Muslim shipping, but who frequently targeted Greek (Christian) ships.[6]

Another factor complicating the categorization of the corsairs is the unconventional form of political authority under which they operated. The Barbary states, as part of the Ottoman Empire, were ostensibly ruled by the sultan's appointees, the pashas. Yet in reality, by the turn of the seventeenth century, these states were under the control of senior military officers acting through their elected leaders, the beys and deys. "Barbary and Turkey acted independently," so that "states which were at peace with Turkey were not necessarily at peace with Barbary, and vice versa." Malta was ruled by the military order of the Knights of the Order of Saint John of Jerusalem, who elected their leader, the grand master. But "the Grand Master owed feudal vassalage to whoever should be the ruler of Sicily, the King of Spain and later the Bourbon Kings." He was also subject to the authority of the pope and later, to that of the king of France.[7]

So, despite their being referred to as "military republics,"[8] there are serious problems in determining who was really sovereign in these lands, and therefore whether the authority under which their privateers operated met the conventional legal requirements of European privateering. By reason of all these complexities, it was quite impossible to determine whether the corsairs were pirates or privateers. These distinctions were meaningless when basic questions about war and sovereignty were unanswerable.

In claiming the sovereign right to authorize nonstate violence during wartime, European state leaders seemed to presume that, in practice, sovereignty and war were unproblematic concepts. As the Mediterranean corsairs demonstrate, this was at best a premature presumption.

ORGANIZED PIRACY

Every generation gets
the pirates it deserves.
(Robert I. Burns, *Muslims, Christians and Jews
in the Crusader Kingdom of Valencia*)

Piracy, as defined in chapter 2, is probably as old as maritime commerce.[9] In this sense, there was nothing new about piracy in the early European state system. What was new was not only the scale and scope of the piracy that emerged in the seventeenth century but the political nature of organized piracy. In several instances, groups of pirates formed communities or quasi-states based on the democratization of politics and violence. This organized piracy presented a threat not only to property but to the developing national state and its way of organizing politics and society.

At this time individuals had particularly good reasons for resisting the nascent European national state.[10] The judicial system was rapidly turning into a mechanism for defending property and for producing and disciplining labor. Capital punishment was expanded with a vengeance. "Beginning at the end of the seventeenth century, but continuing into the eighteenth, the death sentence was extended to cover all sorts of offenses, even those of the most trivial sort." France applied the death penalty to almost any form of larceny, while in England the number of crimes punishable by death increased from fifty in 1689 to two hundred in 1800. Again, these crimes were mostly some form of theft. By 1800, "at least in theory, English property was protected by the most comprehensive system of capital punishment statutes ever devised."[11]

But instead of executing people in droves, states found it more productive to impose forced labor on the misbehavers. The need for labor at home, in the military, and in the colonies meant that "incarceration in workhouses, galley slavery and transportation to bleak, colonial areas served a much more rational end than did execution." Prerevolutionary France sent seven times as many convicts to the colonies as it executed. Some states that had no colonies sold their convicts to others. "In the eighteenth century German authorities sent some of their prisoners to North America as slaves, while somewhat later, Prussia sent convicted felons to Russia to labour in Siberia."[12]

It is not surprising, then, that resistance to European states and society was fierce nor that it took the form of an attack on property. Piracy was not simply or always an economic crime—the theft of private property. It was also a political act—a protest against the obvious use of state institutions to defend property and discipline labor.

This chapter focuses on the major instances of organized piracy in order to characterize the nature of the threats it posed to states and property. It also demonstrates how the state's insistence on authorizing nonstate violence helped to produce situations that threatened its own authority.

Buccaneers

In the seventeenth century, French political and religious refugees settled on Hispaniola and eked out a living providing hides, tallow, and dried meat to visiting ships in exchange for guns and ammunition.[13] Spain drove these buccaneers from Hispaniola both because their settlement was illegal and because they provisioned non-Spanish ships, all of which Spain regarded as pirates. With Spain's having destroyed their cattle herds and driven them from their home, the buccaneers turned to attacking Spanish shipping from the island of Tortuga.[14] This new base attracted adventurers of several nationalities, especially English and French, whose governments were enemies of Spain. "From about 1630, and for the next eighty years despite Spanish efforts to dislodge them, the people of Tortuga lived in something akin to a pirate 'republic' known as the Brethren of the Coast."[15]

The real heyday of English buccaneering began with the British seizure of Jamaica from Spain in 1655. To defend this colonial outpost from recapture by Spain, "the governor freely issued letters of marque to 'Frenchmen' from Tortuga, Dutch adventurers, and then, increasingly, to English rovers."[16] It was from Jamaica that Henry Morgan launched his devastating attack on Panama.[17] While the Spanish charged that Morgan was a pirate, "the English agreed with Morgan that he and his buccaneers were legal privateers."[18] However, in 1670 Britain and Spain had signed the Treaty of America, by which Spain recognized British sovereignty in Jamaica[19] in exchange for British agreement to restrain its depredations on Spanish possessions.[20]

When news of Morgan's attack on Panama reached Europe, Britain was forced to arrest the Jamaican governor and call Morgan home "to answer for his offences against the King, his crown and dignity."[21] Neither man was punished. The governor was returned to Jamaica as chief justice and Morgan, a popular hero, was knighted and later named lieutenant-governor of Jamaica and a judge on its vice-admiralty court.[22] When William of Orange made peace with Spain in 1689, buccaneering declined, since the rich Spanish shipping was no longer a legitimate target and the brotherhood was shattered as "English and French buccaneers found themselves on opposite sides of the conflict."[23] By 1690 organized piracy had vanished only to be revived three years later on a scale unprecedented in history.

Madagascar I

In 1693 a North American privateer captured a Mogul ship carrying, in addition to luxury goods, £100,000 in gold and silver coins.[24] On the heels of this event, European and American pirates poured into Madagascar. While the ships of the Mogul and the East India Company provided the targets, North American merchants supplied the economic support to the pirates.[25] Some North American traders set up shop on Madagascar, exchanging colonial products for the luxury items captured through piracy. Corrupt colonial officials allowed the latter to enter their ports without customs inspections, and some even invested in pirate expeditions. North American shipbuilders could barely meet the demand for pirate trade vessels.[26]

A fundamental difference between the Madagascar pirates and others was that the former came close to constituting an independent nation. Madagascar pirate ships operated under a consistent set of rules specifying the rights and duties of the crews. These rules more or less expressed the laws of the Madagascar "commonwealth." But there was more:

> Another strong sign of an evolving nationalism was the loyalty pirates showed to their fellow outlaws. In fact, pirates were more loyal to each other than they were to their country of origin or to their religion or even to their own race. The evidence for this abounds. English, American and French pirates sailed together and fought effectively together in Henry Every's crew, despite the fact that France was at war with England and her colonies. Irish Catholics and Protestant Scots worked alongside each other without friction aboard scores of pirate vessels, despite the religious antagonisms that divided their nonpirate countrymen.

These pirates also developed their own customs, language, food, and flag. An East India Company petition to the British government noted that most of these pirates were English and warned "that if the present generation of pirates on Madagascar should become extinct, 'their Children will have the same Inclination to Madagascar, as these have to England, and will not have any such affection for England.' "[27]

At one point, rumors circulated in Europe that a French pirate had established a socialist republic in Madagascar. Piracy in this period had not only a strong antiauthority aspect to it but was also often rooted in a rejection of the class system of European society. For example, in trying to recruit a merchant seaman, one pirate captain is reported to have said:

> They villify us, the scoundrels so, when there is only this difference: *they* rob the poor under the cover of law, forsooth, and *we* plunder the rich under the protection of our own courage; had ye not better make one of us, than sneak after the arses of those villains for employment?

Clearly, Europeans viewed the Madagascar pirate "commonwealth" as a formidable quasi-state. And their fears were not without foundation. In the words of one pirate captain, "*I am a free prince* and have as much authority to make war on the whole world as he who has a hundred sail of ships and an army of a hundred thousand men in the field."[28]

It was East India Company complaints that drew the attention of the British government to the Madagascar pirates. The company's problem was that since most of the pirates were English speaking, the Mogul of India charged that they were acting in collusion with the company. When one of his ships was captured by an English pirate, the Mogul seized East

India Company property and imprisoned fifty of its employees, including the manager. After this incident, the Mogul declared that Europeans trading with India would be responsible for the safety of his ships.[29]

The company appealed to London for permission to prosecute pirates and for help from the Royal Navy. Both of these requests were denied, though the government did offer a reward for the capture of the pirates who had attacked the Mogul's ship. Thus the company was forced to attempt to protect the Mogul's ships by escorting them with its own armed merchant vessels. This only led the pirates to attack the company's vessels, which they had previously avoided doing. Of course the company found it particularly galling that it was American colonial corruption which supported the Madagascar pirates.[30]

The first major military assistance provided by Britain for the war against piracy came in the form of Captain Kidd's privately financed privateering expedition (1696–99). His failed mission was not inconsequential, since it demonstrated the futility of private efforts to suppress piracy and "helped to convince many of those in power that only a determined effort by the Royal Navy and an honest effort by colonial officials to enforce the king's writ at sea and ashore would eradicate piracy in the eastern seas."[31]

In 1698 the Treaty of Ryswick produced a lull in the war between Britain and France, allowing the British government in 1699 to send four naval vessels to Madagascar. Finding fifteen hundred pirates in one fortified and blockaded harbor, the Royal Navy commander—in hopes of avoiding a costly battle—sent an emissary to offer the pirates amnesty. Reluctant to take on the navy, most pirates accepted the offer. Those who did not dispersed among the native population. In the course of its subsequent year-long cruise in the eastern waters, the Royal Navy encountered not a single pirate ship. "By the middle of 1701 the pirate nation had all but disappeared."[32]

It was given new life, however, by the War of the Spanish Succession, in which the British Crown authorized privateering against Spanish and French shipping. Madagascar pirates now became "lawful brigands of the queen of England." After the war, thousands of men with up to ten years' experience in sea raiding—and often in nothing else—turned to piracy. With the Royal Navy still patrolling the Madagascar area, many of these pirate trainees moved to the Bahamas.[33]

The Americas

The suppression of piracy in the Americas entailed a two-pronged strategy: eliminating the colonies' propensity to engage in pirate trade and destroying the pirate stronghold in the West Indies. Reasons for colonial support for piracy were numerous. Pirates supplied goods otherwise unobtainable under the Navigation Acts. Luxury goods, especially from the East, were made available at bargain prices. Trade in pirated goods helped the colonies maintain a balance of trade with England, and provisioning pirate ships was a thriving business. Financing pirate voyages provided an investment opportunity for wealthy individuals with excess capital. Bribes, gifts, and protection money obtained from pirates supplemented the rather meager incomes of colonial officials.[34]

ELIMINATING COLONIAL SUPPORT

A crucial problem for Britain in suppressing piracy in the Americas was the weak judicial system in the colonies. Under the system established in 1536 with the first Act of Piracy, piracy trials could be held only in England, necessitating the transport of the accused, evidence, and witnesses from colonial areas to England. Time-consuming and expensive, this procedure led to "a general ignoring of the law, or the holding of what might be termed illegal trials for piracy in the colonies."[35] Apparently, large numbers of captured pirates "escaped" from colonial prisons,[36] but those who did stand trial were often acquitted by colonial juries who were reluctant to impose the death penalty on the accused.[37] Colonial magistrates and governors accepted bribes, or "exacted tribute," from pirates in exchange for the latter's freedom.[38]

Colonial support for piracy began to erode in mid-1699. By that time there were so many pirates off the southeast coast of the United States that there was not enough "glamorous plunder" for all, and they began seizing colonial commodities, like tobacco.[39] Moreover, the surveyor-general of the customs in the American colonies sent a report to the British government that described in great detail the corruption of colonial officials and its contribution to the problem of piracy.[40] It was probably the Captain Kidd affair that finally focused the British Parliament's attention on North America and led it to take seriously reports of the sorry state of affairs there.[41]

In 1699, Parliament passed the second Act of Piracy, which provided for the establishment of vice-admiralty courts in the colonies. Thus, persons charged with piracy would no longer have to be taken to England for trial and would be subject to admiralty laws rather than local, civil law. This act also provided that if a colony "refused to co-operate in working this system it would lose its charter. Another Act of the same sessions provided that each governor should be liable to punishment in England for offenses against the laws of the realm."[42]

In addition to these efforts at facilitating the prosecution of piracy, two other steps were taken. First, the Crown replaced the corrupt governor of

New York, Benjamin Fletcher. Protection and privateering commissions could be purchased from Fletcher, who "openly consorted with and entertained notorious pirates, some at his dinner table."[43] The governors of Pennsylvania, Massachusetts Bay, New Jersey, Delaware, and Maryland, as well as local merchants, were also intimately involved in piracy and competed with each other for the pirates' favor.[44] As Fletcher's replacement, the king selected the earl of Bellomont, naming him "not only governor of New York, Massachusetts, and New Hampshire, but also captain-general of all the military and naval forces in Connecticut, Rhode Island, and New Jersey as well."[45] Bellomont, "with special orders for putting down piracy,"[46] would be "the most powerful royal governor ever to serve in the colonies."[47]

Arriving in 1698, Bellomont's first challenge was to overcome the pro-piracy sentiment that pervaded both officialdom and the merchant community. Initially, the local customs collector, sheriff, and constables all refused to comply with Bellomont's orders to seize pirated goods, and the merchants resisted all his attempts to suppress the pirate trade. In response, Bellomont compiled such a mountain of evidence attesting to Fletcher's corruption that the latter was forced to defend himself against charges of piracy in Britain. Bellomont was then free to fire Fletcher's cronies from various public offices in New York. Meanwhile, the New York merchants sent a representative to England to protest Bellomont's actions, arguing that there was no organized pirate trade in New York and that Bellomont's ostensibly anti-piracy moves were a smoke screen for a pro-Dutch political agenda.[48] They requested that London recall Bellomont and send back Fletcher.[49]

This kind of protest was indicative of the success Bellomont's policies had achieved in suppressing the pirate trade. He forced New York pirate traders out of business by seizing their ships, which were loaded with plunder purchased from pirates, and dismissed pirate traders from political appointments.[50] The governor of Virginia and other colonial officials also joined in the anti-piracy campaign, so that by 1701 the pirate trade had "all but withered away."[51]

DESTROYING THE WEST INDIES PIRATE BASE

Despite this successful suppression of the colonial supporters of piracy, there remained the problem of eliminating the pirates themselves. Under the leadership of Henry Jennings, who was expelled from Jamaica for provoking a diplomatic incident with Spain, pirates established a base in the Bahamas (at New Providence) in 1716. "Within a few months this 'Pirate Republic' boasted a population of 2,000 desperate men." These pirates preyed on shipping in the West Indies, Virginia, and the Carolinas. Though the actual damage and disruption these pirates caused was small in comparison with that of the Madagascar pirates, for example, the British government's concern was considerable.[52]

One strategy was to offer inducements for individuals to give up piracy. A royal proclamation offering a pardon to those who would surrender themselves was read in New Providence in December of 1717. Upwards of 450 pirates, including Jennings, turned themselves in, but these small numbers indicated that further government action was required.[53]

Even before the September 1718 deadline for surrendering, the government decided to send Woodes Rogers, "a seaman of great repute," to eradicate the Bahamian pirates. The Royal Navy men-of-war which had been dispatched to the Caribbean and North America proved ineffectual. For one thing, the commanders refused to take orders from the colonial governors, who were most familiar with the pirates' operations. Moreover, naval commanders found that they could make a great deal of money by exploiting the merchants' fear of piracy. They could charge a fee for either escorting merchant ships or transporting the cargo themselves. When it became apparent that the Royal Navy was not up to the job, a group of English merchants leased the Bahamas from the Crown and petitioned the Crown to appoint Rogers as governor.[54] Their intention was to eradicate the pirates and repopulate the islands with European farmers and artisans.[55]

Rogers's reputation was such that on learning of his impending arrival, about half the Nassau pirates abandoned the region. Those who remained apparently believed that the Royal Navy would soon depart and Rogers, as the governor of a basically worthless colony, would soon fall into the pirate trade business to support himself.[56] Rogers arrived in July of 1718. The month before, Spain had driven English logwood cutters out of the Yucatán so that nine out of ten of the three thousand pirates in New Providence were unemployed cutters.[57]

With only one hundred soldiers and four Royal Navy men-of-war under his command, Rogers could hardly rely on force to suppress the pirate community. As an added incentive for people to voluntarily give up piracy, he allowed those who would accept the government's pardon to keep their ill-gotten gains. This was especially appealing to the more successful pirates, "who had already made their fortunes in the sweet trade and who were therefore now amenable to a more lawful life." For those who were not so fortunate, Rogers offered free plots of land. Neither this nor his attempt to recruit pirates into a militia proved successful, since pirates were not accustomed to the tedious work or discipline entailed in ordinary occupations.[58] Perhaps Rogers's most successful action was to neutralize two of the best-known pirate captains by granting them pardons and issuing them privateering licenses to defend New Providence.

His plan to establish a self-sufficient colony suffered a serious setback, however, when an epidemic killed most of the settlers and drove the Royal Navy from Nassau. With the departure of the Royal Navy, many pirates returned to their old ways, and Rogers faced the prospect that all his accomplishments would shortly come undone.[59]

The execution of two particularly famous pirates—Blackbeard and Bonnet—in the Carolinas provided a new deterrent to piracy.[60] At the same time, though he was not authorized by the Crown to do so, Rogers decided to try piracy cases in his own court rather than send suspects to Jamaica.[61]

At about this time, war broke out between Britain and Spain. The British Crown offered a new amnesty to Caribbean pirates and induced them to enlist as privateers against Spain. During the war, Rogers was able to rebuild the island's defenses, which, when no longer needed against the Spanish threat, were equally valuable against pirates. By mid-1729, piracy had been eradicated from the Bahamas. The remaining unreformed pirates moved to Jamaica and Hispaniola or to Madagascar.[62]

Madagascar II

Several successful pirates who departed Nassau upon learning of Rogers's appointment as governor sailed to Madagascar and set up bases there in 1718 and 1719. Their intention was to prey on Indian and East India Company shipping along the coast of Africa and on the Red Sea and Indian Ocean. Their success in attacking East India Company shipping led the company to appeal to the British government for help. This time the government responded quickly by sending four men-of-war to Madagascar. Both the company and the British government feared the reestablishment of a pirate base on Madagascar.[63]

Though the navy did not capture a single pirate, its mere presence drove most of the pirates out of the region. In fact, the danger of pirates' repeating their Madagascar-based exploits of the 1690s was practically nonexistent. Without the big pirate trade brokers and corrupt officials who had been eliminated from the North American colonies, there simply was no large and ready market for pirate plunder.[64] Moreover, the British Parliament enacted a law in 1721 that made trafficking with pirates and furnishing them with supplies crimes of piracy. Another law provided that merchant sailors who resisted pirate attacks would be rewarded and those who did not resist would be punished. Together with the suppression of markets for pirated goods, these laws contributed to the demise of eastern piracy and to driving unreformed pirates to the only remaining region where they might survive—the western coast of Africa. Nevertheless, the Golden Age of Piracy was effectively suppressed by 1730.[65]

This historical overview of European piracy reveals just how culpable states were in perpetuating it. The tediously repetitive process went like this: The state would authorize privateering, which was legalized piracy, during wartime. When the war concluded, thousands of seamen were left with no more appealing alternative than piracy. The state would make some desultory efforts to suppress the pirates, who would simply move somewhere else. With the outbreak of the next war, the state would offer blanket pardons to pirates who would agree to serve as privateers, and the process would start all over again.[66]

Thus, the practice of privateering produced the problem of piracy, as well as the difficulties in deciding the status of the corsairs. In this period, large-scale piracy was a European problem. It was Europeans who organized piracy. It was Europeans who were the main targets of piracy. And it was Europeans who provided the economic and legal infrastructure that supported piracy. At the heart of these matters was the process of state-building. Privateering reflected state rulers' efforts to build state power; piracy reflected some people's efforts to resist that project.

PROBLEMS WITH MERCENARISM

Mercenarism or, put differently, buying an army from the international system, did not present as many or as severe problems for states as did the other practices examined in this chapter. Many of the problems associated with the private contractors of earlier years were eliminated with the shift toward state "contracting." For example, no eighteenth-century leader faced the catastrophe that befell Milan's Duke Ludovico in 1500. His seven thousand Swiss mercenaries refused to fight the invading French army, which employed six thousand Swiss mercenaries. On the eve of battle, captains for the Milanese- and French-Swiss met and agreed that, because only the latter had official canton approval to serve, the former would abandon Ludovico.[67] Interstate agreement to sell or lease troops to one another eliminated this and other traditional drawbacks associated with mercenarism.

One problem that interstate agreements did not eliminate was desertion. In the U.S. War for Independence, for example, five thousand of Britain's German mercenaries deserted and settled in the United States.[68] In some cases desertion undoubtedly had something to do with the supplying state's methods of garnering its subjects for a mercenary force. For example, the prince of Waldech, in raising an army for Britain, "had to escort a disarmed regiment of his own subjects with mounted Jägers to the embarkation port to prevent desertions."[69]

But if the state's right to buy and sell armies was well established, the right of individuals to enlist in a foreign service was not settled. At issue was the state's responsibility for the actions of its subjects or citizens. Could a state claim neutrality in a particular international conflict while people within its jurisdiction chose to serve in the armed forces of one of the belligerents?

This was the essential problem posed by the mercenary. Was he to be regarded as a market actor, pursuing private ends through the sale of his labor? Or was he a political actor for whose actions his home state could be held accountable? But defining the problem of mercenarism in this way came only with the practical development of the concept of neutrality.

Contemporary neutrality, as a practice and a concept, is two-dimensional. On the one hand, the law of neutrality specifies the rights and duties of states. According to Hall,

> The belligerent is held to be under an obligation to respect the sovereignty of the neutral; the latter is under an equal obligation not to aid, and within certain limits to prevent others from aiding, the enemy of the belligerent in matters directly bearing on the war. If a wrong is done the only remedy is international.[70]

In other words, the rights and duties of neutral and belligerent *states* are the subject of international law. A neutral state has a passive duty to not provide assistance to either belligerent and an active duty to prevent the use of its territory for hostile acts. If a state violates these rules, the injured state seeks recourse through diplomatic channels.

The second aspect of neutrality involves the relationship between the belligerent state and individuals residing within the jurisdiction of the neutral state. Since "the only duty of the belligerent state is to beings of like kind" (i.e., other states), international law does not regulate the behavior of belligerents vis-à-vis neutral individuals or vice versa.[71] However, since the activities of individuals under its jurisdiction may threaten the neutral state's claim to neutrality, it devolves to the individual state to specify the rights and duties of individuals under its jurisdiction. These are embodied in neutrality laws, which are municipal laws. These laws "define the acts which the neutral state believes will compromise its *neutrality*, and provide the means for prosecuting and punishing those who commit such acts." As such, "they are strictly domestic laws and have no direct international effect."[72]

Municipal law can, however, indirectly produce an international effect. If a state's neutrality laws place tighter restrictions on individuals than is customarily done, other states will expect those laws to be enforced equally with regard to all belligerents. "So long also as the law is administered at all, foreign nations will each expect to reap the full benefit which has accrued to another from its operation; and any failure on the part of the neutral government to make use of its powers gives a ground for suspecting unfriendliness."[73] In other words, a lack of consistency in the enforcement by a neutral state of its municipal law suggests to other states a breach of its neutrality.

Despite protests from international law experts, then, there is a linkage between municipal and international law. International law reflects the universalistic customary practices of states, but the ultimate source of those practices is the individual state. Conversely, municipal law reflects the particular state's interpretation of more or less universalistic customary practices of the state system.

But this relationship between the two dimensions of neutrality is new; it emerged only in the nineteenth century. "Until the latter part of the eighteenth century the mutual relations of neutral and belligerent states were, on the whole, the subject of the least determinate part of international usage."[74] First used in an official document in 1408, the term *neutrality* originally denoted nonparticipation in war.[75] A declaration of neutrality meant only that the state would not directly engage in combat, and therefore that it claimed a special status in relation to the belligerents.

Up until the end of the seventeenth century, the rights and duties of neutrals were embodied in bilateral treaties of defensive alliance or of simple peace and friendship in which states agreed to limit their assistance to enemies of their treaty partners during wartime. Yet the principle of and practices associated with neutrality were so ill-defined that in his 1625 *Law of War and Peace*, Grotius "gave the subject no serious consideration." Grotius wrote that

> It is the duty of those who stand apart from a war to do nothing which may strengthen the side whose cause is unjust, or which may hinder the movements of him who is carrying on a just war; and in a doubtful case, to act alike to both sides, in permitting transit, in supplying provisions to the respective armies, in not assisting persons beseiged.[76]

As late as the end of the seventeenth century, there was no conception of neutrality as implying either impartiality or abstention. In fact, "powerful belligerents were so in the habit of performing acts of war within the territory of neutrals that there was little thought of the injured belligerents holding the neutral to account for them."[77]

Several treaties made in the late 1600s suggest that the most a state could expect from a neutral treaty partner was that "the latter should refrain from giving active help to the enemy of the belligerent, and should prevent his territory from being continuously used for hostile purposes." Such treaties might or might not stipulate what obligations to control its subjects that state had. So in practice, states not directly participating in a war were constrained only by their treaty obligations to the participants and their desire to remain outside the hostilities. Moreover, even eighteenth-century scholars of international law, such as Bynkershoek, Vattel, and Wolff, "say nothing indicating how far in their view a nation was bound to watch over the acts of its subjects."[78]

Apparently the first real practical challenge to this conception of neutrality came in 1788. At the same time as it was assisting Russia against Sweden according to its treaty obligations, Denmark "declared itself to be in a state of amity with Sweden." Sweden claimed that Denmark's assistance to Russia was inconsistent with the rights and duties of a neutral state, but Sweden's view was unique. Other states continued to make treaties based on the notion that nonparticipants could give assistance to their allies.[79]

According to Hall, three principles of neutrality did emerge during the eighteenth century.[80] First, a neutral could not commit any act that favored one belligerent's prosecution of the war. Second, belligerents were to respect the sovereignty of neutrals. Finally, a neutral should restrain other states and private individuals from using its territory and resources for hostile purposes, a much less fully recognized principle.

Underlying this emerging conception of sovereignty was the recognition that military service was not a pure international market commodity and the mercenary was not simply an economic actor. By the early years of the nineteenth century it was clear that individuals did not simply respond to market forces but to political concerns. A state's ability to procure military labor did not depend only on its ability to pay but on the popularity of its cause. For example, U.S. citizens were willing to serve the cause of republican France against the British, despite the U.S. central state's desire for neutrality in the Napoleonic Wars.

The full implications of this erosion of market incentives is illustrated by the British debate on a statute regulating the foreign enlistment of their subjects. The British government, the great employer of mercenary armies, took up the question of its own subjects' mercenary activities. According to its 1814 treaty with Spain, Britain agreed to prevent its subjects from serving with the armies of Latin Americans fighting for their independence.[81] "For the first time, Britain was a neutral in a great maritime war,"[82] and had to determine what kinds of controls over its subjects' military activities would be consistent with its claim to neutrality.

Britain's problem was that large numbers of British officers, demobilized from the previous war, had joined in the Latin American cause. In response, the British government notified these officers that their half-pay would be suspended if they joined a foreign army. This action proved inadequate as

> the disposition to enter into the service of the insurgents continued, and recruiting for their service was openly practised in the country. Soldiers were raised, regiments formed, uniforms of various descriptions prepared, considerable bodies openly embarked for South America, and it became necessary to think of some more effectual means of prevention.[83]

Extant British law forbade enlistment with a "foreign prince, state, or potentate," but not with insurgent groups.

Granting the belligerents equality of access to British military manpower was no solution, as it would not guarantee equality of outcome. This was expressly noted by Lord Bathurst during Parliament's debate on the Foreign Enlistment Act of 1819. As he put it (paraphrased by Hansard):

> Let it be supposed that we were engaged in a contest with our own colonies. . . . If, in the event of such an occurrence, France, who had, like ourselves, plenty of half-pay officers who would be glad to be employed, and plenty of disbanded soldiers, who would be eager also to be employed, should, whilst professing the most perfect neutrality, allow these officers and soldiers to enter into the service of our revolted colonies, and vessels for the same service to be fitted out in her ports, would it be very gratifying to us to be told by the French government, "we permit you in the same way to employ our officers, to enlist our soldiers, to fight your battles with your colonists, and to fit out our vessels for the same service, but unfortunately your cause is so unpopular in France, and the cause of liberty has so much the ascendant, that not a man will enlist under your banners, nor a vessel be furnished to you by its owners"—could this for a single moment be considered as a neutrality? and yet this was what had been proposed by those who had opposed this bill, to be the conduct to be adopted on our part.[84]

The act, which passed in 1819, forbade "any natural-born Subject" of the British Crown from enlisting in the army of any foreign entity, including that of "any Person or Persons exercising or assuming to exercise the Powers of Government in or over any Foreign Country."[85] This language was designed to cover insurgent groups, such as the Latin Americans.

Mercenarism reflected the democratization, marketization, and internationalization of military service. The effectiveness of this system is underscored by the fact that it flourished for about five centuries and persists in highly attentuated form to this day. Again the question is why such a successful practice was abandoned.

The answer offered here is that it produced unintended and undesirable consequences for interstate politics. The problem did not come from the demand side; states like Great Britain were more than happy to hire foreigners to fight their wars. Instead, the problem emerged on the supply side; a state that allowed its citizens or subjects to serve in a belligerent's military could not claim neutrality. In short, states began to hold one another accountable for the international actions of individuals under their sovereign jurisdictions. It was no longer acceptable to disclaim responsibility on the basis that individuals were pursuing their private interests. The threat was real; belligerents could reject the state's claim to neutrality and draw it into their war.

PROBLEMS WITH MERCANTILE COMPANIES

Of all the practices invented by the seventeenth-century state, those of the mercantile companies are the most interesting. Though the companies successfully spearheaded European imperialism in Asia, Africa, and America, they sometimes confronted state rulers with complex dilemmas. Armed with sovereign powers as they were, mercantile companies proceeded to exercise violence not only against "non-Christian" peoples, but against each other, against European states, and even against their home states.

Intercompany Conflicts

In 1618 the Dutch and English companies were engaged in open warfare in the Malay Archipelago. The English company's siege of the Dutch fort at Jakarta was broken by the arrival of a Dutch fleet that went on to attack English factories and ships all over the archipelago.[86]

Military conflict between the two companies was temporarily reduced by an accord in 1619. With this agreement, the Dutch company turned over large shares of the East Indian spice trade to the English company while the latter was to help pay for overhead expenses and contribute ships for a "defense fleet." The Dutch had reason to reach some accord with the English in the East Indies, since their truce with Spain was about to expire and they did not feel they could simultaneously fight the English company and Spain. Though formal peace between the companies was imposed, the Dutch commander who had just repulsed the English attack on Jakarta was furious and did what he could to sabotage the accord.

Moreover, the English company was slow to produce the defensive military aid it had agreed to provide. Nevertheless, the two companies did cooperate in the destruction of Portuguese fleets off the coast of India in 1621 and 1625.[87]

Relations between the Dutch and English companies were strained by the so-called Amboina Massacre, in which the Dutch governor of Amboina ordered the execution of the English company's chief factor on Amboina, nine other Englishmen, a Portuguese national, and ten Japanese mercenaries. The Dutch governor charged the group with planning to kill him and seize the Dutch company's fort. Families of the victims received compensation from the Dutch in 1654.[88]

In at least one instance a company's military force was turned on itself. Rebelling against the new governor's policies, the English East India Company's garrison at Bombay staged a coup d'état in 1683. "Their commander, Richard Keigwin, a former naval officer, imprisoned the deputy governor and, having been elected governor by popular vote, proceeded to govern the town 'in the name of the King.'" The king responded by sending a warship to secure Keigwin's surrender.[89]

Intercompany violence in Canada resulted from the Montreal-based North West Company's attempts to break the Hudson's Bay Company's fur trade monopoly. The North West Company, founded in 1783 by a group of merchants, "was not a chartered corporation and had no rights as such." Moreover, "it was never incorporated, and it was not a limited liability company," but what was known as a "common-law company." In essence it was a partnership for joint action without corporate responsibility.[90]

Open conflict between the two companies was sparked when the Red River Colony attempted to expel the North Westers. The North West Company had opposed the settlement of this colony from the beginning since it would be situated "across the vital route by which all North West transportation moved." Nevertheless, in 1811 the Hudson's Bay Company granted the colony 116,000 square miles of land, and soon Scottish settlers moved in.[91] In 1815 the North West Company instigated attacks on the colony that virtually destroyed the settlement. The Hudson's Bay Company organized "a shock brigade" of one hundred troops in Montreal, the colony's leader gathered a party of one hundred Swiss mercenaries demobilized after the War of 1812, and a fresh group of settlers prepared to resettle the colony. Meanwhile the North West Company planned its final assault on Red River, which resulted in the 1816 massacre of nearly all the settlers who had returned. The North West Company partners were arrested, bringing this incident to an end. Skirmishes between the companies continued until 1821, when the companies merged.[92] Thus ended intercompany conflict in Canada.

An obvious question this survey raises is the degree to which these extra-European conflicts coincided with wars in Europe. As the following discussion suggests, the companies' policies toward other Europeans in non-European regions generally did not reflect the stance of their home states. Company behavior was quite independent of European interstate relations.

Company Wars and European State Wars

Many of the companies' military engagements with other European states or companies did indeed coincide with war between their home states in Europe. The Dutch were at war with Spain and Portugal from 1618 to 1648, so the Dutch companies' attacks on Spanish and Portuguese posts in the East, the Americas, and elsewhere were consistent with their state's policy. And much of the conflict between the English and French companies in the East occurred during the Seven Years' War.

The companies did not, however, always comply with their obligation to not make war with other Christian princes without their sovereigns' permission, as their charters specified. In the eighteenth century, "European national wars spread more actively to the colonies, although neither in their beginnings nor their endings did they coincide between Europe and the other continents."[93]

The command ship of the English company's third expedition to the East (1608) was captured by the Portuguese, "despite the fact that England and Portugal were then at peace."[94] The joint Persian-English East India Company attack on the Portuguese at Hormuz (described below) occurred while England and Portugal were at peace. Thus, before the British government could give the company permission to assume the trade in that region, it had to determine whether the company had committed piracy. After the company paid the lord high admiral and the king ten thousand pounds each, on the grounds that they were legally due a share in the prizes, the company was given control of the Persian trade.[95]

The military conflicts between the Montreal French and the Hudson's Bay Company began before the Nine Years' War. France's "unprovoked attack" on a Hudson's Bay Company post in 1682 "in profound peace naturally raised an outcry in England, and the piratical expedition had to be disowned by the French King, who even promised satisfaction to the company."[96] The English East India Company's wars with France in India occurred between 1748 and 1756, when England and France were "at peace" in Europe.

Most of the Dutch company's conquest of the Malabar coast occurred after a peace accord was ratified in Europe in 1622.[97] When the Portuguese protested, the company "promised to restore the towns upon payment of sums far beyond Portugal's ability to pay."[98] Dutch East India Company attacks on the Portuguese in the East continued for a year after the 1641 truce between the Dutch and Portuguese was ratified in Europe. In fact a Dutch company fleet had to be sent to enforce the truce, its commander forcing his company colleagues to pay damages for the delay.[99]

Indeed, the directors of both the Dutch East and West India companies had argued against the acceptance of Portugal's peace proposal. The East India Company directors argued

"that the Honourable Company had waxed great through fighting the Portuguese, and for this reason they had now secured a monopoly of most of the seaborne trade in Asia: that they expected on average yearly return of between seven and ten millions; and that if they were allowed to continue in the same way, the above return would increase sharply." For the Dutch, as for other merchants of the period, war paid off handsomely.[100]

The Dutch company refused to return the island of Pularoon,[101] which they had taken in 1651, to the English "despite treaty obligations to return it."[102]

That the Dutch East India Company asserted its independence from state policy is not surprising, given the attitude of its governors. In 1644 the Seventeen told the States-General that "the places and strongholds which they had captured in the East Indies should not be regarded as national conquests but as the property of private merchants, who were entitled to sell those places to whomsoever they wished, even if it was to the King of Spain, or to some other enemy of the United Provinces."[103] In keeping with this attitude toward private property, the Dutch West India Company sold the island of Surinam to the city of Amsterdam in 1670.[104]

While they were willing to wage war when their states were at peace in Europe, the companies sometimes attempted to prevent European wars from spilling over into their areas of operation. For example, during the War of the Spanish Succession (1701–13), "the three rival East India Companies (i.e., Dutch, English and French) managed to maintain a kind of neutrality among themselves."[105] And as we will see, the French and English East India companies at least tried to impose neutrality in the East during the War of Austrian Succession. To a large extent, then, the companies carried on their own conflicts with each other independent of the state of relations between their home states in Europe. There was, however, a third target of company military actions—namely, European states themselves.

The Companies versus European States

The earliest target of the mercantile companies' violence was the Portuguese state. When the Dutch East India Company began its penetration of the Eastern trade, it frequently used military force to oust the Portuguese from their dominant position. The company's first territorial possession in the East Indies was a fort captured from the Portuguese in 1605.[106] In the following year, the company's second fleet defeated the Portuguese in the Strait of Malacca, but failed to capture the city of Malacca. Its third fleet was defeated by the Spanish in the Moluccas.[107] Between 1612 and 1615, the English East India Company succeeded in defeating Portuguese fleets off the west coast of India. As these victories occurred "in full view of Moghul officials," the Mogul was persuaded to permit the English company to trade at Surat, thus giving the company its first toehold in India.[108]

In 1621 the shah of Persia requested English East India Company assistance in seizing Hormuz from the Portuguese. The company agreed on the condition that they "were to have half the spoils, be forever free of customs, and share half the customs duties at Hormuz." In the following year, the joint English-Persian force took Hormuz and a Portuguese stronghold on a nearby island. An indication of the size of these battles is the death toll, which exceeded one thousand on the English-Persian side alone.[109]

During the 1630s the Dutch renewed their assault on the Portuguese, attacking them "everywhere from Goa and Malabar to Ceylon and Malacca." In 1635 the Dutch company instigated an annual blockade of the Portuguese stronghold at Goa, paralyzing Portuguese trade.[110] At the same time, the Portuguese, realizing they could not exclude both the English and the Dutch, signed a truce with the president of the English East India Company in Surat.[111] The Dutch company's capture of Malacca in 1641 "really dealt a mortal blow to the Portuguese empire in Asia."[112] As its English counterpart did with the Persians at Hormuz, the Dutch company fleet cooperated with Sinhalese forces in an effort to drive the Portuguese from Ceylon.[113] By 1657, after an eighteen-month siege of Colombo, the Dutch had completely driven the Portuguese from Ceylon. Between 1658 and 1663 the Dutch company seized control of all Portuguese ports on the Malabar coast of India.[114]

As France began its attempt to penetrate the East Indian trade, its company came into conflict with the Dutch company. Because the French companies were state enterprises, its conflicts with the other companies were not intercompany but, as in the Portuguese case, state-company conflicts. In 1672, after seizing the town of San Thomé,[115] the French found themselves under siege by the Dutch at sea and by the locals on land. Driven from San Thomé, the French continued to suffer at the hands of the Dutch company, which made prize of their ships and block-aded French shipping at Surat. In 1693 the Dutch seized the French fort at Pondichéry, on the east coast of India, so that after 1703, the French were not trading but simply making prizes of Dutch Indiamen.[116]

When war between England and France was declared in 1744, the French and English East India companies pressed for neutralization in the East,[117] but were unsuccessful largely because "the French and English naval commanders could not oblige them." Besides being obligated to fight, officers "felt very strongly the lure of prize money and the other private perquisites of their profession in the eighteenth century."[118] What followed was a succession of wars known as the Carnatic Wars.[119]

The First Carnatic War was sparked by the English company's seizure of French ships off the coast of India. In response, a French fleet from Mauritius laid siege in 1746 to Madras until the English surrendered. A large English fleet from England retook Madras in 1748 and laid siege to the French settlement at Pondichéry. The Treaty of Aix-la-Chapelle ended the war and returned Madras to the English.[120]

This war marked the beginning of a new phase in Eastern conflicts as it

> brought to India more European troops, stores, and artillery than had ever been seen there before. Moreover, the war had brought for the first time appreciable numbers of professionally trained military officers, not only En-glish and French, but Swiss and German mercenaries as well. Even the Euro-pean infantrymen, though recruited from slums and jails in the usual man-ner, were not as bad as the riffraff with which the East India companies had been manning the tiny garrisons of their factories.[121]

Hostilities were renewed in 1749 when the French and English backed opposing aspirants to the governorships of the Carnatic and Deccan. In this, the Second Carnatic War, there apparently were more shows of force than real battles. The French laid siege to Trichinopoly, where the leading opponent of their favorite candidate had taken refuge. Meanwhile the British promised the captive to "prepare for a full-scale offensive" against the French and their candidate. Though the English company sent a de-tachment to Trichonopoly, the French siege was not lifted until 1754. The English also occupied the capital of the Carnatic "without any serious opposition." The balance of forces between the two companies resulted in a stalemate that was broken through the intervention of the companies' directors in Europe.[122]

Exasperated with the cost of the military buildup, the directors ordered their people in India to negotiate a settlement. In the course of the negoti-ations the French state decided that it was not in its best interest to fight the English in India. The company, being a creature of the French state, was thus forced to make large concessions to the English company. This produced a treaty between the companies in 1754.[123]

> The treaty concluded peace between the two rivals and outwardly acknowl-edged the balance of forces between the two companies, by agreeing to leave each company in possession of the territories which it had actually occupied at the time of the treaty, and enjoining them not to interfere in the quarrels of the Indian rulers.[124]

The Third Carnatic War began in 1756 with the outbreak of the Seven Years' War in Europe. The English company immediately seized an important French settlement in Bengal and, in retaliation, the French attacked English establishments on the east coast of India. This time the French state "resolved to strike an important blow in India" and sent reinforcements to the French company. With the return of the English fleet from Bengal to southern India, the war began in earnest. The French seized numerous English forts and settlements but failed to take Madras, due to a lack of money and the naval commander's refusal to sail against the English stronghold as the army commander wished. An English attack on the French fleet in 1758 drove the latter from the Indian Ocean.

Meanwhile the French continued to seize English settlements, leaving the English company with only three posts in the Carnatic. In late 1758 the French laid siege to Madras by land, but the siege was ended early in the next year with the return of the English fleet. An English army then advanced southward along the east coast, driving the French from the Deccan and attacking them in the Carnatic. A major defeat of the French naval forces led the French fleet to leave India for good. In 1761 Pondichéry surrendered and the remaining French settlements on the Malabar coast fell to the English. "Nothing was left to the French in India."[125]

It is interesting to note that the fall of Pondichéry provoked conflict between the English company and its home government. Despite the fact that government military forces were largely responsible for driving out the French, the company's governor at Madras demanded that Pondichéry be turned over to the East India Company as its property. The army and naval officers on the scene refused. After the company threatened to withhold "subsistence either of the King's troops or of the French prisoners," the government acquiesced. Henceforth, the government and company agreed that the company would receive territories taken by government forces, but would reimburse the government for the expense.[126]

Mercantile companies also used military force against European states in the Western Hemisphere. In 1686 the Montreal-based Compagnie du Nord convinced the governor of New France to send a military force to capture the Hudson's Bay Company's forts. In quick succession, the company's three forts fell to the French. To retake them, the company sent two warships under the command of its "first and only Admiral." When the French defeated this force, the company in 1693 sent four ships, armed with 82 guns and 213 marines, which recaptured Fort Albany. The following year the French took the York Factory, which was recovered ten months later by the English through the actions of three Royal Navy frigates. "In the summer of 1697, the king of France dispatched the most formidable fleet ever sent to Hudson Bay." There it engaged an English fleet composed of two Hudson's Bay Company armed freighters and a Royal Navy man-o'-war. In "the greatest Arctic sea battle in North American history," the French won a decisive victory and retained the York Factory until it was returned to the Hudson's Bay Company by the Treaty of Utrecht.[127]

A particularly fascinating incident occurred when the Hudson's Bay Company turned its guns on the English state's official forces. In 1741 George II approved a Royal Navy expedition to search for the Northwest Passage. Since the fleet would have to spend the winter on Hudson Bay, the Royal Navy pressured the company into agreeing to accommodate the fleet through the winter. Yet "the intensity of the HBC's proprietary impulse" was such that when the two ships arrived at the company's fort, the company's factor "promptly fired a volley across the ships' bows." The naval commander eventually negotiated permission to house his crew in a company building.[128]

Dutch West India Company privateer fleets attacked Spanish and Portuguese vessels in the Western Hemisphere. In 1624 and 1627 the company attacked Bahia and in 1628 captured the Spanish silver fleet. "The enormous booty of eleven million guilders not only earned the shareholders a dividend of 75 per cent, but also put the directors in a position to devise grand new schemes." A large expedition captured Recife in 1630, marking the beginning of the company's attempts to convert itself "from a privateering company into a colonial power." Company efforts to expand its territory in Brazil were strenuously resisted by the Portuguese, necessitating a substantial increase in the company's military expenditures. As a result the States-General were compelled to subsidize the company beginning in 1631. With Portugal's achievement of independence in 1640, the Portuguese nationals living under Dutch rule revolted, and the Dutch were quickly driven to only a few fortifications on the Brazilian coast. A relief expedition sent by the States-General saved Recife from falling to the Portuguese in 1646. From this point, the company was completely dependent on state military support.[129]

While no doubt incomplete, this catalog of instances of company military conflicts with European states indicates the extent and intensity of the companies' military actions against their own and other European states. The unintended consequences of delegating sovereignty to the companies included the companies' use of violence against each other, European states with which their home states were at peace, their home states, and even their fellow company employees. Some companies used violence to procure wealth and defend their private property, which, in several cases, consisted of entire countries. Others engaged in piracy or privateering, both for profit and to weaken their home states' enemies.

Again, at the heart of these practices was the state-building process. To attain the wealth and power promised by overseas expansion, states empowered nonstate actors to exercise violence. State economic and military capabilities alone were insufficient or their use and expansion politically constrained. Turning to the market and nonstate actors was a way to evade these constraints. As an incentive to nonstate actors to undertake foreign adventures, state leaders granted them sovereign powers that placed the mercantile companies literally above the law. They engaged in piracy, extortion, subversion, and war in contradiction of any domestic or international law in the European state system. Violence was blatantly deployed in the defense of private property. Instead of interests taming passions, interests were pursued with passion. So much for the *doux commerce*.[130]

One problem was that the private property interests of the companies often conflicted with the political interests of the state, as when the Dutch East India Company claimed the right to sell its territory to enemies of the United Provinces, or when the British East India Company demanded that the Royal Navy cede Indian territory to the company. When push came to shove, the companies used violence against their home states.

State leaders were direct beneficiaries of the wealth and power generated by the mercantile companies. Plausible deniability served them well—but only to a point. As we will see in the next chapter, the contradiction between granting sovereignty to nonstate actors and disclaiming state responsibility for their actions emerged as a major political issue within the European state system. By the midnineteenth century, balance-of-power calculations among European states necessitated the abandonment of the fiction that nonstate actors could govern entire subcontinents as their private property.

CONCLUSION

The authorization of nonstate violence nicely served state interests for several centuries, yet it also generated a host of problems. At the heart of these problems were fundamental issues of authority. If a sovereign ruler had the authority to commission privateers, then the corsairs raised the question of who was to be recognized as sovereign in North Africa and Malta. If nonstate violence emanated from territory over which no recognized ruler claimed sovereignty, pirate commonwealths raised the question of who should be held accountable for their actions. If the state could delegate its sovereign powers to nonstate actors, the mercantile companies raised the question of who was sovereign over the territories that the companies claimed as their private property. If individuals could join the foreign army of their choice, then mercenaries raised the question of who had the sovereign power to make war.

These practices also weakened the links between a state's declared policy of being at peace or at war with another state and the actions of its subjects beyond its borders. Pirates went about their business regardless of the conflicts among their home states. Their targets were selected on the basis of their wealth and vulnerability, not their home state's policies. Mercenaries served foreign causes for economic or political reasons, regardless of their home states' declared position on a particular conflict. Mercantile companies fought wars with each other and even used violence against their home states when it served their economic or political interests. Their actions sometimes coincided with official state policy but were more often independent of war and peace conditions prevailing in Europe.

Finally, the unintended consequence of authorizing nonstate violence was the empowering of individuals to act independently of their home state. As all of these cases indicate, the ties between the state and its subjects were tenuous; given the chance, individuals would express their independence from state goals, interests, and policies, and go their own way. Ultimately, pirates, mercenaries, and mercantile companies challenged the sovereignty of the nascent national state itself.

CHAPTER FOUR

Delegitimating State-Authorized
Nonstate Violence

BY THE NINETEENTH CENTURY, European state rulers were aware of the problems outlined in chapter 3. At the same time, the principal cause of those problems—authorizing nonstate violence—was a customary practice that it had been going on for hundreds of years. Eliminating problems caused by historically legitimate practices would be inherently difficult. Even if state rulers could agree that a particular practice was a problem, the solution was not obvious. In most cases, resolution of the problems came as an unintended outcome of day-to-day diplomacy.

This chapter focuses on the context in which each practice was delegitimated at the interstate level and on the particular solution state rulers settled on in each case. Analysis of each instance of nonstate violence is aimed at determining (*a*) why one or more states came to regard that practice as a problem and (*b*) how new norms governing the practice were developed. The problems of nonstate violence were eliminated when states stopped authorizing it. As this chapter illustrates, the process was ad hoc. The eradication of nonstate violence was not a goal but the unintended consequence of interstate politics.

THE ABOLITION OF PRIVATEERING

Analytically, the easiest case to understand is that of privateering. European states negotiated an end to the practice, producing a formal international agreement to give up the right to authorize this form of nonstate violence. Yet this outcome was neither foreordained nor simply the result of the powerful imposing their interests on others. As we will see, there was at least one alternative approach to dealing with privateering. The solution that was chosen resulted from a bargain involving real trade-offs between states of vastly different power capabilities.

As we have seen, problems with privateering became evident early on, but perhaps the first major protest against privateering that produced results was lodged by Spain. When Spain and Britain's James I made peace but Raleigh continued his depredations in Spanish America, the Spanish ambassador protested and Raleigh was arrested and later executed.[1] Yet after 1744, when British merchants became major investors in privateering,[2] the same old abuses recurred. The next major protest by a victim of British privateers was made by Prussia. In response to a British privateer attack on one of his subject's ships, Frederick seized money loaned him by English subjects (the Silesian loan), and used the interest to indemnify the injured merchants.[3]

Another source of protest was English insurance companies. With British privateers out of control in 1758, insurance company losses mounted. The government responded by placing a minimal size on privateering vessels and requiring that privateers post a proper security. This eliminated the "little fishermen-privateers," who were most out of control, and improved the conduct of the larger ones.[4] Moreover, the British government itself suffered from its privateers' attacks on neutral and even British commerce. A British naval historian has remarked that during the Seven Years' War, "the action of our privateers was outrageous beyond endurance." Some of these "went so far as to capture vessels which had just been released by our own prize-courts."[5] It seems that "nothing but the most strenuous exertions, penalties by Act of Parliament, cajolery by Government, pay in return for submission to naval discipline, restoration of prizes, enabled Britain to pacify the neutrals."[6]

The next major challenge to the practice of privateering came with the Armed Neutralities of 1780 and of 1800. When the British seized two Russian ships carrying hemp and flax and detained them for a year, Catherine II issued a document on 26 February 1780 "which declared that all neutral vessels might, of right, navigate freely from port to port and along the coasts of nations at war; which laid down the principle of Free Ships Free Goods, and defined contraband so as to exclude materials of naval construction, besides denouncing as invalid all 'paper' or ineffective blockades." Other neutrals, including Denmark, Sweden, Austria, Portugal, the Two Sicilies, and Holland, adopted the Russian declaration, and since they agreed to defend the principles with force if necessary, their arrangement became known as the Armed Neutrality. The second Armed Neutrality grew out of the renewal of this agreement in December of 1800. This led to an Anglo-Russian convention of June 1801, by which Russia gave up its insistence on the principle of free ships, free goods and Britain gave up the Rule of 1756, "conceding the immunity of convoyed vessels from search by privateers."[7]

So while friendly states, neutrals, and insurance companies periodically defined privateering as a problem, their protests only resulted in the imposition of tighter controls on privateering. It was only when the greatest commercial and military naval power—Great Britain—defined privateering as a problem that it was permanently abolished.

On 16 April 1856, the governments of France, Britain, Russia, Prussia, Austria, Sardinia, and Turkey signed the Treaty of Paris. Attached to this document was the Declaration of Paris, whose intent was "to establish a uniform doctrine" on "Maritime Law in time of War." With this, the signatories declared that

1. Privateering is, and remains abolished;
2. The Neutral Flag covers Enemy's Goods, with the exception of Contraband of War;
3. Neutral Goods, with the exception of Contraband of War, are not liable to capture under Enemy's Flag;
4. Blockades, in order to be binding, must be effective, that is to say, maintained by a force sufficient really to prevent access to the coast of the enemy.[8]

The agreement provided that states not attending the Congress of Paris be invited to accede to the Declaration, and that the provisions would be binding only on those states which signed or acceded to it. At the suggestion of Count Walewski, president of the Congress and formulator of the Declaration, the signatories also agreed that the four principles were indivisible,[9] and thus "that the Powers which have signed or may accede to it shall not enter for the future, into any arrangement concerning the law of neutrals in time of war, which does not rest on all four of the principles of the said declaration."[10] This last resolution "was not to have any retroactive effect nor to invalidate existing conventions."[11]

In the view of some international legal experts,[12] the Declaration reflected more of a travesty of than a contribution to international law. The third and fourth principles were well established in international law and "perfectly settled" in prior practice.[13] In other words, these two were simply declarations of what was already embodied in international law. What legal scholars find objectionable is the Declaration's linkage of these established elements of international law with the first two principles, which, in effect, *created* new international law. While all but two states accepted the principle that neutral flags protect enemy goods (principle 2), one of those two states was Britain.[14] Britain had traditionally exerted its right as a belligerent to make prize of enemy goods on neutral ships, regarding it as a mainstay of its naval supremacy. During the House of Lords' debate on the British government's decision to sign the Declaration of Paris, one critic stated that the government proposed to

surrender a right [i.e., to seize enemy goods on neutral ships] which belonged to us, which was established as a right by all jurists of earlier days, which was recognized by all jurists of modern times, which has been upheld by every statesman of importance in this country down to the latest, and which it was reserved for the present Government to throw away, although Pitt and Grenville and Canning successively declared it to be the mainstay of the naval power of England.[15]

Thus, the second provision of the Declaration could hardly be regarded as an established element of international law when the world's most powerful naval power regularly asserted its right to the contrary.

Even worse was the statement that "privateering is and remains abolished." As the U.S. State Department put it,

> The right to resort to privateers is as clear as the right to use public armed ships, and as uncontestable as any other right appertaining to belligerents. The policy of that law has been occasionally questioned, not, however, by the best authorities; but the law itself has been universally admitted, and most nations have not hesitated to avail themselves of it; it is as well sustained by practice and public opinion as any other to be found in the Maritime Code.[16]

In fact, at about the same time as the Declaration was being formulated, a text on international law was published in France which declared that

> the issuing of letters of marque, therefore, is a constantly customary belligerent act. Privateers are *bonâ-fide* war-vessels, manned by volunteers, to whom, by way of reward, the Sovereign resigns such prizes as they make, in the same manner as he sometimes assigns to the land forces a portion of the war contributions levied on the conquered enemy.

It is true that neither France nor Britain had issued letters of marque during the Crimean War. This meant that they had not authorized privateering since the Napoleonic Wars—a period of more than forty years.[17] But of course this unilateral and voluntary decision on the part of only two states not to engage in privateering in one war was not sufficient to make privateering a violation of international law.

The explanation for this attempt to link the reaffirmation of well-established principles with the creation of new and controversial ones is simple: The Declaration of Paris was the result of a political deal. On one side were all the lesser, and usually neutral, naval powers whose interest it was to end the British practice of interdicting neutral ships in search of contraband. With no international agreement on what constituted contraband, British admiralty courts, in accordance with the government's policy of harassing neutral commerce, tended to apply a rather broad definition of contraband.[18] This practice provoked the Armed Neutralities of 1780 and 1800.

On the other side was the British government, whose principal interest was in abolishing privateering. As Lord Palmerston argued in a letter to the queen:

> With regard to the proposal for an engagement against privateering, it seems to the Cabinet that as Great Britain is the Power which has the most extensive commerce by sea all over the world, which Privateers might attack,

and has on the other Hand the largest Royal Navy which can do that which Privateers would perform, Great Britain would find it for her Interest to join in an agreement to abolish Privateering. In Fact during the last war with France though the French Navy was cooped up in its Ports British Commerce suffered very materially from French Privateers fitted out in Foreign Ports.[19]

Not only had French privateers inflicted considerable damage on British commerce during the Napoleonic Wars, but at the outbreak of the Crimean War, Britain learned that the Russians were seeking U.S. permission to issue letters of marque to U.S. citizens.[20] Privateering was "the weapon of the weaker naval Power,"[21] and as such was the only real threat to British naval supremacy.

What Count Walewski did in proposing the new principles of naval warfare, and in making their adoption indivisible, was to offer a package that addressed the major concerns of both sides. None of the seven powers was averse to the prohibition on privateering. France's naval power was second only to that of Britain, so its reliance on privateering was diminishing.[22] Traditionally, Russia, Prussia, Austria, and Sardinia were not privateering states, so they had no objection to ending the practice, and Turkey, as a sort of junior member of the European state system, was not in a position to object to what the "powers" decided.[23] The ban on privateering was apparently a price worth paying for Britain's abandoning its right to interdict neutral ships in search of enemy contraband.

Though it is not clear exactly what motivated Count Walewski to propose the Declaration, it is certainly the case that he seized the opportunity to formulate a deal consistent with the major interests of each state, but which at the same time did not violate the interests of any. Lurking in the background, however, was a third issue, which the Declaration ignored, in large part because the major proponent of a change in this aspect of international practice—the United States—was not a participant in the congress. This was the issue of exempting the private property of a belligerent's *subjects* from seizure on the high seas. The U.S. position was that it would agree to a ban on privateering only if this exemption were adopted as a principle of naval warfare. And, indeed, when invited to accede to the Declaration of Paris, the United States declined.[24]

By 1854 the United States had signed treaties with some twenty countries which provided that free ships make free goods (principle 2) but which did not ban privateering (principle 1).[25] At the same time, the United States circulated a proposal to all the maritime powers asking them to assent to the free ships, free goods principle. However, apparently most of these states consulted with the British, who, of course, counseled them to reject the U.S. proposal unless a ban on privateering were

TABLE 4.1
Accessions to the Declaration of Paris

State	Year
Anhalt-Dessau-Coethen	1856
Argentine Confederation	1856
Baden	1856
Bavaria	1856
Belgium	1856
Brazil	1858
Bremen	1856
Brunswick	1857
Chile	1856
Denmark	1856
Ecuador	1856
Frankfort	1856
Germanic Confederation	1856
Greece	1856
Guatemala	1856
Hamburgh	1856
Hanover	1856
Haiti	1856
Hesse-Cassel	1856
Hesse-Darmstadt	1856
Lubeck	1856
Mecklenburg-Schwerin	1856
Mecklenburg-Strelitz	1856
Mexico[a]	
Modena	1856
Uruguay[b]	
Nassau	1856
Netherlands	1856
New Grenada	1856
Oldenburg	1856
Parma	1856
Peru	1857
Portugal	1856
Roman States	1856
Saxe-Altenburg	1856
Saxe-Coburg-Gotha	1856
Saxe-Meiningen	1856
Saxe-Weimar	1856
Saxony	1856
Sicilies	1856
Spain[a]	
Sweden and Norway	1856
Switzerland	1856

TABLE 4.1 (cont)

State	Year
Tuscany	1856
United States[c]	
Wurtemberg	1856

Source: Edward Hertslet, *The Map of Europe by Treaty* (London: Butterworths, 1875), 2:1284.

[a] Mexico and Spain acceded to all provisions except that dealing with privateering.

[b] "Uruguay assented, subject to Ratification" by its legislature.

[c] As Indicated in note 24, the United Sates, it is believed, never acceded.

included. Prussia actually gave that response to the United States. Clearly the British were setting up a scenario in which the United States would be alone in its defense of privateering.[26] As Britain's secretary of war put it, "If the Americans stood out on a question of privateering against a Resolution adopted by the Congress, they will be isolated on a point in which the whole civilized world will be against them."[27] And indeed, as of March 1858, forty-two of the forty-six states invited to accede to the Declaration of Paris had done so (see table 4.1).

In this case, state leaders knew precisely what they wanted to achieve. They intended to abolish privateering and did so with a formal international agreement. Against five hundred years of customary practice, they gave up the right to authorize this form of nonstate violence. An alternative to this approach, which the United States and twenty other states supported, was to reduce the problems created by privateering by narrowing the range of legitimate targets to state property. In other words, the state's right to commission privateers would remain, while private property would be exempt from attack. It is difficult to predict how things would have turned out had the U.S. position been adopted. Undoubtedly states would have found a way to disguise their property as being private and, therefore, not subject to attack. Clearly, though, the ban on privateering was not a foregone conclusion; expanding state regulation and control was a viable option.

Privateering after 1856

The extent to which states complied with the ban on privateering is a separate issue. Five years after the Declaration of Paris, the Civil War in the United States began. In this situation, the attitude of the U.S., British, and French governments "underwent a change which can only be described as remarkable."[28] For the first time, the U.S. government found itself in the position of being the stronger naval power (vis-à-vis the Confederate states), and the French and British in the role of neutrals. The United States attempted to accede to the Declaration of Paris, thereby forcing Britain and France to treat Confederate privateers as pirates.

This effort failed, since Britain and France had already recognized the Confederacy as a belligerent and had declared their neutrality in the war. With the Confederate states as bona fide belligerents, the Washington government could not "sign away their belligerent rights."[29] As nonsignatories to the Declaration, the Confederate privateers were entitled, under international law, to be treated as "armed vessels of a belligerent."[30] So although the United States did not commission privateers during the war, the Confederacy did, though these were legally considered to be "commissions in the 'Confederate navy.'"[31]

The next post-1856 case involving the issue of privateering was the Spanish-Chilean War (1865–66). Here it was agreed that although Chile had acceded to the Declaration, it was legally permitted to commission privateers for use against Spain, which was not a party to the agreement.[32]

Prussia's announced intention to raise a "volunteer navy" for use in the Franco-Prussian War provoked the French to ask the British government whether this might not constitute a violation of the ban on privateering. The Law Officers of the Crown were of the opinion that "there were substantial differences between a volunteer navy as proposed by the Prussian Government and the privateers which it was the object of the Declaration to suppress."[33] Since the volunteer navy was not in fact formed,[34] the issue in this case was moot.[35]

In the first case of an important interstate maritime conflict after 1856, the Spanish-American War of 1898, neither party engaged in privateering. After Congress declared war, the United States issued a presidential proclamation in which it declared that it would abide by all of the provisions of the Declaration of Paris, including the ban on privateering.[36] Spain maintained its right to issue letters of marque but limited itself to organizing "for the present a service of auxiliary cruisers of the navy composed of ships of the Spanish mercantile navy which will co-operate with the latter for the purposes of cruising and which will be subject to the statutes and jurisdiction of the navy."[37]

On the whole, then, compliance with the Declaration of Paris's ban on privateering was such that "the right to use them has now almost disappeared from the world."[38]

THE DELEGITIMATION OF MERCENARISM

Mercenarism became an issue in interstate politics during the Napoleonic Wars. For U.S. state leaders, the prime objective was to avoid being drawn into the war, a goal that required a strict policy of neutrality. In its War for Independence, the United States had signed a Treaty of Amity and Commerce with France, which "bound the United States to admit into its ports French ships with their prizes of war" while excluding other countries' ships bearing prizes captured from France, and to grant asylum to only French warships.[39] With the outbreak of war in 1793, the United States faced the question of how to fulfill its treaty obligations to France without being drawn into the war itself.

This became a practical problem when the French minister in Charleston began engaging U.S. citizens as privateers—naval mercenaries—to attack English shipping. He also instigated or supported a number of schemes in which U.S. citizens would "liberate" Louisiana and other territories from Spain.[40] There is some evidence that the British were supporting similar plans for attacks on French territory in America.[41]

When an English ship was seized and condemned as legal prize by the French consul in Charleston, British statesmen protested to the United States that the seizure was illegal and that privateering for France was a violation of U.S. neutrality.[42] The British also suggested that the United States might consider France's granting of commissions to *American* privateers as a violation of U.S. sovereignty.[43] While the French contended that their activities complied with the terms of the Franco-American Treaty of 1788, Secretary of State Jefferson disagreed. He argued that while the treaty forbade countries other than France to fit out privateers, sell their prizes, or buy provisions in U.S. ports, it did not grant France the right to do so. In other words, Jefferson contended that excluding everyone but France from privateering activities was not equivalent to granting France permission to do so. U.S. control over French privateering was a separate question that the United States could decide based on the particular context and circumstances.

More germane to the present discussion is Jefferson's argument that "the granting of military commissions, within the United States, by any other authority than their own, is an infringement on their sovereignty, and particularly so when granted to their own citizens, *to lead them to commit acts contrary to the duties they owe their own country*."[44] In other words, while France was violating U.S. sovereignty, it was also undermining the U.S. central state's control over its citizens.

The U.S. view of the concept of neutrality was officially and publicly enunciated in President Washington's address to Congress in December of 1792, and was put into practice in August of 1793. On 7 August, Jefferson requested that France "effect restitution of all prizes taken by (such) privateers and brought into the ports of the United States," and asserted that henceforth the United States would prevent French privateering activities within its jurisdiction. In a September letter to the British, Jefferson accepted U.S. responsibility for compensating Britain for the three vessels captured by French privateers, but asserted that since the United States had begun enforcing its neutrality on 7 August, it would not make compensation for vessels seized after that date. And, indeed, the United States did begin taking active steps to terminate French privateering; it arrested privateers, interrupted the sale of prizes, detained ships, and issued instructions to customs officials to enforce U.S. neutrality. Thus, "there is no evidence that after August 7, 1793, other privateers were fitted out in the ports of the United States."[45]

U.S. Neutrality Laws

These policies were codified in the Neutrality Act of 1794.[46] The act prevented "citizens or inhabitants of the United States from accepting commissions or enlisting in the service of a foreign state, and [served] to prohibit the fitting out and arming of cruisers intended to be employed in the service of a foreign belligerent, or the reception of any increased force by such vessels when armed."[47] Moreover, it forbade anyone (with two exceptions)[48] in the United States from enlisting people in the service of a foreign state and prohibited all persons in the United States from "setting on foot" military expeditions against states with which the United States was at peace.[49]

A subsequent act, passed in 1817, added colonies, districts, and people to princes and states as foreign entities to which the U.S. neutrality laws applied.[50] All U.S. neutrality laws were collected into the Neutrality Act of 1818, which, with some amendments, remains the law of the United States.[51]

The neutrality laws made it a high misdemeanor for a U.S. citizen to accept and exercise a commission to serve another state engaged in war with a state friendly to the United States.[52] They also prohibited all residents of the United States from enlisting in a foreign military service and from hiring other residents to enlist. These laws did not prevent a citizen from leaving the country to join a foreign army. Moreover, they did not forbid individuals from inducing others to go abroad in order to enlist in a foreign army, since this would have violated the free-speech guarantees of the U.S. Constitution.[53] To violate these provisions of the neutrality laws, a U.S. citizen would have to accept *and exercise* a commission within the jurisdiction of the U.S. state. An individual violated the enlistment provisions only if he enlisted or hired others to enlist in a foreign army while in the United States.

The neutrality laws also made it illegal for individuals within the jurisdiction of the U.S. central state to begin, "set on foot, or provide or prepare the means for a military expedition against a state with which the United States is at peace." This seems to preclude individuals from raising an army within the United States even if it is not done to serve the interests of a foreign political entity. In other words, individuals cannot raise a military force with which to pursue their own private interests. "The Neutrality Act of 1794 was the first domestic law in the world to deal specifically with the problem of hostile expeditions against foreign countries, and it served as a model for England and other nations."[54] This provision produced its own enforcement problems, as we will see in chapter 5.

In summary, the neutrality laws forbid anyone other than the U.S. central state from raising an army within the territory of the United States to attack a state with which the United States is at peace. They prohibit individuals from selling their services as soldiers to another state while within the jurisdiction of the United States. Individuals are also forbidden from hiring others into the service of a state when the transaction is completed within the United States. Finally, individuals are prohibited from organizing military expeditions against foreign political entities in their own private interests. In short, no one can raise an army within the jurisdiction of the United States with the intention to commit hostile acts against a state friendly to the United States.[55]

The Globalization of Restrictions on Mercenarism

International law experts regard the U.S. Neutrality Act of 1794 as a watershed in the development of the concept of neutrality.[56] For the first time, the rights and duties of a neutral state were permanently codified in municipal law. Previously these rights and duties were spelled out in bilateral treaties, proclamations, and edicts that were of a temporary nature, dealing with particular states, wars, and forms of assistance. In short, neutrality was not so much a principle as a set of policies related to specific states and wars. It was the United States that first attempted to specify a *universal* doctrine of neutrality and to institutionalize practices consistent with the doctrine.[57]

TABLE 4.2
Legal Restrictions on Foreign Military Service

Country	Year	Proscribed Activities
Argentina	1921	General
Austria	1803/52	Recruitment
Belgium	1807	Enlistment
Bolivia	1834/1903	General
Brazil	1890	General
UK/Ireland	1819/70	Recruitment + enlistment
Australia	1874	Recruitment
Canada	1937	Recruitment + enlistment
Chile	1874/1934	Recruitment + enlistment
Colombia	1936	General + recruitment
Costa Rica	1889	Enlistment
Cuba	1936	Recruitment
Czechoslovakia	1920	Enlistment
Denmark	1803/19	Recruitment + enlistment
Dominican Republic	1884	General
Ecuador	1906	General
El Salvador	1904	Recruitment
France	1804	Enlistment
Germany		
Hanover	1840	Recruitment
Reich	1871	Recruitment
Greece	1834	Recruitment
Guatemala	1889	General
Haiti	1826	General
Honduras	1906	Recruitment
Iraq	1924	Enlistment
Italy		
Sardinia	1859	Recruitment
Tuscany	1853	Recruitment + enlistment
Papal States	1832	Recruitment
Unified	1864/1912	Enlistment
	1938	Recruitment + enlistment (military men only)
Liberia	1914	Recruitment + enlistment
Luxembourg	1879	General
Mexico	1886	Enlistment
Netherlands	1881/92	Recruitment + enlistment
Nicaragua	1891	General
Norway	1902/37	General + enlistment
Panama	1922	Recruitment
Paraguay	1910	Recruitment
Peru	1924	General

TABLE 4.2 (cont)

Country	Year	Proscribed Activities
Poland	1932	General
Portugal	1852	Recruitment + enlistment
Spain	1882	Recruitment + enlistment
	1932	Recruitment
Sweden	1804/1904	Recruitment + enlistment
Switzerland	1853/59	Recruitment + enlistment
Turkey	1936	Recruitment
Russia	1845	Enlistment
United States	1794	Recruitment + enlistment
Uruguay	1889	Recruitment
Venezuela	1912/26	Recruitment
Yugoslavia	1924	General

Source: Francis Deàk and Philip C. Jessup, eds., A Collection of Neutrality Laws, Regulations and Treaties of Various Countries, 2 vols. (Washington, D.C.: Carnegie Endowment for International Peace, 1939).

Evidence that U.S. neutrality practices became "the standard of conduct which is now adopted by the community nations"[58] is presented in table 4.2. Between 1794 and 1938, forty-nine states enacted some form of permanent legal control over their citizens' or subjects' foreign military service. Many others passed controls of a temporary nature.

Britain instigated a major wave of antimercenarism legislation in the late nineteenth century. In response to the Franco-Prussian War, the British instituted the Foreign Enlistment Act of 1870. It was the government's recent and unfortunate experience in the American Civil War that led it to believe that new legislation was needed.[59] The new act prohibited enlistment by any British subject in the military service of any state "at war with any foreign State at peace with Her Majesty."[60] So, unlike the 1819 legislation, the act of 1870 applied not only to natural-born Britons but to all subjects of the British Crown. Moreover, while the 1819 law prohibited foreign enlistment per se, that of 1870 applied only to states involved in war or civil conflicts.

The act of 1870 specified that its provisions were to be extended to all British dominions and that it would be "proclaimed in every British possession by the governor thereof as soon as may be after he receives notice of this Act."[61] Within seven years, fourteen colonies had officially adopted the act, and by 1928, twenty-four had the laws in place.[62]

In 1816 there were twenty-three members of the interstate system, of which thirteen were members of the central system, or what I term *leading states*. As table 4.3 indicates, all states in the central system, save

Sweden and Turkey, imposed restrictions on mercenarism during the nineteenth century. Among members of the interstate system, only the pre-unification German states and the Two Sicilies did not impose permanent laws restricting mercenarism.

As table 4.2 shows, three approaches to exerting new authority were used. Sixteen states banned the recruitment of their citizens or subjects for foreign military service, and eight forbade their citizens or subjects from enlisting or serving in a foreign military organization (at least not without state permission). Thirteen states prohibited both practices. The remainder enacted statutes of a more general nature, prohibiting acts that could threaten retaliation from another state. Penalties for violations of these laws included fines, imprisonment, internal or external exile, and loss of citizenship.

These restrictions were new to the state system. Before 1800, only Britain, the Netherlands, and the United States had enacted permanent legislation regulating foreign military service.[63] In the late-eighteenth century, Venice, the Two Sicilies, and the Papal States issued edicts that forbade their subjects from enlisting in the armies of states currently engaged in war, but these restrictions were not made permanent until well into the nineteenth century.[64] While at most three states had laws restricting foreign military service in 1800, by the midnineteenth century one-third of the states had placed restrictions on foreign military service. By 1938 nearly seven out of ten states had such restrictions in place.[65]

There is variation across states in the amount of authority and control exerted. For example, citizens of a state that proscribes recruitment only may still be free to leave its jurisdiction and enlist in a foreign army. The penalties accrue only to agents who recruit for a foreign army within the state's jurisdiction. Many states' restrictions on recruitment and/or enlistment apply only when the activity is not authorized by the state. Presumably such states could grant permission to individuals to recruit for or enlist in a foreign army. Even more ambiguous, and therefore perhaps more of a deterrent, are the laws forbidding acts that endanger state security. At one extreme, only activities that resulted in some violent reprisal against the state would be included, while at the other, only the imagination of the authorities would limit the definition of a threat to state security.

These caveats notwithstanding, legal restrictions on foreign military service represent the assertion of new forms of state control over the use of violence in the international system. To enact legislation constraining foreign military service is to claim the authority to decide when, where, and why to use violence in the international system. "The law of neutral-

TABLE 4.3
Leading States of the Nineteenth Century and Antimercenarism Laws

Member of		
Central System	Interstate System	Antimercenarism Laws
United Kingdom		1819/70
Netherlands		1881/92
France		1804
Switzerland		1853/59
Spain		1882
Portugal		1886
Germany		1871
	Bavaria	None
	Prussia	None
	Baden	None
	Saxony	None
	Wurttemberg	None
	Hesse, Electorate	None
	Hesse, Grand Duchy	None
Austria-Hungary		1803/1852
Italy (Unified)		1865
	Sardinia	1859
	Papal States	1832
	Two Sicilies	None
	Tuscany	1853
Russia		1845
Sweden		1904
Denmark		1803
Turkey		1936
	United States	1794

Sources: For interstate and central system members, J. David Singer and Melvin Small, *Wages of War, 1816–1980, Augmented with Disputes and Civil War Data* (Ann Arbor, Mich.: Inter-university Consortium for Political and Social Research, 1984), 29–33; for legislation, see data in table 4.2.

ity, unlike the law of war, did not emerge until the rise of nation-states and the assumption of these nations of the authority and power to wage war."[66] In other words, such legislation reflects a definition of state sovereignty expanded to include greater authority over the exercise of coercion beyond the state's borders. At the same time, these statutes necessarily limit the state's authority to draw on the coercive resources of the international system. As more and more states place restrictions on foreign military service, it becomes increasingly difficult for a state to simply buy an army from the international system.

Explaining the Decline of Mercenarism

What accounts for U.S. action in this case and the rest of the world's adoption of similar controls? As we have seen, mercenarism was delegitimated in the context of war and in conjunction with the institution of neutrality. Neutrality is a particularly interesting practice because it is not an objective fact but a claim whose viability depends fundamentally on an intersubjective understanding, a set of expectations among statesmen about the proper behavior of a neutral state. A state cannot simply proclaim its neutrality in a particular war and then proceed to define its rights and duties according to its self-interest in that situation. To make good its claim to neutrality, a state must adopt policies that other states will interpret as consistent with neutrality. States assess another state's neutrality by comparing the latter's policies with the customary practices of neutrals. In other words, to make good their claim to neutrality, states imitate the customary practices of neutral states.

Practices that have been eliminated as inconsistent with neutrality cannot be resurrected at will. Belligerents will simply deny the neutrality of a state that strays from customary practice, and reject its claim to special status in the war. Ultimately, the "neutral" can be drawn into the war. So, in a very real sense, neutral states are coerced into adopting the customary practices of neutrality; belligerents threaten to bring them into the war if they do not.

Thus, according to one explanation (hereafter referred to as the *neutrality argument*), U.S. neutrality policy became universalized because it created new expectations about the behavior of neutral states. At issue were the kinds of controls belligerents could expect a neutral state to exert over its citizens or subjects during wartime.

If the essence of the delegitimation of mercenarism were a redefinition of neutrality, we would expect states to successively implement the norm as they confronted a particular war, and decided to assert and defend a claim to neutrality. In a study of this kind, it is not possible to examine the circumstances under which each and every state adopted its antimercenarism legislation in order to determine whether it was a direct result of a wartime neutrality policy. There are, however several pieces of empirical evidence that undermine the neutrality argument.

First, as did the United States, the states listed in table 4.2 instituted permanent and universal restrictions on their citizens' mercenary activities. An argument which says that U.S. practices of neutrality became customary still cannot account for why other states did not simply adopt them on a temporary basis, that is, until the particular war was over. Moreover, many of these laws do not simply ban mercenarism during wartime but define mercenarism as a violation of the law under any circumstances.

Second, the British case raises doubts about the strength of the ties between its legislation and the issue of neutrality. On the one hand, it appears that the neutrality issue was importantly involved in the institutionalization of Britain's antimercenarism laws. Its 1819 legislation was implemented in the context of the wars for Latin American independence and the act of 1870 in the context of the Franco-Prussian War. Yet the language of the earlier act is suggestive of something other than a strict concern with defending Britain's neutrality. It prohibited only natural-born British subjects from enlisting in any foreign army; it did not apply to all subjects, much less to all individuals within the British state's jurisdiction. Moreover, in contrast with the 1870 act, the prohibition applied to all foreign states, not just those involved in war. While the language of the 1870 act was expressly designed to protect the British state's neutrality, that of the 1819 act implies that it was wrong for a British national to serve in any foreign army.

Third, the lack of correlation between war and the implementation of the legislation by new states does not confirm the neutrality explanation. Most of the Latin American states entered the state system during the nineteenth century.[67] If neutrality were the key to the antimercenarism norm, we should expect to find the Latin Americans adopting it at about the same time, as they collectively confronted a world or hemispheric war.

Table 4.4 presents the Latin American states in order of their entry into the state system, the dates on which they adopted their restrictions on mercenarism, and the wars that were underway on those dates. Table 4.5 lists all the wars that occurred in the Western Hemisphere between 1816 and 1980, and their participants. As table 4.4 indicates, only two of the twenty states adopted the antimercenarism norm at the same time as a war occurred. Even if we include the three cases in which the norm was implemented within a year or two of the onset or termination of a war, we still cannot explain fifteen of the twenty cases. It is especially significant that among those states which had not passed the legislation before 1914, none implemented it during World War I. Interestingly, five states enacted their restrictions in the interwar years.

This analysis suggests that the relationship between war and the imple-

TABLE 4.4
The Latin American States and Antimercenarism Laws

State	Achieved Statehood	Enacted Legislation	War at Time of Legislation
Haiti	1815	1826	No
Paraguay	1815	1910	No
Argentina	1816	1921	No
Chile	1818	1874	No
Colombia	1819	1936	No
Mexico	1821	1886	No (Central American, 1885)
Brazil	1822	1890	No
Peru	1824	1924	No
Bolivia	1825	1834	No (Texan, 1835–36)
Uruguay	1828	1889	No
Venezuela	1830	1912	No
Ecuador	1830	1906	Yes (Central American, 1906–7)
Costa Rica	1838	1889	No
Nicaragua	1838	1891	No
Honduras	1838	1906	Yes (Central American, 1906–7)
Guatemala	1839	1889	No
El Salvador	1841	1904	No
Dominican Republic	1844	1884	No (Pacific, 1879–83; Central American, 1885)
Cuba	1902	1936	No
Panama	1903	1922	No

Sources: For statehood, Arthur S. Banks, *Cross-National Time-Series Data Archive User's Manual* (Binghamton: State University of New York, 1975), 47–52; for legislation, see data in table 4.2; for wars, see data in table 4.5

Note: Since a state might adopt this legislation in anticipation of an impending conflict, I have included wars occurring immediately following on the legislation, where appropriate.

mentation of the norm by Latin American states is completely random. Neutrality does not appear to explain the globalization of antimercenarism laws.

Another explanation (hereafter referred to as the *state-building argument*) is that controls on mercenarism had less to do with neutrality than with enhancing state authority over people. In this period, states were attempting to form mass, national armies, a process that entailed the state's claim to a monopoly on its citizens' or subjects' military service. Still, U.S. neutrality laws prohibited not only service with a foreign army but the formation of private armies.[68] In short, the U.S. central state claimed a monopoly on the authority to organize violence within its borders, even if it were organized for deployment beyond those borders.[69]

TABLE 4.5
Wars in the Americas

War	Dates	Participants
Texan	1835–36	
Peru-Bolivia	1841	
Mexican-American	1846–48	
La Plata	1851–52	Brazil, Paraguay, and Uruguay vs. Argentina
Franco-Mexican	1862–67	
Ecuadorian-Colombian	1863	
Spanish–Santo Domingo	1863–65	
López	1864–70	Brazil, Argentina, and Uruguay vs. Paraguay
Spanish-Chilean	1865–66	
Pacific	1879–83	Chile vs. Peru and Bolivia
Central American	1885	Guatemala vs. El Salvador, Nicaragua and Costa Rica
Cuba	1895–98	Cuba vs. Spain
Spanish-American	1898	U.S. vs. Spain
Central American	1906–7	Guatemala vs. El Salvador and Honduras
World War I	1914–17	
Chaco	1932–35	Paraguay vs. Bolivia
World War II	1939–45	
Football	1969	El Salvador vs. Honduras

Source: J. David Singer and Melvin Small, *Wages of War, 1816–1980, Augmented with Disputes and Civil War Data* (Ann Arbor, Mich.: Inter-university Consortium for Political and Social Research, 1984), 15–18.

"The fundamental purpose of the Neutrality Act . . . lay . . . in strengthening the authority of the central government vis-à-vis its citizens, particularly with respect to warfare." The act was meant to secure the central state's exclusive authority to make war.[70]

That such authority was in jeopardy is illustrated by the U.S. central state's failure to convict mercenaries before passage of the Neutrality Act. In 1793 Gideon Henfield was indicted by a federal grand jury for serving on a French privateer that had attacked British ships. At his trial, two Supreme Court justices and a federal judge found that "the acts of hostility committed by Gideon Henfield are an offence against this country, and punishable by its laws."[71] Yet the jury found him not guilty. The popular press applauded the jury, claiming it had "upheld the right of free men to enter the lists on the side of liberty and against oppression" and rejected the notion that federal courts could punish violations of common and international law.[72] In contrast, this verdict concerned

Washington so much that it led him to consider calling a special session of Congress.[73]

It is not known whether other indictments were sought during 1793 but "in general, where enforcement during the 19th century was lax, this laxity was primarily due to massive public support for the violators of U.S. law."[74] The Neutrality Act provided the central state with the legal basis for making its claim, against its own citizens, to a monopoly on war-making authority. As we will see in chapter 5, enforcing that claim was a major preoccupation of the nineteenth-century U.S. central state.

Antimercenary regulations reflected a new relationship between states and people. This was made explicit in the laws adopted by a number of states. Great Britain, at least initially, forbade natural-born British subjects from serving in a foreign army. According to France's 1804 Civil Code, Frenchmen who enlisted in a foreign army were subject to the loss of their status as Frenchmen.[75] This was reasserted in its 1927 Nationality Statute. Belgium (1807),[76] Costa Rica (1889), Iraq (1924), Italy (1912), and the Netherlands (1892) adopted similar measures. Laws enacted by the Swiss in 1859, the Russians in 1845, and the Portuguese in 1886 punished foreign military service with the loss of political rights.[77]

This also explains the Latin American cases. Those states, like the United States in 1793, were weak. They adopted antimercenarism laws to prevent their citizens from intriguing with other states or forming their own armies.[78]

Interstate relations or systemic forces were responsible for the decline of mercenarism. An international institution—namely, the institution of neutrality—empowered state-builders to implement new controls on their citizens or subjects, thereby monopolizing authority to make war. State leaders did not set out to eliminate mercenarism since most of them benefited from it. Instead, their common interest in building state power vis-à-vis society produced an international norm against mercenarism.

Mercenarism after 1794

The last instance in which a state raised an army of foreigners was in 1854, when Britain hired 16,500 German, Italian, and Swiss mercenaries for the Crimean War. None of these troops actually saw combat, since the war ended before they reached the theater of battle.[79]

Bolívar recruited between 5,000 and 6,000 Britons for the Spanish colonies' War for Independence. Germans, especially Bavarians, were recruited for the War of Greek Independence in 1823. In the 1830s, several thousand mercenaries were employed in dynastic struggles in Portugal and Spain.[80] Brazil hired Irish and German mercenaries to fight in its 1830 war with Argentina.[81]

In 1853 Mexican President López de Santa Anna hired German Baron Stutterheim to recruit troops in northern Germany "to reinforce his army with reliable elements against an impending *coup de main* by disloyal sections of the armed forces." López Santa Anna was overthrown before the mercenaries could provide assistance.[82]

In 1860 an American mercenary, Frederick Townsend Ward, organized the Foreign-Arms Corps, which was composed of Filipinos and Western mercenaries, to help suppress the Taiping Rebellion. This force ceased to function in 1861. Ward then formed the Shanghai Foreign Legion, made up of mercenaries from eighty countries including the United States, Great Britain, Denmark, and Norway. Following the defeat of this force, Ward reconstituted the Foreign-Arms Corps, this time with Chinese soldiers. Ward was granted an official rank in the Chinese military hierarchy and, by the time of his death in 1862, had organized his forces into the "Ever-Victorious Army." Charles "Chinese" Gordon, a British officer, took over this army in 1863 and continued to use it in suppressing the Taiping uprising. Later Gordon accepted a post in the Egyptian army in the Sudan.[83]

Certainly, this is not a complete list of nineteenth-century cases of mercenarism. It does illustrate the trend away from the employment of foreigners in state armies, however. Yet mercenarism continues to exist, if not thrive, in the twentieth century. The question is whether or not it is right to claim that the antimercenarism norm has had any real effect. Has mercenarism simply disguised itself or taken on a new form? Do twentieth-century practices really differ from those of the eighteenth century and, if so, how? In the following section I attempt to come to grips with these issues.

Twentieth-Century Mercenarism

Contemporary mercenarism takes one of four forms. First, foreigners may be permanently employed, thus constituting a portion of the state's regular standing army. There are two variants of this anomaly. Foreigners may join an army individually and without their home state's complicity, as in the case of the French Foreign Legion. Or, like the Gurkhas, they may be recruited under an interstate treaty or contract. Third, individual foreigners may be hired directly by a state for use in a particular conflict.

This ad hoc recruiting of individuals was used, for example, in the Congo, Nigeria, and Angola. Finally, a state may pay a per capita charge for the use of another state's troops, as the United States did during the Vietnam War. Each of these anomalies is examined below.

STANDING ARMIES

In the 1980s eighteen states employed foreigners in their regular standing armies. Only one, the United Arab Emirates (UAE), relied almost exclusively on mercenaries. Its soldiers were recruited from foreigners—especially Omanis and Yemenis—living in the UAE or abroad and officers were obtained from Britain, Pakistan, and Jordan.[84]

Until 1970 the Omani army was wholly mercenary, and until 1977 its chief of staff was British.[85] In the late 1970s one-half of its officer corps was British and one-third of its troops were Pakistani.[86] All senior naval officers, the internal security chief, and the commander of the army were British. The air force, police force, royal guard, and secret service were all led by British officers. In 1981 three out of five infantry battalions were Pakistani.[87] Officers in the Qatar army are mostly Britons and Pakistanis either seconded[88] or under contract to Qatar.[89] "The majority of the enlisted ranks are recruited from the bedouin tribes who move freely between Saudi Arabia and Qatar."[90] In the 1970s, one-third to one-half of the Kuwaiti army was made up of Iraqi and Saudi tribesmen.[91] Some foreign officers served in Bahrain under contract.[92]

"In Saudi Arabia Pakistani officers serve in all the different formations of the armed forces, viz., in the army, the national guard and the palace guard."[93] From the 1950s to the 1980s, "a considerable number of Pakistanis (had) served in the Saudi armed forces on an individual basis, particularly in technical positions."[94] Following the Mecca Uprising, "the ruling family quietly initiated plans to use three specially trained Pakistani brigades (with a total strength of 12,000) as a special royal guard."[95] Pakistan has also supplied combat troops to Saudi Arabia, though the Saudi government has repeatedly denied it. According to a 1980 agreement, Pakistan could supply up to "10,000 military men, including some combat troops"[96] as part of an agreement in which Saudi Arabia would provide $1 billion in annual aid.[97] The Pakistanis were to wear Saudi uniforms and "practically be integrated into the Saudi army."[98] It was reported that as many as 30,000 Pakistanis were operating in Saudi Arabia in 1982.[99]

Gurkhas serve in the armies of India and Britain under the Kathmandu Agreement of 1947.[100] In 1815 the British East India Company began recruiting Nepalese into its army, and the following year Britain and Nepal signed the Treaty of Segauli, which gave Britain the right to recruit

Nepalese subjects.[101] In 1947, in preparation for Indian independence, Nepal agreed to allow the division of Gurkha forces between the armies of India and Britain[102] and to allow both to recruit Gurkhas so long as they were accorded the "same rights of pension and gratuity on retirement as applicable to the citizens of those countries."[103] Nepal insisted that Indian and British Gurkhas receive the same pay and that Gurkhas never be forced to fight Gurhkas, Hindus, or civilians.[104] As of 1980, 6,000 to 8,500 Gurkhas were serving in the British army and 75,000 to 100,000 in the Indian army.[105]

With the granting of independence to Brunei in 1983, the issue of what to do with British Gurkha forces arose again. Gurkhas remain in Brunei, as do 60 to 150 British officers,[106] but the terms of the agreement under which they serve the Brunei government are—perhaps understandably—secret.[107] Politically, the Gurkhas presented a touchy issue: If the Gurkha contingent remained under British control, it would look like a colonial force; if it were placed under the command of the sultan, it would appear to be protecting the sultan from his own people.[108]

Ghana's army includes volunteers from francophone states to the north.[109] French officers serve in the Ivory Coast and Cameroon armies, and Greek officers are seconded to the army of Cyprus.[110] After gaining independence in 1978, the Solomon Islands recruited soldiers from Fiji and hired British officers.

The French Foreign Legion is the only standing military force that is composed of multiple nationalities whose loyalty to their employer is unquestioned.[111] After five years of service, its members are eligible for French citizenship.[112] While seventy nationalities served in the 1975 Foreign Legion, over one hundred were represented in 1983.[113] Legion strength peaked in 1940 at 45,000 troops.[114] Today the Legion provides eight regiments, or about 8,300 men, to the French army.[115]

Despite its name, troops of the Spanish Foreign Legion, "apart from a few Portuguese, [are] recruited almost entirely from Spaniards." The Legion supplies three regiments to the Spanish army.[116]

According to one source, in 1981 Libya recruited thousands of Pakistanis into its Islamic Legion, which was later sent to Lebanon.[117] However, since the Pakistani recruiting agents "deceived most of their compatriots by giving them the impression that they would be employed in civilian jobs,"[118] it is not clear how many actually served as soldiers once they arrived in Libya and learned the truth.

South Korea's entire army is commanded by a foreigner. Under the terms of the 1950 Taejon Agreement, South Korean President Rhee placed all Republic of Korean forces under the Unified Command of the United Nations forces.[119] This agreement remains in force today. Since the commander of these forces has always been an American, in effect,

TABLE 4.6
Foreigners in Current Standing Armies

Employer	Suppliers
United Arab Emirates	Jordan, Oman, Pakistan, North Yemen, Britain
Oman	Britain, Pakistan
Qatar	Britain, Pakistan, Saudi Arabia
Kuwait	Iraq, Saudi Arabia
Bahrain[a]	
Saudi Arabia	Pakistan
Britain	Nepal
India	Nepal
Brunei	Nepal
Ghana	Francophone North Africa
Ivory Coast	France
Cameroon	France
Cyprus	Greece
Solomon Islands	Britain, Fiji
France	All states
Spain	Portugal
Libya	Pakistan
South Korea	United States

Sources: See notes to text.
[a]Though there were foreigners employed by Bahrain, I was unable to determine their home (supplier) state(s).

ultimate operational authority over the Korean army is exercised by a U.S. citizen.[120]

Table 4.6 summarizes the previously described employment of foreigners in current standing armies. These cases fall into three categories.

Twelve of these are a direct result of imperialism.[121] From the eighteenth century until 1971 Britain provided for the "defense" of the Persian Gulf.[122] Britain withdrew from Kuwait in 1961 and from the UAE, Qatar, and Bahrain in 1971. This historical relationship helps to account for the large number of British officers in the region's armies. The Solomon Islands, a former British colony, employs officers from Britain as well. Gurkha forces that serve in the armies of India and Brunei are descended from the British imperial army in India.

French officers serve in the former French colonies of Cameroon and the Ivory Coast. Of course, the French Foreign Legion is itself a remnant of the French imperial army. Greeks serve in Cyprus's army for obvious historical and political reasons.

A second set of cases displays the characteristics of eighteenth-century European mercenarism. Spain's small contingent of foreign troops is recruited from Portugal. Ghana's foreign recruits are obtained from

French-speaking Africa. But the most dramatic instances of mercenarism are the Middle East states that obtain military manpower from Pakistan. Indeed, Pakistan's role in the Middle East is in some ways comparable to that of Switzerland in seventeenth-century Europe. These rich, but peripheral, states, then, buy armies from a poor but ideologically compatible supplier.

Finally there is the unusual case of South Korea whose army is under the command of the United Nations. This is obviously a remnant of UN participation in the Korean conflict and the previous U.S. occupation of Korea.[123]

AD HOC FORCES

Ad hoc foreign forces have been raised to fight in several twentieth-century conflicts.[124] Perhaps the most famous case is the Spanish Civil War. Some 35,000 foreigners—mostly Europeans—volunteered to serve in the Spanish Civil War. Though some volunteers did serve with the Nationalist forces, most of the foreigners who fought for the Nationalists were regular soldiers of the Italian and German armies. Republican volunteers were generally motivated by ideology and were poorly paid.[125]

Africa has been the site of the most publicized cases of mercenary activity in recent years. French, South African, Rhodesian, Spanish, Italian, British, and Belgian mercenaries served in the Congo, on both sides of the conflict, from 1960 to 1968.[126] They never numbered more than several hundred.[127] Recruiting missions were sent to Belgium and France in 1960 and recruiting offices opened in South Africa in 1961.[128] Some Congoese mercenaries—about forty-five Frenchmen—were subsequently hired by the Royalists in the Yemeni Civil War.[129] Mercenaries also served in Oman.[130]

Mercenaries fought for both the federal government and the Biafran separatists in the 1967–70 Nigerian Civil War. On the federal side, foreigners—Britons, Egyptians, Rhodesians, and South Africans—served primarily as pilots. These numbered between twelve and twenty throughout the war.[131] Mercenaries played a slightly larger role in the Biafran effort, with Americans, Germans, Frenchmen, and South Africans providing the bulk of the recruits.[132] Pretoria-based Mercenaire International supplied mercenaries to Biafra and to Yemen.[133]

In 1975 the French mercenary, Denard, was hired by the opposition to overthrow the president of the Comoro Islands, which he did. Three years later Denard was hired by the deposed president to overthrow the president he had helped to put in power. Following this success, Denard was named defense minister, commander-in-chief of the army, and chief of police. Though he converted to Islam, became a Comoro Islands citizen, and adopted a Muslim name, he was forced to resign. Outraged at his presence, the Organization of African Unity (OAU) had threatened to boycott the Comoro Islands.[134]

In June 1976 two American citizens, an Argentine resident of the United States, and ten British subjects were tried in Angola for mercenarism and other crimes. Three Britons and one American were executed, and the remainder sentenced to prison terms ranging from sixteen to thirty years.[135] Perhaps 1,000 white mercenaries—American, British, French, Dutch, German, Portuguese, Cuban, and Belgian—served in Angola.[136]

Between 250 and 300 Americans and more than 1,000 other foreign nationals—mainly British, Australian, Portuguese, and Greek—were recruited into the Rhodesian army in the mid-1970s.[137] Though these were enlisted into the standing army of Rhodesia, they are included in the ad hoc category because they were recruited for the civil war.[138]

During the Vietnam War, the United States paid the South Korean, Philippine, and Thai governments for the use of their troops. Under separate agreements with the three governments, the United States agreed to pay an overseas allowance, a per diem for each soldier, plus an additional allowance according to rank. Moreover, the United States agreed to pay basically all expenses associated with deploying these forces in Vietnam and with securing their replacements in the home army. This is in contrast with U.S. agreements with Australia and New Zealand, which fully reimbursed the United States for its administrative and logistical expenses. The U.S. payments to the Thai government led the Thai press to label the arrangement as mercenary.[139]

In 1966 General Westmoreland also investigated the possibility of hiring British Gurkhas who, at that time, were scheduled to be phased out of the British army. Though Britain's subsequent decision not to phase them out before 1969 made the issue moot, it is unclear whether the United States would have hired them anyway. According to U.S. military historians, "besides American antipathy toward the use of mercenaries" and the reluctance of Gurkhas to serve non-British officers, U.S.-employed Gurkhas could have become "the focal point of a new Communist propaganda campaign."[140]

Table 4.7 presents a list of employers and providers of ad hoc mercenary forces. Most cases of ad hoc recruitment involved the hiring of individuals from Western industrialized countries by Third World states or rebel groups in the context of civil wars or independence struggles. Foreigners were generally recruited for their special expertise in unconventional warfare or for their technical skills. Again, former imperial powers were the principal suppliers, and in several cases these states were clearly involved or strongly implicated in the initiation or manipulation of the conflict.

TABLE 4.7
Foreigners in Twentieth-Century Ad Hoc Forces

Conflict	Suppliers
Spain	All states
Congo	France, South Africa, Rhodesia, Spain, Italy, Britain, Belgium
Yemen	France
Oman[a]	
Nigeria	Britain, Egypt, Rhodesia, Germany, South Africa, United States, France
Comoro Islands	France
Angola	United States, Britain, France, Netherlands, Germany, Belgium, Portugal
Rhodesia	Britain, Australia, Portugal, Greece
Vietnam	Thailand, Philippines, Korea

Sources: See notes to text.

[a]I was unable to determine the home (supplier) state(s) of the foreigners involved in Oman.

One major exception to this pattern is the Spanish Civil War. Volunteers from at least twenty-nine and as many as fifty-three countries served in the Republican Army during the Spanish Civil War.[141] Most of these came from Europe. This case is usually explained in terms of an ideological commitment to antifascism.

Another anomaly is U.S. payments for allied troops in the Vietnam War. While Australia and New Zealand bore the costs of sending their troops, the United States paid the costs of deploying Korean, Philippine, and Thai troops, as well as a per diem, overseas allowance and death benefit for each soldier.

In sum, foreigners play a minor role in most twentieth-century standing armies. Of the more than 150 states currently in existence, 3 former imperial powers and only 12 former dependencies continue to employ foreigners. The major anomalies are Libya, the Gulf states, South Korea, and the Vietnam War—instances of rich peripherals buying armies or of hegemon-led collective interventions.[142] Mercenaries continue to be used on an ad hoc basis for "small" wars, though their participation is often more in response to their home states' political goals than to the blind forces of the international market for mercenaries.

In the eighteenth century, a typical army obtained 20 to 30 percent of its troops and officers from abroad. Both the provision and purchase of foreign troops were virtually universal practices in the European state system. The nineteenth century marked the transition from this norm to the twentieth-century citizen army. Large mercenary forces were not raised after the midnineteenth century. Since then, mercenaries have been either individual soldiers of fortune or government-sponsored or -sanctioned agents employed for their leadership or technical expertise.

When we compare the twentieth century with the eighteenth, it is clear that several eighteenth-century practices have been eliminated. States no longer allow other states to directly recruit within their territories, nor do they provide troops to commercial enterprises, as the Germans did for the Dutch East India Company. They do not lease their armies to other states, and they do not directly subsidize other states' armies. On the other hand, what I have termed twentieth-century anomalies can be seen as "disguised mercenarism." Saudi Arabia does not directly pay Pakistan for the use of its troops; it receives the troops in exchange for an overall package of foreign aid. Philippine, Korean, and Thai troops were not formally "leased" by the United States for use in the Vietnam War; the United States simply defrayed all the costs associated with their deployment and replacement in the home army. Today real states do not buy mercenaries.

Mercenarism persists for three main reasons. First, no state can be expected to exert total control over all individuals residing in its jurisdiction. It is difficult to see how the soldier of fortune could be eliminated, short of a country's sealing its borders.[143]

Second, most states did not ban foreign military service per se but instead retained the right of the executive to authorize it. So, for example, "the English statutes provided that enlisting or recruiting constituted crimes only when done 'without leave or license of his Majesty.'"[144] As a result, some states continue to authorize their citizens' or subjects' service in foreign armies during peacetime. State-contracted military services persist, particularly in formerly formal imperial relationships.

Finally, the Cold War sparked a decline in the enforcement of neutrality laws. In a world in a permanent state of war with no neutrals, the U.S. Neutrality Act and British Foreign Enlistment Act "are virtually dead letters." France's prosecution of mercenaries has also been half-hearted.[145]

I want to emphasize that eliminating mercenarism is not a matter of enforcing international law; the laws in question are municipal laws. The Great Powers' failure to enforce their municipal law has led some Third World leaders to seek an international ban on mercenaries, so far to no avail. In light of mercenary activities in Africa, Nigeria in 1976 submitted to the United Nations a proposal for formally outlawing mercenarism.[146] An ad hoc committee has since drafted a definition of mercenarism for inclusion in the Geneva Conventions. The debate has been couched in terms of individual liberties versus world peace. Western states argue that an effective ban on mercenarism would entail substantial violations of their citizens' basic rights, especially freedom of speech and movement. Third World states argue that mercenaries pose a threat to world peace, and Western states cannot simply disclaim responsibility for the mercenary activities of their citizens.[147]

My argument is that twentieth-century practices described in this chapter reflect the delegitimation of mercenarism that occurred in the nineteenth century. They appear to us as anomalies precisely because they are only marginally legitimate. As the incident with the Thai press suggests, the charge of mercenarism is always lingering in the background, and may serve as a propaganda tool. Statesmen must create legitimating devices, such as foreign aid in place of direct subsidies, because the latter practice is not legitimate. Moreover, since the norm was implemented, no state has attempted to reinstitute eighteenth-century practice by reversing or even challenging the norm. In the twentieth century, foreign aid, mutual defense pacts, and per diems have replaced eighteenth-century subsidies, leases, and direct recruiting.

THE DEMISE OF THE MERCANTILE COMPANIES

Mercantile companies were eliminated through a variety of processes. A common route to extinction was through bankruptcy. The French companies, for example, were doomed from the start due to undercapitalization. Alternatively, companies such as the various British Africa companies failed through a combination of mismanagement, undercapitalization, and the inability to sustain the overhead associated with defending their ships and maintaining their forts.[148] Massive corruption by its employees and the decline of the "country trade"[149] also contributed to the bankruptcy of the Dutch East India Company, which was dissolved in 1796, its territories and debts taken over by the Dutch revolutionary state.[150]

Another not uncommon road to extinction was through merger. For example, the North West Company, which was founded in 1779 by opponents of the Hudson's Bay Company,[151] was merged with the Hudson's Bay Company in 1821.[152] And the New East India Company, formed in 1698 by opponents of the (original) East India Company, merged with the latter in 1702.[153] In both cases, the mergers resulted from the realization that the intercompany competition was proving ruinous to both.[154]

Interestingly, as early as 1610 the Dutch East India Company proposed a merger with the English East India Company. The English rejected the offer, saying that "in case of joyning, if it be upon equall Terms, the Art and Industry of their People will wear out ours."[155] In 1644, when "the Dutch East India Company was fighting tooth and nail with the English East India Company for permanent supremacy over Eastern trade, 'the merchants of Amsterdam, having heard that the Lord Protector would dissolve the East India Company at London, and declare the navigation and commerce to the Indies to be free and open, were greatly alarmed; considering such a measure as ruinous to their own East India Company.' "[156] Apparently the presence of another monopolistic company, even as threatening a competitor as the English company, was preferable to throwing the region open to all English merchants.

At least one company met its demise directly through interstate politics. The Dutch West India Company, formed to break the Spanish-Portuguese monopoly of South American trade, never recovered from the loss of Brazil, whose control it had seized from Portugal in the 1620s and 1630s. It was the 1661 peace treaty between the United Provinces and Portugal that, among other things, recognized Portuguese sovereignty in Brazil while it opened the Americas to Dutch shipping. "The West India Company ceded all claims to Brazil in exchange for a lump sum of eight million guilders."[157] This marked the demise of the Dutch West India Company,[158] which went bankrupt in 1674.[159]

Yet another way a company could be eliminated was by the Crown's revocation of its charter. This was the fate, for example, of the Virginia Company, which had been licensed in 1606 to establish a colony between what today are New York and South Carolina. This was James I's way of establishing a royal colony in Spanish territory "under the guise of a private venture." Though the company received great support from the English people, the form of government it should adopt for its colony was from the beginning a source of conflict between the king and Parliament. The king wanted "to build a colonial empire which should be dependent upon himself for its government and which should add to the royal revenues," not subject to parliamentary control. On the other hand, many company leaders wished "to establish a more free government in Virginia."[160]

Under its initial charter of 1606, the colony was a royal colony; the king wrote the constitution, appointed the members of the company's governing council, and controlled policy. Reformers in the company apparently "planned to secure from the King successive charters each more liberal than its predecessor," succeeding by 1617–18 in allowing the colonists to establish a parliament. In 1621 the company prepared a new charter that provided for "the establishment of a government in the colony far more liberal than that of England itself." After the Privy Council reviewed the document, the king imprisoned the head of the company. Then when the king's candidates for company treasurer were soundly defeated, "the King decided that the charter must be revoked." In 1624 the company's patent was revoked, "the London Company practically ceased to exist, and Virginia became a royal province."[161]

Though the Hudson's Bay Company's monopoly was challenged in the

1730s, its privileges remained intact for two hundred years. One important reason for this immunity to attack was that the company was not regarded as source of revenue for the Crown. Indeed, in return for the company's charter, "Charles II required the Company merely to yield and pay two elks and two black beavers 'whensoever and as often as wee our heires and successors shall happen to enter into the said Countryes Territoryes and Regions hereby granted.' " As late as the mideighteenth century, the British regarded the company's territories as worthless, with some suggesting that they "might serve as an English Siberia, where we might hold our convicts" and turn the worst offenders over to the Eskimos as slaves. What the company supplied the British state was not revenue but a block to first French and then U.S. expansionism.[162]

From their inception, the companies that were based on a trade monopoly were targets of domestic opposition from free traders.[163] The English East India Company was subject to intense criticism by other merchants and producers, particularly when its charter came up for renewal. As Mukherjee and others point out,[164] these struggles between various economic groups were augmented, if not superseded, by the political struggle between the Crown and Parliament. Through its prerogative to grant monopoly rights, the Crown availed itself of a source of revenue beyond the control of Parliament.[165] In addition to the regular payments to the Crown that the companies were required to make, the Crown was not averse to extorting bribes or "loans" from them by licensing "interlopers" or otherwise threatening to erode their monopoly.[166] Members of Parliament, too, were susceptible to bribery,[167] though it is not clear how much this influenced Parliament's acquiescence in the renewal of company charters.[168]

Charles II, who depended on Louis XIV for an allowance, knew that a royal grant of monopoly could also reduce the Crown's dependence on foreign sovereigns.[169] Thus, Parliament's attacks on the monopolies largely reflected the Parliament's will to exert greater control over the Crown. Some argue that parliamentary attacks on such royal grants of privilege "formed the central issue in the outbreak of the seventeenth century revolution."[170] At any rate, some companies—most notably the English East India Company—met their demise when their opponents succeeded in getting their monopoly privilege revoked.

The Dutch East India Company avoided the fate of the English East India Company for two reasons. First, the company was itself an amalgamation of numerous independent companies that had competed with each other for control of the Eastern trade. Their cutthroat competition ended after Dutch politicians negotiated "the fusion of the competing pioneer companies into one monopolistic corporation," the Dutch East India Company.[171] No important merchant with an interest in Eastern trade was excluded, so the Dutch company was much more nearly a national monopoly than was the English company.[172] Opposition to the company's policies was confined to the small shareholders, and their impotence reflected the second reason for the company's success in defeating its opponents. Their powerlessness vis-à-vis the company's directors was aptly expressed in a 1622 pamphlet that said, "If we complain to the regents and the magistrates of the town, there sit the directors, . . . if to the admiralties there are the directors again. If to the States-General, we find that they and the directors are sitting there together at the same time." It was this relationship between the company's directors and the political leaders that was "the chief reason why they (the directors) were able to sidetrack or to ignore criticism of their conduct by disgruntled shareholders, and to consolidate their own position as a self-perpetuating oligarchy accountable to nobody."[173]

The English East India Company was not so fortunate. Its sovereign powers were challenged in 1766 when a committee of the House of Commons was established to investigate the company's activities in India. Parliament confronted the problem of liquidating "the great expence incurred by the government in assisting the company in its military enterprises in the middle of the century."[174] A central if underlying issue in this debate was the company's role as a financial institution. "For the company had come to be regarded as a permanent source of revenue, like some other departments of the public service; and it may have been feared that, unless their yearly dividends were kept under control, all available profits might be distributed amongst the shareholders, and nothing left for the State."[175]

During the inquiry

> The relation between the public, and the territory now held by the Company in India, called for definition. It was maintained on the one hand, as an indisputable maxim of law, supported by the strongest considerations of utility, that no subjects of the crown could acquire the sovereignty of any territory for themselves, but only for the nation. On the side of the Company, the abstract rights of property, and the endless train of evils which arise from their infringement, were vehemently enforced; while it was affirmed that the Company held not their territories in sovereignty, but only as a farm granted by the Mogul, to whom they actually paid an annual rent.

Though the issue of company sovereignty was not directly resolved, the parliamentary act of 1767 required the company to pay the British government £400,000 a year "in consideration of holding the territorial revenues for two years." This arrangement was renewed for five years in 1769.[176] By 1773, however, the company was in such dire financial straits that it not only could not make the £400,000 payment but had to borrow £1.4 million from the government.[177]

When the government proposed to stop the company from sending an expensive "commission of supervision" to India,[178] the company argued that this would violate its property rights. The government responded that the company's privileges "to which the term property, in its unlimited sense, could not without sophistry be applied, were insufficient to set aside that for which all property is created—the good of the community."[179] In 1784 Parliament enacted the Pitt Bill, which "was the beginning of the end" for the East India Company.[180] Among other things, the act placed the company under a Board of Control composed of six members of the Privy Council appointed by the king. The president of the board was "essentially a new Secretary of State." The board's "sphere of action extended to the whole of the civil and military government, exercised by the Company; but not to their commercial transactions."[181] Thus, the government approved the company's political actions and issued orders to India "which would be sent out in the name of the company.[182]

In 1813 the company's charter was renewed but its monopoly was limited to the China and tea trade.[183] More importantly, the government for the first time formally claimed sovereignty over the company's territories:

> In the act renewing the Company's privileges in that year the territorial acquisitions were continued under its control "without prejudice to the undoubted sovereignty of the crown of the United Kingdom, etc. in and over the same." But at what moment that sovereignty came into being still remained a riddle.[184]

International politics played the key role in raising the problematic nature of the company's sovereignty. The issue of the East India Company was raised in the context of postwar peace negotiations between the European powers. The question of British sovereignty in India was evaded in the Treaty of Paris (1763), the Treaty of Versailles, and the Treaty of Amiens.[185]

The problem was that the company exercised four different forms of sovereignty. In Bombay, which was ceded to England by the Portuguese, the company exercised sovereignty under the authority of the English Crown. Second, in places like Madras, the company was granted sovereignty by Indian rulers in exchange for revenue. Third, the company exerted de facto sovereignty, in the Carnatic for example, where the de jure Indian rulers served at the pleasure of the company. Finally, in Bengal, the company exercised sovereignty over territories taken by conquest.[186]

This complex mix of company sovereignty proved problematic for English statesmen in their peace negotiations with the French and Dutch. The problem, as stated by Cornwallis in 1786, was that "from this complicated system . . . founded on grants conferred and powers assumed, of sovereignty exercised though not avowed, many difficulties arise in all negotiations with foreign nations." The English government's failure to assume formal sovereignty was due to the company's fear that "such claims would provoke or hasten interference by the ministry" and the Crown's unwillingness "to assail the legal rights of the Company." Finally, the 1814 Treaty of Paris and English convention with the Netherlands

> placed the position of the English Governnment in India beyond question internationally. Both refer specifically to the British sovereignty in India, which was then for the first time acknowledged by the French and the Dutch. . . . Thus the claim put forward by the legislation of 1813 was in the following year formally announced to the diplomatic world of Europe and recognized by the two powers principally interested in the East.[187]

The company's monopoly was ended entirely in 1833, and it was directed "to wind up its commercial affairs." As of 1834, then, "the company ceased to be a commercial organization and became solely the agency through which Britain governed India."[188] Over the course of the seventy-five years following enactment of the Pitt Bill, the company was stripped of its sovereign powers. This process was completed with the Act of 1858, passed following the Indian Revolt. According to this act

> the territories under the government of the East India Company and all its other property except its capital stock and future dividends were vested in the crown, together with all the governmental powers that had previously been exercised by it. The company and the Court of Directors and Court of Proprietors were to be replaced in the government of India by a Secretary of State for India assisted by a "Council of India," the Board of Control being abolished.

Queen Victoria then "announced the replacement of the company by the English government." The company was dissolved in 1874, and the queen became empress of India in 1877.[189]

A final possible mode of extinction, unique to the Hudson's Bay Company, was for a company to be transformed from a seventeenth-century mercantile company into a modern corporation. The Hudson's Bay Company, founded in 1670, is "the oldest continuous capitalist corporation still in existence." Its charter was never successfully challenged in its first two hundred years. Granted the usual political powers and economic privileges of the seventeenth-century mercantile companies, the Hudson's

Bay Company came to govern one-twelfth of the earth's surface, a "king-dom" whose size was exceeded only by Russia, Britain, and the United States.[190] The company was not obliged to colonize nor to Christianize the Indians, and was permitted "to continue or make peace or Warre with any Prince or People whatsoever that are not Christians."[191] It was for-bidden from making "war against another Christian monarch without his [the king's] permission" and from taking over "territory claimed by any other Christian Prince." The charter did make vague reference to the company's duty to explore the territory for a Northwest Passage. When the company failed to do so, its opponents, in 1749, seized upon this and forced the company to launch some exploratory expeditions.[192]

Though its monopoly on the fur trade was challenged by individuals and companies in England and the Americas, the company's sovereign powers did not come under strong challenge until the 1850s. As the expi-ration date of the company's trade monopoly in the Northwest Territo-ries (1859) approached, the basic political issue in Britain and Canada was "whether the prairies should go to the United States or to Can-ada."[193] The British government's principal aim was to stem American expansionism by colonizing the Northwest Territories and firmly estab-lishing state sovereignty in the region.

Tensions between the United States and Britain had recently been exac-erbated by British efforts to recruit in the United States for the Crimean War. This had "made the problems of defence paramount" at the same time the British government wanted to reduce its military commitments in North America. Yet "the Canadian government was in no position to assume such responsibilities."[194]

For its part, the company wanted to stop the expansion of American and Russian traders, who were threatening its fur trade monopoly.[195] Moreover, the company had for decades wanted to rid itself of its admin-istrative responsibilities in the Red River Colony. It had repurchased the colony's land grant in 1834, and the colony "continued to irritate the commissioned officers who felt that its administrative costs as borne by the Company reduced their fur trade profits."[196]

Meanwhile the Province of Canada expressed a "growing desire . . . to extend its rule and to settle some of the Company's territory," stating that "the western boundary of Canada extended to the Pacific Ocean." Added to this were the desires of the Europeans who had settled in the North-west Territories. Some criticized the company's rule, claiming that their grievances fell on deaf ears and demanding that they be incorporated in "that glorious fabric, the British Constitution" before "American expan-sion engulfed them." And of course there were the free traders, who wanted an end to the company's fur trade monopoly.[197]

It was the growth of U.S. power that led this mercantile company to be defined as a problem by the British state. By the mid-1860s,

American ambitions were ill concealed and well known. The great increases in military and naval strength which the American Civil War had necessitated, and the determined policy which that war revealed gave reasonable cause [for Canadians] . . . to call attention to the amazing and unprecedented growth of the military power of their neighbors.[198]

During the Civil War, Canada's relations with the Northern states were strained when Canadian soil was used as a "base for attacks upon the North," and the North threatened to abrogate its 1854 Reciprocity Treaty with Canada. The United States made good its threat and abrogated the treaty in 1865. In the following year came the "Fenian scare":

Following the close of the Civil War the Fenians in the United States conceived the unhappy notion that the way to free Ireland was to attack Britain in her American provinces. Their threats of invasion were voiced openly for months, and in the spring of 1866 they gathered in menacing numbers, armed and well officered, on the Canadian and New Brunswick borders. While the invasion on the Niagara border, when it came in June, proved a fiasco, and on the New Brunswick border the United States authorities finally prevented hostilities, great excitement if not panic prevailed in the provinces.[199]

These events suggested that Britain and British North America were threatened by the United States, not only economically but militarily. The problem was that neither the company nor the Province of Canada had the resources to deal with this threat, and the British state did not want to assume the burden.

Finally, in 1869 the colonial secretary negotiated an agreement in which "the Company was to be paid £300,000 and to be allotted one acre for every twenty acres of land opened for settlement. It was also to retain its existing posts and surrounding land and it was to surrender all its territorial rights to the British Government."[200] Moreover, the British government agreed to guarantee the loan with which Canada would purchase the land.[201] Thus, in 1870 the Northwest Territories and Rupert's Land were incorporated into the Canadian federation, and the company agreed to surrender its trade monopoly.[202] Most importantly, the Deed of Surrender provided that "the said governor and company do hereby surrender to the Queen's Most Gracious Majesty, all the rights of government, and other rights, privileges, liberties, franchises, powers, and authorities, granted or purported to be granted to the said governor and company" by the original charter, and "also all similar rights which may have been exercised or assumed by the said governor and company in any part of British North America." It also specified that nothing in the British North America Act of 1867 "shall prevent the said governor and company from continuing to carry on in Rupert's Land or elsewhere trade and commerce."[203] Thus the Hudson's Bay Company "relinquished the administration of the Country"[204] and was transformed from a seventeenth-century mercantile company, with the sovereign powers of a state, into a purely economic enterprise.

Though the company never gave up its original royal charter, subsequent supplemental charters completed its transformation into a modern corporation.[205] Because it still operates under a royal charter, it is exempt from the Companies Act of Great Britain,[206] under which limited liability corporations are organized.[207] Governance of the company remains with the board of directors in London.[208]

CONCLUSION

Authorized nonstate violence was eliminated in an ad hoc, piecemeal fashion. There was no generalized assault on nonstate violence per se, much less a single method for ending those practices. Privateering was eliminated through a formal international agreement. Mercenarism's demise came through changes in municipal law. It was initiated by the United States in the late eighteenth century but was not completed for another hundred years, during which time most other states adopted legislative restrictions similar to those of the United States. The mercantile company, as an institution with coercive power, was never formally banned; the individual companies either went bankrupt, were taken over by the state or, in one case, were converted into a purely economic enterprise.

The state's right to authorize nonstate violence per se was not addressed. Instead, particular practices were eliminated as they provoked interstate conflicts. A key finding of this study is that the impetus for this change in state authority came from other states. Nonstate violence was not delegitimated by society or domestic political actors but by European statesmen. System-level political forces were responsible.

An interestsing question is why the approaches were so different. Power cannot explain the divergent outcomes. Great Britain questioned the legitimacy of mercenarism and privateering, both customary practices, but proposed an international ban only on the latter. Moreover, everyone followed the lead of the weak U.S. central state in permanently eliminating mercenarism, while the strong British state ended the mercantile company in response to threats and demands from weaker states. There was no hegemon making rules or institutions to shape state practices.

Another interesting question is why this all occurred in the nineteenth century. The authorization of nonstate violence had been a legitimate practice for up to six hundred years (in the case of privateering), so why was it suddenly abandoned after 1800? Answers to these questions will be offered in chapter 6 but, first, we need to understand how states dealt with unauthorized nonstate violence, the focus of the next chapter.

CHAPTER FIVE

Suppressing Unauthorized Nonstate Violence

STAMPING OUT unauthorized nonstate violence was not a mere mopping-up operation. In practice, determining which states were responsible for quashing piracy entailed resolving fundamental questions about sovereignty. Who was sovereign where, and for what violent acts could states be held accountable? Once Europeans had resolved these issues, the antipiracy norms were spread to extra-European regions, where political rulers were charged with implementing those norms or risking the loss of their sovereignty.

The establishment of a republican government in the United States generated a new form of extraterritorial violence—nonstate military expeditions against neighboring territories. Like privateering, this form was not always a purely nonstate-actor operation but often enjoyed state authorization, support, or tolerance. What was different in this case, however, was that the violence was directed at territories where state sovereignty was recognized by Eureopean rulers.

The issue to be resolved here was this: In a republican polity, like the United States, where popular sovereignty was claimed, to what extent was the state to be held accountable for its citizens' actions beyond its borders? From the beginning, the U.S. central state was charged with responsibility for violent acts emanating from its territory. This expectation that the state would effectively police its own people and borders empowered the weak and fragmented U.S. central state to monopolize authority over the deployment of violence in and from its territory.

PIRACY

In chapter 4 the conversion of privateering from "patriotic piracy"[1] into "a Kind of Piracy which disgraces our Civilisation"[2] was revealed. Here we will examine how piracy was transformed from an "honorable crime"[3] to a crime against the human race.[4] There simply is no question that piracy was a legitimate practice in the early European state system. Pirates brought revenue to the sovereign, public officials, and private investors. They weakened enemies by attacking their shipping and settlements. They supplied European markets with scarce goods at affordable

prices. They broke competing states' trade monopolies. The most successful of the British pirates were knighted and/or given important posts in
the Royal Navy or the British Admiralty.[5] By the early eighteenth century,
however, pirates were being hanged en masse in public executions.

It is not clear whether piracy is a crime under international law or, if it
is, when it was outlawed.[6] A defining characteristic of the pirate is that his
violent acts are not authorized by a state. Thus, if piratical acts are divorced from state authority, and therefore responsibility, they do not
come under the rubric of international law, which deals only with sovereign states.[7] Whether or not piracy is a violation of international law, it is
agreed that states do have the right, if not the duty,[8] "to discourage piracy
by exercising their rights of prevention and punishment as far as it is
expedient."[9] Piracy is a unique practice that, under international law,
states have the right but perhaps not the duty to prosecute. States can
prosecute foreigners for committing acts of piracy against foreigners, but
there is no liability implied in not doing so.

As the preceding chapters have demonstrated, it is assuredly *not* the
case that piracy was always and everywhere treated as a crime, and that
it flourished only so long as states lacked the capacity to suppress it.
Rather, the campaign against piracy was preceded by a change in the
state's attitude from one in which individual violence was an exploitable
resource to one in which it was a practice to be eliminated.

As we saw in chapter 2, the absence of political authority is a key
element in the definition of piracy. An equally interesting element is that
the violence must emanate from the sea. This is not a trivial distinguishing
feature of piracy because, unlike the cases in which violence emanates
from land, no state today is sovereign over the high seas. It is important
to recognize that the issue of sovereignty on the high seas was not resolved until the turn of the nineteenth century. In other words, the absence of sovereignty over the oceans is not a timeless feature of the international system but something that emerged in the course of the eighteenth century:

> Down to the beginning of the nineteenth century then, the course of opinion
> and practice with respect to the sea had been as follows. Originally it was
> taken for granted that the sea could be appropriated. It was effectively ap-
> propriated in some instances; and in others extravagant pretensions were
> put forward, supported by wholly insufficient acts. Gradually, as appropria-
> tion of the larger areas was found to be generally unreal, to be burdensome
> to strangers, and to be unattended by compensating advantages, a disinclina-
> tion to submit to it arose, and partly through insensible abandonment, partly
> through opposition to the exercise of inadequate or intermittent control, the
> larger claims disappeared, and those only continued at last to be recognized

which affected waters the possession of which was supposed to be necessary to the safety of a state, or which were thought to be within its power to command.

So while states generally considered the seas as objects for appropriation until the middle of the seventeenth century, by the turn of the nineteenth century, all but a handful of claims to sovereignty had been abandoned.[10]

The question is, If no state is sovereign—that is, exerts authority—over the high seas, who is responsible for individual acts of violence launched from the sea? If individual states do not assert jurisdiction over the seas, then "unless complete lawlessness is to be permitted to exist, jurisdiction must be exercised either exclusively by each state over persons and property belonging to it, or concurrently with other members of the body of states over all persons and property, to whatever country they may belong." Clearly, the former has become the normal practice of the modern state system.[11]

But we are concerned here with how this came to be the modern practice, and this entails answering the question: Why did one or more states come to regard piracy as a problem?

The first state to define piracy as a problem, and one within its own empire, was Britain. Formerly a great beneficiary of piracy, the British state was, in the early eighteenth century, faced with a situation in which the British East India Company was demanding the British Royal Navy's protection against British pirates who were operating in collusion with British colonists to plunder British commerce in the East. Rather than providing protection for this trade, the Mogul of India demanded that the company assume responsibility for the safety of his ships. In his view, the pirates were English speaking and therefore were probably operating in concert with their countrymen in the company. The problem was that once the company began convoying the Mogul's ships, the pirates no longer saw any reason to refrain from attacking the company's ships right along with the "Moorish" ones. In essence, it was the Mogul who defined British piracy as a problem for the British company to deal with and the British company that in turn defined it as a problem for the British state's attention.

But sending the Royal Navy to patrol the Eastern waters merely motivated the pirates to move to the Bahamas. In order to permanently resolve the piracy problem, Britain had to put its own house in order. American colonial markets for pirate booty had to be suppressed. Colonial legal systems were strengthened, corrupt officials replaced, and a new government for the Bahamas established. Pirate attacks on the Americans' own shipping contributed to the decline in colonial support for piracy.

Having suppressed piracy in the Americas, the British state found it had merely succeeded in driving the pirates back to Madagascar. This time company complaints about them led to the quick dispatch of Royal Navy vessels to the region. So in the case of major, organized piracy, it was the Mogul of India who alone among those who defined piracy as a problem, was able, through his pressure on the East India Company, to define piracy as a problem for the British state. And the problem was mainly caused by British subjects in the British empire. Piracy was now delegitimated, but the issue of which states were responsible for eliminating which pirates was not resolved.

The Mediterranean Corsairs

The circumstances under which the Mediterranean corsairs were defined as a problem were more complicated. Again, though the North African states benefited from the activities of the Barbary Coast corsairs, the most important of the corsairs were Europeans. Here then it was impossible for one state, as a victim of corsair attacks, to hold another European state responsible, as the Mogul did in the case of the Madagascar pirates. Adding complexity to the corsair issue was the fact that the European states were dealing with ostensibly sovereign states so they were never able to determine definitively whether the corsairs were pirates or belligerent warships. Again, the European states initially treated this violence as a potentially exploitable resource, provided one could buy protection for oneself and leave one's competitors to bear the attacks. It is clear, however, that the leading European states had defined the Barbary corsairs as a problem by 1814. For a variety of reasons, including strategic concerns, the Europeans were unable to launch a concerted campaign against them, leaving it to the French to unilaterally stamp them out.

Three approaches were used in attempting to suppress the Barbary corsairs. Many states negotiated treaties with the individual states, securing protection from corsair attacks with the payment of cash and/or commodities. As England, France, Spain, Holland, and Sweden did during the seventeenth century, the United States signed such agreements in the eighteenth century.[12] "Venice paid 22,000 gold sequines and an annual tribute of 12,000 gold sequines for peace; the young Republic of the United States paid $642,500 and an annual tribute of $21,600 in naval supplies; Hamburg, Sweden, Denmark and Naples also paid handsomely for protection." In its 1796 treaty, the United States also agreed to provide "the gift of a thirty-six-gun frigate." These treaties were not easily enforced, in part because of the difficulty of establishing the national identity of European ships. For one thing, many of the Barbary corsair personnel could not speak or read English or French, so it was difficult for them to verify the passports carried by European vessels. In addition, English ships employed Spanish sailors and Italian and French ships used Genoese crews. Barbary officials found it difficult to believe that a ship flying the French flag but whose crew could not speak French was really French, or a ship with an Italian-speaking crew was really English.[13]

"Had all, or even three or four, of the wronged powers agreed to combine their forces, they could at any time have wiped out the North African pirates."[14] Three factors prevented this.

First, European states viewed the Barbary corsairs as a tool with which to gain advantage in their competition with other European states—in war or in commerce. By paying protection money, a European state could dominate Mediterranean trade while its rivals would be open to attack by the corsairs.[15] Second, European state leaders must have had a somewhat ambivalent attitude toward corsair activities, since the people who purchased their prizes were "those same English, French or Dutch merchants who had sailed to buy just these goods in the normal run of commerce"— only it was much cheaper to purchase these goods in prize auctions than at their point of origin.[16]

The third factor inhibiting European cooperation had to do with the second strategy for dealing with the corsairs: the application of brute force. Though states repeatedly took unilateral military action against the corsairs' port bases,[17] proposals for concerted action generally failed. At the 1814 Congress of Vienna, the British admiral proposed that a multinational naval force be formed and sent to destroy the Barbary corsairs, though nothing came of this.[18] Instead, in 1816 the British informed the dey of Algiers that the Congress of Vienna had abolished piracy and slavery, and "demanded the Algerians accept this decision and free its Christian slaves." This outraged the Algerian population, which physically attacked the English emissaries. In reprisal, a joint Anglo-Dutch naval force destroyed the Algerian navy.[19] However, "scarcely was the fleet out of sight of the Mediterranean than the pirates were at their old ways again."[20] At the 1818 Congress of Aix-la-Chapelle the powers again agreed to send a multinational force, but this also failed because "Britain feared the presence of Russian warships in the Mediterranean."[21]

Unilateral military action by the United States in 1803 and the Anglo-Dutch attack in 1816 temporarily reduced corsair activities, but it was the French who put a permanent end to the Barbary coast corsairs. By the turn of the eighteenth century, French and English naval power in the Mediterranean was great enough to deter the corsairs from risking a war with either power by attacking its ships. Yet, the full force of these naval powers was not turned on the Barbary states, despite the "pinpricks and petty annoyances" they experienced from the corsairs and the pleas from

Christian Europe that the corsairs be destroyed. Though Britain and France surely enjoyed seeing their trading rivals bear the brunt of corsair attacks, it is also true that both powers were almost constantly at war during the eighteenth century. Moreover, it was not clear that the benefits of wiping out the corsairs would exceed the cost, which would go far beyond that of simply bombarding the coastal bases.[22]

The third and ultimately successful approach to eliminating the corsairs was to impose European sovereignty over the Barbary states. In 1830, a French army of thirty-seven thousand men invaded and captured Algiers.[23] What provoked the invasion was a dispute between the French government and the dey over a debt owed the dey by some French merchants. The French decision to invade Algiers was approved by Russia and the two German powers, but was opposed by England and, of course, the Ottoman Empire.[24] The French occupation of Algiers led Tripoli and Tunis to "come to heel" and thus "to retain their independence for a further 50 and 80 years respectively."[25] So, in the end, it was only through the establishment of European state sovereignty in North Africa that the Barbary corsairs were suppressed.

Malta

In contrast with their Barbary counterparts, the Maltese corsairs were suppressed not by their victims but by their supporters. Europeans had three ways of exerting influence on the Maltese. Because of its dependence on Sicily for corn, Malta was susceptible to threats of a Sicilian grain embargo. Secondly, since the Order of Saint John was originally "created during the Crusades with charters from the Pope," the pope exerted considerable influence, backed by the threat of excommunication. Finally, the Order, in its war against the Muslims, depended on contributions that were often in the form of land. Since these lands "were scattered all over Europe, the Order depended on the goodwill of European sovereigns."[26] Pressure from all of these actors, exerted in furtherance of their individual interests, eventually squeezed the Maltese corsairs out of business.

The corsairs got into trouble on three counts. First, though they were supposed to attack only Muslims, many persisted in capturing Christian—mainly Greek—ships. This led to repeated conflicts with the pope, whose mandate against attacking Greek Christians ended the practice in 1732.[27] A second set of problems stemmed from the fact that the Maltese were Frenchmen. On the one hand, this meant that France was susceptible to reprisals by the corsairs' victims. On the other, when France was allied with Turkey, the Maltese were effectively prohibited from attacking Turkish ships. All of these factors contributed to a situation in which France consistently narrowed the Maltese corsairs' range of targets.

The third problem was that the French, who wanted to dominate Mediterranean trade themselves, became major carriers of Muslim goods. Maltese corsairs were thus deprived of a major source of booty. Though the corsairs asserted the right to search friendly (i.e., French) ships for enemy (i.e., Muslim) goods, the French king prevailed in ordering a stop to this practice. As a result of these restrictions, no corsair licenses were issued between 1749 and 1751.[28]

The Maltese found various ways to "cheat" on these restrictions—such as sailing under the flag of the prince of Monaco or claiming that high winds had carried them into the restricted areas of the Mediterranean—so their activities continued through the eighteenth century. As in the case of the Barbary corsairs, however, it was the establishment of French sovereignty over the island that brought Maltese corsairing activity, for all practical purposes, to an end. In 1798, Napoleon took over Malta and abolished privateering.[29]

In the end, then, the corsairs—whether privateers or pirates—were eliminated only with the imposition of European sovereignty on these "military republics." Real sovereign states, as defined by Europeans, did not engage in, support, or condone piracy.

Piracy outside Europe

At the end of the seventeenth century, a veritable "dynasty of pirates" had been established on the Malabar coast.[30] This "federation" was controlled by a native family, the Angrias, who had achieved de facto independence from the Indian empire by 1698. From here the "pirate king" launched attacks on British East India Company ships with impunity until 1729. In that year, the Angrian "king" died, leaving five sons whose quarrels produced a twenty-year lull in Malabar coastal piracy. One son emerged as the leader in 1749 and resumed the attacks on British shipping. Portuguese and Dutch merchants were also targets. Once the English had established sovereignty over all of India, the Angrias offered to give passes to English ships—an offer the British rejected. Instead, in 1755 and 1756, the Royal Navy seized the Angrias' major forts. Their leader surrendered and spent the rest of his life in prison.[31]

In the Middle East, the most significant center of piracy was the southeast shore of the Persian Gulf. These pirates, the Joasmees, first began attacking English shipping in 1778. The king of Oman proved more effective at controlling piracy in this region than did the British government at Bombay, but his death in 1804 led to further attacks on British ships. An

Arab fleet under British command was sent and secured the pirates' surrender. As a result, in 1806 Bombay and the Joasmees signed a treaty by which the Joasmees agreed to stop attacking English ships in return for the right "to trade at English ports between Surat and Bengal." The pirates shortly broke the treaty by attacking a British East India Company ship. Though they were captured, tried, and found guilty, the pirates were released by the Bombay government. This apparently encouraged them to commit further depredations on British ships. Finally, the governor-general at Calcutta sent a fleet that destroyed the pirates' bases and most of their ships. Less than a year later, the Joasmees had not only regained control of the gulf but began attacking trade in the Red Sea and along the Indian coast. The Joasmees were finally suppressed in 1819 when a large British-Omani naval fleet and four thousand soldiers effectively destroyed the Joasmees' bases and fleet.[32]

Chinese pirates made costly attacks on British and Portuguese ships in the China Seas at the beginning of the nineteenth century. One pirate, at the peak of his career, employed seventy thousand men organized in six large squadrons. The emperor's efforts to buy him off failed, and imperial fleets sent against him were defeated three times in two years. In 1810, the huge pirate fleet fell victim to a mutiny by its admirals. One squadron of 160 ships and eight thousand men surrendered to the emperor, who pardoned them. Eventually the leader of the pirate fleet took advantage of a general pardon and surrendered as well. "The government gave each pirate money for starting life ashore," gave the pirates two towns to live in, and bestowed an imperial commission as a major on the former second-in-command of the pirate fleet.[33]

One last significant instance of piracy was based in the Malay Archipelago. In 1813 the leader, the so-called Prince of Pirates, began attacking English ships, taking forty ships over the next sixteen years.[34] When a U.S. merchant ship was seized in 1831, the United States sent three hundred marines, who destroyed the pirates' forts. In the 1840s, Borneo was the source of the worst piracy. After a successful British naval expedition against the pirates' inland bases, the sultan of Brunei ceded to Britain the island of Labuan "for the suppression of piracy and the encouragement and extension of trade."[35] But since the Brunei state depended on the slave trade and piracy for much of its revenues, the sultan's opponents overthrew him and replaced him with "a puppet of the pirates."[36] British naval forces sailed to the capital and, finding that the sultan's court had fled, "the Admiral issued a proclamation that 'if the Sultan would return and govern his people justly, abstain from acts of piracy and keep his agreement with the British government, hostilities would cease,' but 'if the same atrocious system was again carried on when the ships left the Coast' he would burn Brunei to the ground."[37] This action was followed in 1849 by a final British naval operation in which more than eight hundred pirates were killed or drowned.[38] This expedition effectively put an end to Borneo piracy.[39]

Another outbreak of piracy occurred during the Greek War for Independence (1821–27), when major pirate bases were established in the North Aegean and in southern Crete. In 1826 alone there were ninety-six cases of Greek piracy. Again, the line between war and crime was blurred, as Greek warships were so poorly provisioned that they seized what they needed from any ship unable to defend itself. Upon defeating the Turkish navy with an allied squadron of British, French, and Russian warships, the British admiral warned the Greek government that the forces used to destroy the Turkish navy could be turned against the Greeks unless their piracy were suppressed. Though both the Greek navy and the pirates seem to have taken the warning to heart, the British in 1828 destroyed the pirate base on Crete and destroyed large numbers of pirate vessels.[40]

The abolition of slavery in the British empire in 1834 provided a major impetus for piracy. Since the demand for slaves in the Americas, India, and the Arab world was unabated, the "illegal" trade in slaves continued. Those states which had outlawed slavery defined trading in slaves as piracy. Though the Royal Navy made a concerted effort to suppress the trade at its sources in West Africa, it was only with the abolition of slavery in the United States that the transatlantic slave trade ended.[41] The Arab slave trade was suppressed only with the policing of the Red Sea and Persian Gulf by France, Italy, and Britain beginning with the turn of the nineteenth century.[42]

Hong Kong had long been a base for piracy. When Britain took it over, the pirates moved inland. Initially the Chinese emperor forbade British gunboats from entering his territorial waters. With the outbreak of civil strife in China in the 1850s, the British forced the viceroy at Canton "to admit that he could not keep his own house in order" and secured his cooperation in suppressing the new outbreak of piracy. The British forces were supplemented with one of the viceroy's war junks, two steamships supplied by a Chinese merchant, and aid from the American commodore and the Portuguese governor of Macao. Even while Britain and China were at war (1856–60), Chinese mandarins continued to assist the Royal Navy in suppressing the pirates. Piracy in China was finally ended through a combination of international coercion, effective prosecution, and a new system of vessel registration adopted by the Chinese at the behest of the British. After 1869, the Chinese themselves took responsibility for protecting local trade.[43]

Norms against piracy developed not through interstate bargaining and negotiation but in conjunction with the practical resolution of problems associated with sovereignty on the high seas. The first practically derived norm was that the state was responsible for quashing piracy within its own territorial waters, that is, where it claimed sovereignty. Evidence for the existence of this norm in Europe can be found as early as the beginning of the seventeenth century. In 1611, the Dutch asked for and were granted permission to send warships into English and Irish harbors "to capture pirates of any nationality."[44] In asking for permission, the Dutch were acknowledging the English state's sovereignty in its own territorial waters. In granting its permission, the English state conceded that it lacked the capacity to meet its sovereign obligations.

By the early nineteenth century, European state leaders charged the state with responsibility for controlling piracy in its own territorial waters. Backed with the threat of coercion, this charge said in effect: You cannot simply disclaim responsibility for piracy in your territorial waters, regardless of who its victims are or how much you may profit from it. To be recognized as sovereign, a state must control piracy within its jurisdiction.

Resolving the issue of who was responsible for piracy on the high seas was more complex. Three solutions were possible. One was for a single state to claim sovereignty over broad stretches of the sea. Spain tried this when the papal bull granted it sovereignty beyond a line "west of the Azores and north of the Tropic of Capricorn." Spain defined anyone trespassing this line as a pirate.[45] This extraordinary claim to sovereignty failed for the simple reason that Spain could not enforce it. If even "legitimate" agents of other European states (e.g., privateers) were deemed pirates, then bona fide pirates could not be identified. This produced a veritable "state of nature," in which Spain was at war with all outsiders. The best Spain could do was to make deals with individual states in which Spain would recognize the legitimacy of some of the other states' claims in the New World in exchange for that state's agreement to control its subjects' violence against Spain.

A second possible way of resolving the problem of violence where no state was sovereign was to charge the home state of the perpetrators with responsibility. The Mogul of India pursued this strategy. If the pirates who attacked his ships were white Europeans who spoke English, then in his view, they were English nationals whose activities were the responsibility of the English mercantile company. Mercantile companies could not simply disclaim responsibility for violence perpetrated by their fellow countrymen. This approach was successful insofar as it provoked the British to at least enforce the anti-piracy norm within the areas over which it did claim sovereignty. By rooting out corruption within its own empire and offering both positive and negative incentives to pirates operating from within its sovereign jurisdiction, Britain did much to suppress piracy in the East.

Yet, the Mogul's approach did not become the norm. It was based on the premise that the national origin of the pirate should determine which state was responsible for his acts in the international system. This proved difficult in two ways. For one thing, as we saw in the case of the Mediterranean, sovereignty and nationality could be entirely divorced. Despite the fact that a ship flew the flag and carried the official documents of the British state—meaning the British state exerted sovereign authority over it—the crew might not include a single British national. The Barbary corsairs assumed that if the seamen were Italians, the ship was Italian, and was fraudulently claiming to be British or French.

A second, and perhaps more serious, problem was raised by the deep-sea marauders. These were Europeans who expressly rejected any ties to their home state and gave their allegiance to pirate "commonwealths," with their radical democratic, even anarchical, mode of governance. As we have seen, neither linguistic or religious differences nor national origin or race was of any relevance to these individuals. The true basis of their unity was their profession, their rejection of European society, and their refusal to recognize themselves as being subject to the sovereign authority of any state.

So neither a state's claiming sovereignty over sections of the high seas nor one state's charging another with responsibility for its nationals produced an effective norm against piracy. European states refused to recognize a claim to sovereignty on the high seas unless it could be enforced— something even the most powerful states found impossible to do. European states also refused to accept responsibility for piratical acts based on the nationality of the perpetrators because there was no firm link between nationality and state sovereignty. According to the norm that did develop, pirates are stateless individuals and therefore, in an international legal sense, do not exist. In essence, the norm says that no state is responsible for the acts of pirates, and therefore no state can be held accountable for them. As a practical matter, then, states are left with the discretion to extend their sovereignty to the high seas and to prosecute pirates if they choose to outlaw piratical acts in their municipal law.

Tracing the globalization of the norm against piracy on the high seas is not easy. My argument is that no clear norm could develop, much less be universalized, until the state system produced a clear definition of what constituted piracy. *And this was impossible so long as states continued to regard individual violence as an exploitable resource.* Simply put, piracy could not be expunged until it was defined, and it could not be defined until it was distinguished from state-sponsored or -sanctioned individual violence. International norms against piracy were universalized only with the delegitimation of the practice of privateering.

This norm was transmitted to areas beyond the European system by a mixture of coercion and imitation. For example, Algiers refused to adopt the norm voluntarily and found the norm imposed on it with the establishment of French sovereignty. On the other hand, China cooperated with the British in implementing the norm in the China Seas.

THE RISE AND DECLINE OF FILIBUSTERING

During the first sixty years of the nineteenth century, the United States produced dozens of adventurers known as *filibusters*.[46] Filibusters were individuals who launched military expeditions from U.S. territory, usually against neighboring states, for a variety of reasons. Some wanted to bring new territory into the United States, others to establish an independent republic, and some to create an independent state under their own dictatorial rule. Leaders of these expeditions included U.S., French, and Spanish-American nationals. Among these were politicians, military officers, and private citizens. In several cases, filibustering expeditions were led by agents of the U.S. central state who appear to have exceeded their orders.

Unlike the other cases of nonstate violence we have so far considered, filibustering was new to the nineteenth-century state system. Moreover, this practice was not only a product of a new state—the United States—but remained a uniquely American phenomenon. Individuals from Western Europe, for example, did not launch private military expeditions to seize territory from the decaying Ottoman Empire. Two factors were primarily responsible for the development of filibustering in the United States. The structural precondition for this practice was, of course, the geographical proximity to the United States of weak states that presented realistic targets for the filibusters. Spain, and later the new Latin American states, simply lacked the capacity to effectively deter individuals in the United States from launching filibustering expeditions. While the weakness of its neighbors was a necessary precondition for U.S. filibustering, it does not explain why filibustering was confined to the Americas nor why it ended so abruptly. After all, as late as the 1920s, the United States was able to "occupy" Nicaragua for more than a decade with a force of only one hundred marines.[47] Weak neighbors persisted long after filibustering's demise.

The second factor that contributed to the filibustering phenomenon, and that accounts for its being peculiar to the United States, was the weakness of the U.S. central state. This ineffectiveness of central state control over the states, its own citizens, and even its own agents allowed filibustering to flourish.

As we saw in the previous chapter, the central state moved to enhance its powers under the guise of the Neutrality Act, which, among other things, prohibited even the planning of hostile expeditions within the United States. The courts have interpreted the statute as applying to

> expeditions against all nations not at war with the United States, not simply expeditions against nations at war with a third country. The statute applies to foreign exiles within the United States as well as to United States citizens. . . . Moreover, the Act has been held to prohibit any type of military enterprise or expedition, not merely an official invasion. Training, the enlistment of men, the contribution of money, clothing or provisions, the furnishing of transportation, and the provision of arms are all overt acts prohibited under the Act.[48]

In our current era of covert operations, it bears emphasizing that these prohibitions applied to the president as well. Federal officials aimed to take the right to make war from individuals; they did not challenge the Congress's exclusive power to declare war, as the Constitution specified. Individuals charged with neutrality act violations, on the other hand, commonly used the defense that the executive branch had authorized their expeditions. The courts responded that the president did not have the power to authorize an illegal act. It seems clear that throughout the nineteenth century, the Congress, courts, and president were united in their support of the neutrality statutes.[49]

When federal officials attempted to take firm action against a filibustering expedition, however, their efforts were usually foiled by state officials, the local citizenry, and often federal employees. Filibusters were lionized by citizens who regarded them as heroes. Grand juries refused to indict and trial juries refused to convict filibustering suspects. State politicians actively supported and sometimes directly participated in filibustering expeditions. Military officers, faced with extreme hostility from local citizens, failed to carry out their orders to prevent the departure of filibusters. So even when the federal government did order the suppression of a filibustering expedition, its orders often fell on deaf ears.

In the following section, I describe several major cases of filibustering to illustrate the efforts of individuals to legitimate their activities, the role of foreign powers in the expeditions, and the U.S. central state's efforts to enforce its ban on filibustering. I first look at cases in which the enterprises were undertaken by individuals acting on their own initiative. The next set of cases are ones in which efforts by Mexico to attract U.S. settlers inadvertently produced filibustering expeditions. Finally, I describe several cases in which filibustering expeditions were launched by officials and agents of the U.S. central state.

Expeditions Launched on Private Initiative

FOREIGN NATIONALS

Two famous filibusters were Venezuelan nationals named Francisco de Miranda and Narciso López. The former sought to liberate "the entire Spanish-American continent,"[50] while the latter wanted to secure Cuban independence from Spain. In late 1784, Miranda, assisted by General Knox, formulated a plan which included the recruitment of five thousand men in New England. Alexander Hamilton provided Miranda with a list of U.S. military officers, including George Washington. Miranda claimed that Washington, Knox, and Hamilton assured him support if he could secure British naval assistance.[51] Nevertheless, "President Adams could not be persuaded [to support Miranda]."[52]

After several years of indecision, Britain hinted that Miranda would enjoy some British naval support in his operation.[53] In 1805, Miranda met with the president and secretary of state, who both "refused to grant any official approbation to Miranda's expedition" but "agreed to look the other way while Miranda's merchant friends put up the money and recruited an expeditionary force in the port of New York." Madison is reported to have said that "the Government would shut its eyes to their conduct, provided that Miranda took his measures in such a way as not to compromise the Government."[54]

Early in 1806, Miranda sailed for Venezuela, and the French and Spanish ministers immediately protested against this violation of U.S. neutrality.[55] The expedition was financed by U.S. and British merchants,[56] including U.S. merchant Samuel Ogden, who provided seventy thousand dollars in money and equipment.[57] Recruits were French, U.S., English, and Polish officers and soldiers drawn from "the dregs of the port [of New York], the unemployed, and some hitherto-disappointed fortune hunters."[58] These men were recruited by Colonel William Smith, the surveyor of the Port of New York.[59] Most of them had no idea of their destination.[60]

U.S. officials responded to the Spanish minister's protests by removing Colonel Smith from office and by indicting Smith and Ogden for violating U.S. neutrality laws.[61] The defense applied for subpoenas of the vice-president, secretary of state, secretary of treasury, secretary of war, secretary of the navy, the postmaster general, the Spanish minister, the senator from Vermont, and the president's son-in-law. President Jefferson "ordered the subpoenas to be ignored, on the grounds that attendance in court would interfere with the performance of official duties."[62]

Both defendants testified to the effect that "the expedition 'was begun, prepared and set forth with the knowledge and approbation of the President . . . and . . . of the Secretary of State of the United States.'" Defense attorneys argued that the charges would not have been leveled had the expedition succeeded. Instead, the defendants would have been applauded by the entire world.[63] The defense also pointed out that federal officials in New York knew all about the expedition but did nothing.[64]

While the judge told the jury that "the defendants' guilt was 'clear and decisive,'"[65] the jury found that "the expedition was prepared in, and sailed from, the port of New York with Administration connivance," and both defendants were acquitted.[66]

Meanwhile, the Spanish minister alerted authorities in Cuba, Venezuela, and Mexico, who repelled the invasion. Sixty prisoners were tried for "piracy, rebellion, and murder." Ten were hanged and the rest sentenced to long prison terms.[67] Jefferson was so upset about the charges of U.S. government complicity in the Miranda expedition that, after leaving office in 1809, he wrote the Spanish minister to say that "I solemnly, and on my personal truth and honor, declare to you that this was entirely without foundation, and that there was neither cooperation nor connivance on our part."[68]

Narciso López, who adopted Cuba as his home country, led three filibustering expeditions against Cuba between 1849 and 1851. López wanted to secure Cuban independence from Spain while preserving the institution of slavery on the island. After participating in an abortive uprising in Cuba in 1848, López fled to the United States, where he began organizing his first expedition.[69]

Command of the expedition was offered to Jefferson Davis and Major Robert E. Lee. Both declined, the latter on the basis that "it would be wrong to take command of the army of a 'foreign power' while he held a commission in the United States Army." Though several American army officers joined, López and another Cuban exile filled the two top command posts. Money was raised from Cuban and American sources, and three ships were procured. Eight hundred men, described as the "most desperate looking creatures as ever were seen would murder a man for ten dollars," were recruited into the filibuster army. No one informed these recruits of the expedition's objective, which was to attack Cuba on 1 September 1849.[70]

Meanwhile, the U.S. government learned of López's activities, and on 11 August President Taylor issued a proclamation warning that participants were liable to a three-thousand-dollar fine and up to three years in prison.[71] Two days earlier the commander of the U.S. naval squadron at

Pensacola had been ordered to prevent the filibusters' departure from Mississippi and, if necessary, to "go to Cuba and prevent a landing." A naval blockade persuaded the eight hundred filibusters to return to the mainland, where they were freed.[72] On 7 September two of the filibusters' ships were seized in New York and arrest warrants issued for five of their leaders.[73]

Though the government took no further steps, the expedition was effectively suppressed. Federal officials were reluctant to do more because López's mission was so popular in the South, particularly in New Orleans. There the press claimed that the president had "denied the doctrine of expatriation which would allow individuals to leave voluntarily their native land to participate in foreign quarrels, whatever their motive." Moreover, the dispatch of the navy to Mississippi territory was regarded as a violation of states' rights.[74] Nevertheless, the Spanish minister of state was satisfied with U.S. government action.[75]

In April of 1850 López renewed his efforts to organize an expedition, this time in New Orleans. He planned to avoid violating the neutrality laws by portraying the filibusters as emigrants bound for California by way of Panama. The men and arms would be brought together on Contoy, an uninhabited island in Mexican territorial waters. López received financial support and assistance in recruitment from the governor of Mississippi. The judge of the Supreme Court of Errors and Appeals of Mississippi signed the Cuban bonds that were sold to raise money for the operation. Three U.S. Army colonels organized regiments in Kentucky, Mississippi, and Louisiana. Arms were procured from the state arsenals of Mississippi and Louisiana.[76]

In April and May, over one thousand filibusters obtained their tickets to Panama and sailed for Contoy.[77] The Spanish consul in New Orleans requested that federal officers detain them, but the request was denied. The administration, however, had already dispatched three war vessels to Cuba to stop any American invasion.[78]

At Contoy many of the filibusters deserted,[79] were captured by a Spanish naval vessel, and were taken to Cuba.[80] On 19 May the remaining filibusters, numbering about 520, landed at Cardenas, Cuba. Finding that they enjoyed little support among the Cuban population, the filibusters departed.[81] A Spanish naval vessel pursued the filibusters to Key West, where the Spanish captain demanded their arrest. Though the filibusters' vessel was seized, local residents helped the men to escape.[82]

Secretary of State Clayton directed U.S. district attorneys in the South to arrest López. On 25 May he was arrested at Savannah but was released because there were no witnesses to testify against him. For the same reason, the district attorney in Mobile failed to arrest López. Finally, on

7 June he was arrested in New Orleans, along with nine of his officers, three American civilian supporters, the governor of Mississippi, the supreme court judge of Mississippi, and the general of Mississippi's state militia.[83]

Meanwhile, the focus of diplomatic attention was on the Contoy deserters who were being held in a Havana prison on charges of piracy. The United States held that the filibusters were not pirates, since piracy could be committed only on the high seas, while the filibusters' acts of violence were committed in Cuba. Moreover, the men captured at Contoy had not intended to commit violent acts against Cuba but were bona fide travelers to Panama.[84] Finally, the United States argued that Spain had no right to arrest people in neutral territory, namely, the territory of Mexico.[85] The United States took the position that the Contoy prisoners "might be guilty of violating American but not Spanish law," and therefore Spain should return them to the United States for prosecution.[86]

Spain contended

> that these persons made part of an expedition fitted out in the U.S. with the
> intention of invading Cuba, burning and sacking her cities, plundering and
> murdering her inhabitants, and committing every act which could put them
> in the rank of buccaneers and pirates, and as such entitled to the protection
> of no government, but worthy only of the execration of mankind.[87]

In the end, a Spanish maritime court found all but three of the Americans not guilty on the grounds that "they were deceived as to the true object of the expedition." The three who were found guilty were given long prison terms but were pardoned and sent back to the United States in November of 1850.[88]

In December of 1850, the case against the sixteen filibusters indicted in the United States, known as the Cuba State Trials, began.[89] After three juries failed to reach a verdict, all the charges were dropped in March of 1851.[90]

López then planned a third expedition to Cuba to be launched in the spring of 1851. President Fillmore spoke against it in his December message to Congress and issued a proclamation against it in April.[91] The day after the proclamation was issued, three of López's American backers were indicted and arrested. This, along with a lack of money and a poorly executed plan, delayed the filibusters' departure. In July, New Orleans received news of a revolution in Cuba and on 3 August, López's last expedition set sail. Included were "about fifty Cubans, twenty or so Hungarians and Germans, one infantry battalion of Americans of 232 men, and an artillery battalion of 122."[92] Also on board were "three ex-employees of the Custom House at New Orleans," one of whom—the nephew of the attorney general—warned López on 1 August that the government would seize his ship on the third.[93] On 23 August, the filibusters were routed by the Spanish, and on 1 September López was executed.[94]

Foreign nationals were not alone in their attempts to launch from U.S. territory military expeditions against other states. U.S. citizens, including public officials, did the same. Two of the most notable were Aaron Burr and William Walker.

"The Burr Conspiracy was incubated in Washington during the winter of 1804–1805." At this time, the plot involved Aaron Burr, vice-president of the United States, and General James Wilkinson, commander of the United States Army, who apparently originated the scheme. They believed that war with Spain was inevitable and that the people of the western United States would, under the two men's leadership, form a volunteer army to take Mexican territory.[95]

For the conspirators the principal problem was to secure financing for the project. Burr approached the British minister to the United States, who wrote to his government:

> I have just received an offer from Mr. Burr, the actual Vice-President of the United States . . . to lend his assistance to his Majesty's government in any manner in which they may think fit to employ him, particularly in endeavoring to effect a separation of the western part of the United States from that which lies between the Atlantic and the mountains, in its whole extent.[96]

Historians generally agree that the idea of detaching the western states was a ploy Burr used to secure British financial and military aid.[97]

Despite what the minister was told, the real aim of the Burr conspiracy was to take Spanish territory in Mexico and establish a new nation.[98] Burr later wrote that he "did hope to establish an empire in Mexico and to become its emperor."[99]

Burr also approached the Spanish minister to the United States with a bizarre scheme:

> The plan was to fill Washington with men in disguise, and when the Colonel [Burr] gave the signal, to seize the President, the Vice President and the substitute President of the Senate, the public moneys and the arsenal. If Washington could not be held, Colonel Burr would take the ships in commission at the Navy Yard, burn the rest, and sail to New Orleans to establish the independence of Louisiana and the West. None of the Spanish possessions were to be molested.[100]

Nevertheless, major financing was not forthcoming from either Britain or Spain. Burr then turned to soliciting funds through a western land-speculation scheme. His plan was to develop a colony in the Louisiana territory on a million-acre tract owned by a Kentucky army officer. While some contend that Burr was sincere about this project,[101] others suggest that "it was a plausible cover for the forces he was gathering. If Burr's expedition were challenged by the U.S. government, it could be presented as a legitimate colonization scheme."[102]

Meanwhile, President Jefferson received a number of reports on Burr's activities,[103] but did nothing. It is not clear whether this was due to his complicity in the conspiracy[104] or to his reluctance to denounce a conspiracy hatched by the man he had appointed governor of the Louisiana Territory—General Wilkinson. "The president had not dared to do anything that would compel his remote military commander to go over to Spain or to combine with Burr in a war of their own, possibly directed against the government of the United States."[105] For fifteen months the federal government did nothing to stop Burr.[106]

In the spring of 1806, the secretary of war ordered General Wilkinson to move his forces from his headquarters in Saint Louis to the lower Mississippi in anticipation of a Spanish invasion. Wilkinson, who was awaiting the arrival of Burr's forces, delayed leaving and arrived at the Sabine River only in late September.[107]

"Wilkinson's plot was now to draw Burr into the West, then to betray him to Jefferson and the country, charging him with treason, the while he made peace with the Spaniards so as to dispatch an emissary to Mexico City to demand a large sum of money from the Viceroy for having saved New Spain from Burr and his 'bandits.'"[108] Following the U.S. War for Independence, Wilkinson secretly had become not only a subject of Spain but an agent of the Spanish government. He had convinced the Spanish that he could lead western settlers to revolt against the U.S. government and place themselves under the authority of Spain.[109]

Why Wilkinson decided to betray Burr and the conspiracy is not clear,[110] but in October Wilkinson wrote the president that he had uncovered a plot to invade Vera Cruz. He did not mention Burr's name.[111]

In September, Burr proceeded to Kentucky and Tennessee to recruit more men.[112] The district attorney in Kentucky informed Jefferson of a plot to disrupt the Union, but since he presented no evidence, Jefferson took no legal action. He did send a State Department official to investigate Burr's activities, and to "put the Governors, etc., on their guard, to provide for his arrest if necessary."[113] In Kentucky, on 5 November, the federal district attorney requested that a hearing be held at which Burr and others would be required to answer charges of treason. Since no evidence was presented, the court denied the motion.[114] Burr then demanded an investigation and was exonerated when the district attorney again failed to produce any witnesses. On 27 November, the district attorney again tried and failed to secure Burr's arrest, and was removed from office.[115] Burr issued a statement denying he had any intention of breaking up the union and claiming he was preparing to take 100 or 150 settlers to the Louisiana Territory.[116]

In the meantime, Jefferson's agent told the governor of Ohio about the plot, and the state militia was sent to seize the boats and supplies Burr had accumulated there. Kentucky's governor sent troops against the expeditionists gathered near Louisville. In both cases, the troops arrived after the filibusters had sailed downriver.[117]

On 27 November, Jefferson issued a proclamation condemning the expedition and ordered officials to arrest the expeditionists who were preparing to sail down the Ohio River.[118] The "President only charged misdemeanor—attack on the Spanish possessions."[119] It was the receipt of General Wilkinson's report on the conspiracy that prompted the cabinet to finally move against Burr. General Wilkinson was instructed to "use every exertion in your power to frustrate and effectually prevent any enterprise which has for its object, directly or indirectly, any hostile act on any part of the territories of the United States, or on any territories of the King of Spain."[120] The government was still not sure whether Burr intended to invade Mexico, detach the western states, or both.[121]

Wilkinson seized on the Burr expedition's threatened "invasion" to establish a military dictatorship in New Orleans. While the governor refused to declare martial law, stating that "many good disposed citizens do not appear to think the danger considerable, and there are others who . . . endeavor to turn our preparations into ridicule," Wilkinson began arresting people without civil authority. He placed three individuals on "a war vessel bound for Baltimore, consigned to the President of the United States." All of the individuals Wilkinson sent were released.[122]

Meanwhile, Congress requested that Jefferson clarify the matter. Was Burr really planning to disrupt the Union or was General Wilkinson creating the alarm for his own purposes? In his 22 January message to Congress, Jefferson said that "Colonel Burr's 'guilt is placed beyond question.'" With this, Jefferson publicly accused Burr of treason.[123]

On 10 January, Burr learned of Jefferson's proclamation and of the governor of the Mississippi Territory's order for his arrest. Burr turned himself in,[124] convinced the grand jury that he only intended to attack Spanish territory, and was exonerated.[125]

Thus, for the third time, Burr was acquitted in federal court. Still the judge refused to release him and ordered Burr to present himself to the judge on a daily basis.[126] Meanwhile, General Wilkinson was attempting to have Burr either kidnapped to New Orleans or assassinated.[127] Burr,

faced with unconstitutional civil prosecution in Mississippi and a court-
martial by Wilkinson in New Orleans, decided to go into hiding.

On 18 February Burr was arrested, charged with the misdemeanor of
planning to invade Mexico and with treason for preparing to wage war
on the United States.[128] Chief Justice Marshall issued his opinion that
there was insufficient evidence for the charge of treason. Only the misdemeanor charge was let stand. Burr was released on bail to await the opening of the next session of the circuit court on 22 May. Jefferson, who was
angry with Marshall's decision, mobilized agents to collect depositions
on and interview witnesses to Burr's treasonous activities.[129] On 2 April,
President Jefferson wrote to Madrid, saying that "no better proof of the
good faith of the United States [toward Spain] could have been given than
the vigor with which we acted . . . in suppressing the enterprise meditated
lately by Burr against Mexico."[130] In June, a grand jury indicted Burr for
filibustering and treason.[131]

Burr's trial lasted a month, ending with his acquittal on the treason
charge on 1 September. Two weeks later he was acquitted of the misdemeanor charge as well. On 19 October, Burr was reindicted on the misdemeanor charge, but "Marshall ruled there was not sufficient evidence
to commit on another charge of treason."[132] Burr went into exile first to
England and then to France, still seeking to obtain support for his conquest of Mexico. Wilkinson was court-martialed for being a "pensioner"
of Spain but was exonerated.[133]

William Walker, the most famous filibuster, began his career with an
invasion of Mexico in 1854.[134] In November he took the governor of Baja
prisoner and proclaimed the independent Republic of Lower California.
When the Mexicans foiled his invasion of Sonora, which Walker intended
to add to his republic, Walker retreated to California. There he was arrested for violating the neutrality laws, but was acquitted by a jury that
needed only eight minutes to reach its verdict.

Walker's better-known expeditions to Nicaragua began in 1854 when,
during his visit to Honduras, Nicaraguan revolutionaries asked that he
organize a force to help them overthrow their government. Walker would
be given land as payment for his services. Since this would violate U.S.
neutrality laws, Walker and his supporters proposed a colonization
scheme and obtained the permission of the U.S. district attorney and the
U.S. Army commander in California. By October of 1855 Walker had
captured Granada and formed a new government with himself as commander-in-chief of the army.

Within days the U.S. minister in Nicaragua recognized Walker's government. When Secretary of State Marcy learned of this he reprimanded
the minister, ordering that he "at once cease to have any communication
with the present assumed rulers of that country." In December, when the

new Nicaraguan minister to the United States requested an interview with Marcy, the latter replied that the president "has not yet seen reasons for establishing diplomatic intercourse with the persons who now claim to exercise the political power in the State of Nicaragua."

Also in December the president issued a proclamation intended to prevent more Americans from going to Nicaragua to join the Walker expedition and ordered district attorneys in port cities to stop people from sailing to Nicaragua to join its army. At this time the administration had good reason to act against the filibusters. Its ongoing negotiations with Britain over the interpretation of the Clayton-Bulwer Treaty were complicated by Walker's activities.[135] Moreover, the United States had recently protested British attempts to recruit Americans to fight in the Crimean War. Accordingly,

> it was Pierce's intention in acting against the filibusters to show that his administration was impartial in enforcing the neutrality laws. He could not wink at the violations, or suspected violations by Americans, while he was prosecuting British agents and planning to demand the recall of the minister to the United States . . . for his part, a leading one, in obtaining the enlistments.

Upon learning that the Nicaraguan minister was recruiting more filibusters, the U.S. attorney in New York warned the minister that he would be arrested and his ship seized if the filibusters left port. These threats came to nothing. Since the filibusters were sailing not on a chartered ship but on a regular commercial passenger ship, federal officials could not claim they constituted an organized expeditionary force. A few arrests were made, but U.S. marshals were able only to delay the filibusters' departure by a couple of days.

In June of 1856, the United States received the new Nicaraguan minister to the United States and directed the American minister to Nicaragua to establish diplomatic relations with that government. What the administration did not know is that the government it proposed to recognize no longer existed. In the meantime, Walker had taken over the government, making himself president. Yet the American minister proceeded to recognize the Walker government without consulting Washington. The following month Walker named as his new minister to the United States an American who had only recently arrived in Nicaragua. This time the administration refused to receive the minister. The president and secretary of state were outraged that the American minister had recognized Walker's government. In September, Marcy recalled the minister.

The other Central American countries agreed in July to cooperate in overthrowing Walker. During the subsequent war, Walker received hundred of recruits from the United States, an act that led the Central American allies to request that the local U.S. naval commander prevent the landing of Walker's recruits at San Juan de Sur. The United States declined, as the president had recently declared that a state of civil war existed in Nicaragua and proclaimed U.S. neutrality. This meant that a U.S. attempt to interdict Walker's reinforcements would favor one side of the conflict.

By April of 1857 Walker's position had become untenable. To prevent the starvation or slaughter of the remaining Americans, the U.S. naval commander persuaded the allies to allow the Americans to leave if Walker would surrender. Walker agreed and was taken to New Orleans, where he was received as a hero.

Walker proceeded to Washington, where he hoped to persuade President Buchanan not to invoke the neutrality laws against his second expedition to Nicaragua. Buchanan met with him on 12 June, but as there is no official record of the meeting, it is not known whether Buchanan approved or condemned the expedition. Of course Walker claimed that the president approved his plans.

Walker's efforts to organize a new expedition led the Guatemalan and El Salvadoran ministers to the United States to protest to the secretary of state "of an expedition 'so publicly and shamelessly proclaimed.'" The secretary responded by ordering officials in port cities to stop any military expeditions from sailing. In November the U.S. district judge at New Orleans issued a warrant for Walker's arrest. Walker was released on bail and sailed for Mobile. There the U.S. district attorney searched his ship and, finding nothing illegal, released it. Walker's second expedition to Nicaragua departed on 14 November, only five-and-one-half months after he had arrived in the United States.

The president, however, had not only ordered officials to prevent Walker's departure but had instructed the navy "to send three ships to Central America to stop filibusters if they escaped from the United States." Walker managed to deceive the navy and landed his troops at San Juan del Norte.

On 6 December Commodore Paulding arrived at San Juan de Norte, secured Walker's surrender, and put him on a ship to New York. Walker arrived on 27 December only to charge that "Paulding had violated neutral territory in arresting him" and to promise that "he would return to Nicaragua as that republic's legitimate president." President Buchanan, however, had gone on record as opposing filibustering. In his first annual message he had stated that "such enterprises . . . can do no possible good to the country, but have already inflicted much injury both on its interests and its character."

The day after his arrival Walker surrendered to the U.S. marshal in New York, who directed him to turn himself into officials in Washington. There Secretary of State Cass told Walker that only the judiciary could hold him. Walker's inability to find someone to whom he could surrender stemmed from the dilemma that he posed for the administration. While it did not want to countenance filibustering, the government's arrest of Walker on neutral territory was of questionable legality.

Though the government eventually undertook three prosecutions of the Walker filibusters, all failed and Walker began to organize his third expedition. When Mobile port officials learned of his intention to sail for Nicaragua on 10 November, they asked the secretary of the navy for advice. "Cobb replied that he could not give explicit instructions but there must be no repetition of the sailing of the *Fashion*, which had carried weapons, the year before." By this time, however, Walker's activities were so well publicized that Buchanan issued a proclamation against the expedition.

The government did thwart the departure of one shipload of "emigrants" bound for Nicaragua, but a grand jury failed to indict Walker for violating the neutrality laws. A second ship managed to elude government officials and sailed for Honduras, from whence Walker planned to launch his invasion of Nicaragua. This group arrived in Belize only to be returned to the United States by a British naval vessel.

January of 1859 found Walker again trying to organize an expedition, but this time in secret. By this time there was no question as to what Walker's intentions were. When a friend told him that future attempts were not likely to succeed in the face of "the declared hostility of the world," Walker replied, "I am not contending for the world's approval but for the empire of Central America." This expedition also failed due to the intervention of government officials. Walker's recruits were arrested by the army near New Orleans, though a grand jury failed to indict them.

Walker began organizing his fourth and final expedition in early 1860. This time he received support from a new quarter. In late 1859, the British government had agreed to turn the Bay Islands over to Honduras. The British settlers who opposed this decided to fight for independence, and asked for Walker's assistance. When the British governor of Belize became suspicious of the steady stream of immigrants from New Orleans, Walker sailed for Honduras, where he seized the town of Trujillo. Two weeks later the commander of a British warship demanded Walker's departure, but Walker escaped. A few days later British and Honduran warships arrived at his new camp and again demanded his surrender. Walker agreed to surrender to the British but, though the British took custody of his men, the Hondurans took Walker. Eight days later he was court-martialed. He was executed the next day.

This set of cases reveals the complex political nature of filibustering. It entailed issues of central state interests, states' rights, citizens' rights, and the central state's capacity to exert control beyond the capital. It is important to note that the U.S. central state did not publicly support any of the expeditions, regardless of whether they were led by a foreign national, a private U.S. citizen, or even the "actual Vice-President of the United States." Yet in several instances, top officials met with the filibusters, providing the latter with the opportunity to claim legitimacy. This produced confusion among state officials, federal employees, and juries as to the extent of the administration's knowledge of and support for the expeditions.

Ambivalence at the top exacerbated federal officials' twin problems of filibustering's popularity in the West and South and of the central state's lack of effective control. Citizens believed they had the right to leave the country to fight for whatever cause they wished. A common aim of the filibusters—expanding the territory of the United States—was widely supported.

These cases also reveal just how tenuous was the central state's control. Some of its own agents participated in filibustering expeditions. At the time they hatched their Mexican scheme, Burr was vice-president and General Wilkinson was commander of the U.S. Army. Federal officials, civilian and military, served as recruiters for filibuster armies.

If federal officials exerted little control over their own employees, they had even less influence on state officials and ordinary citizens. Time and again we see state officials actively participating in filibustering enterprises, failing to cooperate in their suppression, and resisting federal efforts as an infringement of states' rights. Finally, federal prosecutions of filibusters repeatedly failed due to the lack of cooperation from citizens. If the government could not convict William Walker of filibustering, though it made three attempts, it is difficult to see how it could have convicted anyone.

Expeditions Inadvertently Invited by Mexico

In the 1850s, French residents of California participated in several expeditions against Sonora, Mexico.[136] Mexico, in light of its recent war with the United States, was seeking to establish defensive colonies along its northern border to deter American expansion and Indian attacks. The Mexican government apparently believed that the California French, being the nearest Europeans, would be the most desirable colonists. By 1851, then, Mexico began courting the French, not foreseeing that "these men, discovering the weakness and wealth of Mexico, might turn against the possessors of the land and government of the country, quite as readily as had Americans in Texas or California."[137]

In 1851, the first of the French filibusters learned that the Mexican consul in San Francisco was organizing people to establish a colony in Sonora, gathered about eighty men, and sailed to Guaymas. As the consul had promised, they were warmly received and were given financial support for their expedition inland. They were also given a land grant in a valley near the northern frontier, where they established their colony. After several months, during which the group suffered a number of Indian attacks, the Mexicans stopped sending supplies. The colonists' leader went to the state capital to ask for aid, but his demands and threats alarmed Mexican officials, who ordered him to leave.[138] He died shortly after returning to the colony, and those members of his expedition who had not already deserted, either returned to San Francisco or settled in Guaymas.[139]

The Mexicans suddenly ended their support of the colonizing expedition due to their fear of its leader. This man's reputation in France was so bad that the French minister to Mexico refused any responsibility for him. Mexican federal officials warned the *commandante general* of Sonora that he might cause trouble and directed him to imprison the Frenchman if he disturbed the peace of Sonora.[140]

The second French expedition, consisting of sixty to eighty persons, arrived at Guaymas from San Francisco in March of 1852. This expedition had been given a concession by the Mexican consul in San Francisco to work some abandoned mines in Sonora.[141] This time, though he allowed them to establish a colony, the governor of Sonora decreed that the Frenchmen would have to serve in the militia and pay taxes.[142] Finding no gold, the expedition soon dispersed.[143]

Since these first two expeditions failed so quickly, and since they had had the support of the Mexican government, it is not clear whether they should be termed filibustering operations. What the Frenchmen's attitude toward Mexican authorities would have been had they succeeded is unknown. The third expedition, however, was unquestionably a filibustering enterprise.

The leader this time was a Frenchman named Raousset. He first went to Mexico City, where, with the assistance of a powerful Franco-Mexican banking house and the French minister to Mexico, he secured a contract to work abandoned mines in northern Sonora. In exchange, his colonists were to defend the frontier against Indian attacks.[144] Back in San Francisco, the French consul, Dillon, helped him recruit two hundred Frenchmen who sailed to Guaymas with him in May of 1852. There Raousset met with resistance from the now wary governor,[145] but did secure permission to take his troops to the mines.

Very quickly the filibuster fell into a disagreement with the governor on the issue of naturalization of the colonists. Believing he could not obtain justice from the governor, Raousset "threw caution to the winds and raised the standard of revolt."[146]

The filibuster's first target was Hermosillo. While the residents tried to stall the French until government troops could arrive, Raousset announced that he would take the city within one hour. "And strangely enough he made good his boast—an hour was sufficient to take the city of twelve thousand persons, garrisoned by a force six times stronger than that of the attackers." The task of occupation proved too much for the French, who departed for Guaymas to procure reinforcements and supplies. There his men repudiated Raousset, and the French consular agent arranged for their return to San Francisco.[147] Thus ended this expedition in December of 1852.

When Santa Anna became president of Mexico, Raousset went to Mexico City to see if he might obtain permission to renew his colonization scheme. These negotiations came to naught, and Raousset returned to San Francisco. There he actively organized an expedition to take Sonora by force.[148] Meanwhile, Walker's filibustering activities alarmed Mexican authorities to the point where they revived the idea of setting up French colonies in Sonora, mainly to defend against filibustering by either Raousset or Walker.[149]

In San Francisco the Mexican consul enlisted the assistance of the French consul in organizing the expedition. The recruits were to serve in the Mexican army for one year and then be given an allotment of land.[150] The consuls chartered a ship to carry the eight hundred men they had recruited to Mexico, but the United States libeled the vessel and indicted the Mexican consul for violating its neutrality laws.[151] According to the Gadsden Treaty, the United States was supposed to cooperate with Mexico in suppressing filibustering, and in light of Walker's activities, the president had issued a proclamation against filibustering in January of 1854.

After some legal maneuvering, the ship was allowed to depart with four hundred French, German, Irish, and Chilean recruits on 2 April 1854.[152] Six weeks later, Raousset set sail for Guaymas to assume leadership of the expedition. At this time Raousset made clear his filibustering aims when he wrote

> Do not be surprised, my friend, to see me embrace all of Mexico; I dare not say that this is in my plans, but it is in the realm of possibility. I am convinced that my work, the establishment of the French in Sonora, will be only the first step of France towards the occupation of this magnificent country.[153]

In Guaymas, after a battle with Mexican troops, the filibusters surrendered. Most of them were taken to Vera Cruz, from whence a French

naval vessel transported them to the French West Indies. Raousset, however, was tried, convicted of treason, and executed on 12 August.

The last French filibuster was a former naval officer exiled after
the 1848 revolution. In late 1855 he "led some two hundred French, Italians and Anglo-Americans from the Golden Gate to La Paz in Baja California, on their way to join the Mexican revolutionists fighting against
Santa Anna." Suspecting the Frenchman had designs on Sonora, the
Mexicans arrested him and his men and sent them to Mexico City. There
they were imprisoned until 1856–57, when diplomatic efforts secured
their release.[154]

The U.S. government's role was, as usual, ambiguous. In January 1854
the secretary of war appointed General John E. Wool as commander of
the Pacific department. Wool was ordered to "use all proper means to
detect the fitting out of armed expeditions against countries with which
the United States are at peace, and . . . zealously cooperate with the civil
authorities in maintaining the neutrality laws." Yet when the general
stopped the filibusters' ship from sailing and persuaded the district attorney to indict the Mexican consul, Jefferson Davis reprimanded him for
exceeding his authority. Of course, since Mexican authorities were actively involved in organizing these expeditions, it was rather difficult for
Mexico and the United States to define them as filibusters. As a result of
Wool's censure, all efforts to halt filibustering expeditions from San Francisco ceased.[155]

In these cases efforts by the Mexican government to attract U.S. residents
to defend the frontier against Indian and filibuster attacks backfired when
the immigrants themselves turned to filibustering. This led to a rather
bizarre situation in which the U.S. government indicted the Mexican consul for violating U.S. neutrality laws. What the consul viewed as a legitimate colonization scheme was seen by the U.S. government as a violation
of its treaty obligations to prevent filibustering expeditions to Mexico.
Here again, though, the federal government's actions were confusing. It
ordered its army commander to suppress filibustering, but when he actually moved against the filibusters, the secretary of war reprimanded him
for exceeding his authority.

Another interesting feature of these cases is the high degree of similar-
ity between the U.S. and French cases. Raousset, like many of his American counterparts, claimed to be working for the occupation of Mexico by
his home state. Despite France's apparent lack of support for Raousset,
the French government did not abandon his men to their fate with Mexican authorities. As the U.S. government frequently attempted to do, the
French government secured the filibusters' release and transported them
to French territory, even though the filibusters had left France to live in

California. The notion that the home state has the right to exert authority over its citizens, or that it has some responsibility to even its wayward citizens, was common to the U.S. and French states.

Expeditions Launched by U.S. Government Agents

While the role of central state officials in the previous cases is ambiguous, a number of filibustering operations were led by employees of the central state. For this reason, it is more difficult for state leaders to deny knowledge of or accountability for the operations.

GEORGE MATHEWS

In late 1810 the Spanish governor of West Florida offered to turn over his territory to the United States unless he received reinforcements by the start of the new year. His existing forces were not adequate to deal with Americans in Baton Rouge and Mobile who were threatening to invade his territory. Congress authorized the president to take possession of the territory if either an agreement were reached with Spain or another foreign power, namely England, attempted to occupy it. Madison then appointed Colonel McKee and General George Mathews to negotiate the transfer of West Florida to the United States.[156]

Meanwhile, the Spanish governor received support from his government and the Mobile filibusters disbanded, so he revoked his offer. Mathews was relieved of his task, but the government gave him "discretionary power to continue his mission with respect to East Florida." Mathews convinced the administration that the residents of East Florida would rise up and declare their independence from Spain. The secretary of state instructed him to take possession of East Florida if the local authorities agreed to surrender it or if a foreign power attempted to occupy it. Army and navy officers in the region were ordered to prepare to assist Mathews if he requested it.

In August Mathews reported to Secretary of State Monroe that the local authorities would not turn over the territory peacefully, and he requested covert military aid to the inhabitants so they could overthrow the government. Monroe did not reply, though "Mathews thought, no doubt,—and justly—that the Secretary's silence gave tacit approval to his measures. Yet he took pains to see that Monroe was thoroughly informed of his plans, and asked plainly enough to be relieved if the government disapproved his policy." Why did the government assume this hands-off policy? "The only reasonable conclusion is that the government wished the plan to proceed under the auspices of Mathews, but preferred to avoid committing itself in any way, so that it might disavow the action of its agents should it prove expedient to do so."[157]

Mathews proceeded to prepare for the seizure of Saint Augustine by an army consisting of local inhabitants, some volunteers from Georgia, and fifty U.S. soldiers. These soldiers were to go not as members of the U.S. army but as individual volunteers. To obtain naval support, Mathews spread a rumor that British troops were approaching. The plan was ruined, however, when the local army commander, Major Laval, refused to allow the fifty soldiers to participate as volunteers.

Mathews's alternate plan was to take Fernandina and Amelia Island. The forces he assembled there on 14 March 1812 consisted of 180 to 350 people. A few were Spanish subjects but most were U.S. citizens. These people, claiming to be the local authorities, then asked the United States to annex their territory. Mathews requested that Major Laval send troops to take possession, but the latter refused.

Meanwhile, several American gunboats "took up threatening positions where they could blockade the harbor and command with their guns the feeble shore defenses."[158] The Spanish commandant at Fernandina, López, then asked the local American army and navy commanders if the United States was supporting the revolutionaries. Both denied it.[159]

López refused to surrender to the revolutionaries, instead offering to surrender to the United States, either in the person of Mathews or to the gunboats. Mathews could not accept the surrender since he could only take the territory through peaceful means. At one point, López took down the Spanish flag and sent it to one of the gunboats. The Americans refused to receive it, so it was "taken back to the city and hoisted up again."[160]

Finally, the Spanish surrendered and Mathews accepted Amelia Island in behalf of the United States. Major Laval was arrested and replaced by Lieutenant Colonel Smith, who sent troops to secure Fernandina and Amelia Island. Mathews, Smith, and the naval commander were all concerned that they had exceeded their orders, and asked their superiors for clarification. The last "begged to be at once informed whether his conduct was approved."[161]

Mathews and Smith continued their conquest of East Florida, and on 21 March Mathews sent Monroe a draft by whose terms the United States would receive the entire province of East Florida.[162] This left federal officials in an embarrassing situation. Monroe publicly disavowed Mathews's actions and dismissed Mathews, writing him that his actions "are not authorized by the law of the United States, or the instructions founded on it, under which you have acted."[163] While the government disavowed Mathews's activities, it did not end its support for the filibusters for twenty-five months.

After firing Mathews, Monroe put the governor of Georgia in charge of negotiating with the Spanish governor for a return to the status quo antebellum. The hitch in these instructions was that the governor was to obtain assurances that the filibusters still in East Florida would not be harmed. Of course, many of the filibusters were the governor's fellow Georgians.

On 3 July the U.S. Senate defeated a bill that would have authorized the occupation of East Florida, and three days later Monroe wrote to the governor "that the President thought it advisable to withdraw the troops."[164] The governor objected to this and said he had sent reinforcements to Colonel Smith. The filibusters wrote to Monroe protesting the proposed troop withdrawal, arguing that the filibusters had been assured from the start that the United States would guarantee their safety.

In January, the Senate again failed to pass a bill authorizing the occupation of East Florida. Meanwhile, Spain agreed to grant amnesty to the insurgents, and the secretary of war ordered the troops in East Florida to withdraw. Despite the filibusters' refusal of a pardon offered by the government of Saint Augustine and their pledge to pursue their cause, the U.S. troops completed their withdrawal on 15 May.

In early 1814 the filibusters made one final attempt to get the United States to annex their territory, but Monroe replied that

> the United States being at peace with Spain, no countenance can be given by their government to the proceedings of the revolutionary party in East Florida, if it is composed of Spanish subjects,—and still less can it be given to them if it consists of American citizens, who, so far as their conduct may fall within the scope of existing laws long enacted and well known and understood, will be liable to censure.

With this action, "twenty-five months after the opening of the revolution in East Florida, the United States finally repudiated all connection with it."[165]

WILLIAM EATON

Another filibuster who was a government official who exceeded his orders was William Eaton.[166] A former army officer, Eaton was appointed U.S. consular agent at Tunis in 1797. As we have seen, at this time the United States was paying protection money to all the Barbary states, and Eaton's task was to renegotiate its treaty with Tunis so that the United States could pay its tribute in cash and not naval stores, as the bey de-

manded. Eaton succeeded in this endeavor, then spent the next four years
in Tunis trying to enforce the treaty and to develop a normal trading
relationship between the United States and Tunis. Meanwhile, Pasha
Yusuf of Tripoli was demanding more money from the United States: "an
initial payment of $225,000 and an annual tribute of $20,000." In reject-
ing the U.S. consul's offer of $30,000 in exchange for waiting for a reply
from the U.S. government, Yusuf appeared to show "a preference for
war."[167]

When the United States failed to comply with his demands, Yusuf declared war on 14 May 1801. At this point Eaton concocted a scheme by
which the United States would overthrow Yusuf and replace him with his
brother, Hamet, whom Yusuf had forcefully replaced as pasha of Tripoli.
Eaton knew that launching such a project would exceed his instructions
from the State Department, so he wrote to Madison, telling him of his
contacts with Hamet and suggesting that the United States support
Hamet's efforts to regain his throne.

In late 1803 Eaton returned to the United States to brief the government and lobby for the use of military force. Persuaded by Eaton's arguments,[168] President Jefferson appointed Eaton naval "agent for the Barbary regencies,"[169] a vaguely defined position of adviser to the commander of U.S. naval forces in North Africa. In addition, the secretary of
the navy directed his commodore to support Eaton's efforts when expedient, and the secretary of state authorized the expenditure of $20,000 in
support of Hamet.[170]

In December of 1804 Eaton proceeded to Egypt, where he raised an
army composed of U.S. Marines,[171] European mercenaries, and hundreds
of Arabs, with himself as general.[172] He finally found Hamet, who was in
exile in Egypt. Eaton made an agreement with him by which the United
States would restore Hamet to his throne in exchange for Hamet's making a new and permanent treaty with the United States. Among other
things, the treaty provided that Hamet would reimburse the United States
for costs incurred in putting him on the throne.[173]

Eaton marched his army six hundred miles across the desert to Tripoli.
Along the way he attracted more volunteers, so that by the time he
reached Derna, Tripoli, he may have had as many as seven hundred men.

With the assistance of U.S. naval bombardment, Eaton's army took
Derna in April of 1805. Eaton planned to proceed to Tripoli, where, with
naval support, he would overthrow Yusuf and secure the U.S. "conquest"
of all of Tripoli by installing the puppet, Hamet, on the throne. Thus, he
urgently requested that the commodore attack Tripoli. As Eaton waited
for a reply, Yusuf's forces counterattacked, setting off a month-long battle for the city.

Meanwhile, the U.S. Navy, believing that Tripoli could be suppressed by sea, had been engaged in a campaign against Tripoli's shipping. In the course of this campaign in late 1803, Tripoli captured an American warship and took its three hundred sailors prisoner. On 3 June, after bombarding Tripoli, the navy secured Yusuf's agreement to release the American prisoners in exchange for a small ransom. On 11 June, the navy brought word of the treaty to Eaton along with orders that he and his "Christian forces" withdraw from Derna. On the night of 12 June, the Americans and Europeans quietly boarded ships, leaving their Arab colleagues to flee to the mountains.

Yusuf offered amnesty to the Arab rebels and the governorship of Derna to Hamet. The U.S. government provided Hamet with about $9,300 in relief and reimbursed Eaton $12,700 for his expenses.[174]

In the United States Eaton was lauded by the president, Congress, and the public for his role in bringing Yusuf to heel. He clearly demonstrated the utility of force in dealing with the North African rulers. Nevertheless, his scheme to overthrow the Tripolitan government and install a puppet ruler using an army with himself as general far exceeded the aims of U.S. officials:

> From the beginning of Eaton's agitation for the utilization of Hamet as a puppet, the government at best had been only lukewarm. The navy had shown little enthusiasm. . . . Commodore Barron . . . authorized the search for Hamet in Egypt and the expedition to Derna, but Eaton clearly misinterpreted his instructions if he believed that Barron had promised to restore Hamet to the throne of Tripoli. The American government was willing to give Hamet the benefit of Eaton's leadership and a small amount of assistance in the hope that he might be able to stir up a revolution in Tripoli; but apparently no one except Eaton, from President Jefferson to Commodore Barron, dreamed of waging a great campaign to ensure Hamet's throne. If he could take the throne, well and good; if he could not, then the United States would benefit by whatever difficulties he might cause the belligerent Pasha.[175]

Filibustering expeditions led by agents of the U.S. state were highly successful, but their ultimate goals were repudiated by federal officials. Both Mathews and Eaton clearly enjoyed the support of the executive branch to a point. In both cases the filibusters achieved their immediate goals only to have their ultimate objectives blocked by the U.S. government. Congress refused to annex East Florida, which Mathews had secured for the United States. The U.S. Navy refused to support Eaton's efforts to place a puppet on the throne of Tripoli.

Both outcomes were the result of U.S. domestic politics. The North-

South conflict led Northern congressmen to refuse to annex East Florida. Eaton's plans for Tripoli were thwarted by the navy, which believed Hamet was incapable of ruling and preferred to deal with the established government, even if Yusuf were its head.

CONCLUSION

Technically, pirates were clearly distinguishable from privateers. Privateers possessed a state's authority to commit violence. They targeted only enemies of the authorizing state. They operated only during wartime. Yet, in practice, who was to say whether the Elizabethan Sea Dogs, the Barbary corsairs, or the Malabar Angrias were pirates or privateers? Moreover, as we have seen, at the end of every war, large numbers of privateers turned pirates only to be granted new privateering commissions on the outbreak of the next war. So long as states insisted on the right to exploit individual violence, piracy could not even be defined, much less suppressed.

Only with this delegitimation of state-sponsored individual violence on the high seas was it possible to clearly distinguish piracy from privateering and criminal acts from acts of war. Only then did it become possible to develop an international norm against piracy and to suppress it. Only then could pirates be defined as stateless persons for whose actions no state could be held responsible but any state could prosecute. Only with the universalization of the metanorm against individual violence on the high seas were the areas of the globe not subject to sovereignty converted from a state of nature into a realm of orderly interstate relations.

Despite their sometimes comical aspects and their frequently disastrous conclusions, the filibustering expeditions were not a trivial aspect of nineteenth-century international relations. As table 5.1 indicates there were at least a dozen more instances of filibustering between 1810 and 1860.

Many expeditions, including Eaton's, Mathews's, and Walker's, succeeded. Eaton did overthrow a foreign government official (the governor of Derna). Mathews did secure East Florida for the United States, and Walker did take over the government of Nicaragua, holding it for eighteen months. If nothing else, the filibusters helped to poison U.S.-Latin American relations to this day. And all three of these, the most successful filibuster operations, were repudiated by the federal government—by the executive, the Congress, or both.

As in the case of mercantile companies, the demise of filibustering was the result of developments both within the United States and in the international system. States defined filibustering as a problem from its very

TABLE 5.1
Other Nineteenth-Century Filibusters

Leader	Target	Year
Jackson	East Florida	1817
Long	Texas	1819
Long-Trespalacios	Texas	1820
Mackenzie-Hunters' Lodge	Canada	1837–38
Flores	Ecuador	1851
Moorehead	Mexico	1851
Brannan	Hawaii	1851
Carvajal	Mexico	1851–55
Quitman	Cuba	1851
Kinney	Nicaragua	1855–58
Crabb	Mexico	1857

Sources: Charles H. Brown, *Agents of Manifest Destiny: The Lives and Times of the Filibusters* (Chapel Hill: University of North Carolina Press, 1980); Isaac Joslin Cox, "Monroe and the Early Mexican Revolutionary Agents," *Annual Report of the American Historical Association for the Year 1911* 1 (1913): 199–215; Edwin C. Guillet, *The Lives and Times of the Patriots: An Account of the Rebellion in Upper Canada, 1837–1838, and of the Patriot Agitation in the United States, 1837–1842* (Toronto: University of Toronto Press, 1968); Joseph Allen Stout, Jr., *The Liberators: Filibustering Expeditions into Mexico, 1848–1862, and the Last Thrust of Manifest Destiny* (Los Angeles: Westernlore Press, 1973), 42–48 and 143–68; Ernest C. Shearer, "The Carvajal Disturbances," *Southwestern Historical Quarterly* 55 (1951): 201–30; and Justin H. Smith, "La República de Río Grande," *American Historical Review* 25 (1920): 660–75.

beginning. This contrasts with the mercantile company case, for example, where we found that states did not define the institution as a problem for two hundred years. What accounts for the different responses is that filibustering, which was directed for the most part at Spain and later the Latin American states, occurred within the European state system.[176] Thus, for example, while Cortés fits the definition of a filibuster in that his conquests were not sanctioned by the Spanish king,[177] he is not considered a filibuster because his actions were directed at extra-European areas whose sovereignty was not recognized. The defining characteristic of nineteenth-century filibustering was that individuals from one sovereign state conducted warlike operations against a second sovereign state with which the first state was at peace. This definition was meaningless where the target territory was not recognized as being under the sovereign authority of a state.

Changes within the United States were also important. The abolition of slavery removed a major motivation for Southern expansion,[178] while the

Homestead Act opened new territory to the land-hungry, and the Pacific Railroad Act reduced the importance of a transisthmian canal. The railroad building boom also attracted the filibusters' former financiers toward more legitimate investments.[179]

Most important, however, was the consolidation and growth of the U.S. central state's authority and power. The state developed the capacity to control military activities beyond its borders. The Civil War reduced the autonomy of the states and greatly augmented the military and bureaucratic capabilities of the federal government. Time and again we see the state executive issuing proclamations and indictments, and arresting, prosecuting, and using military force against filibusters. In some cases these actions effectively deterred expeditions. For the most part, however, local officials actively subverted the central state's antifilibustering policies. Moreover, ordinary citizens not only refused to convict filibuster leaders but openly supported and even celebrated them.

In most instances it is simply impossible to determine whether U.S. state actions were sincere efforts to suppress filibustering or were simply gestures made to appease other states. Clearly state leaders were not averse to giving the expeditions a wink and a nod, leaving themselves free to disavow failure or exploit success. Of course on several occasions this backfired, as with Eaton and Mathews, when the administration was forced to repudiate highly successful operations. The interesting, and ultimately unanswerable, question is whether the U.S. central state could have suppressed filibustering if it had really been committed to doing so.

But again, the central issue is not explaining enhanced state capabilites but the ends to which they were applied. At the most basic level, the U.S. central state's struggle with the filibusters reflected the state's effort to expand and enforce its control over individuals within its territorial jurisdiction. State rulers sought and obtained the exclusive authority to form an army and use violence against other states. The international institutions of sovereignty and neutrality empowered the central state to expand and enforce that authority.

CHAPTER SIX

Conclusion

THE STATE'S MONOPOLY on external violence came very late and through a process spanning several centuries. For three hundred years nonstate violence was a legitimate practice in the European state system. In the course of the nineteenth century nonstate violence was delegitimated and eliminated. The evolution of sovereignty in the realm of extraterritorial violence was toward a state monopoly on authority over its use. In terms of the analytical framework presented in chapter 1 (see table 1.1), external violence was shifted to boxes 1 (state allocation) and 5 (state ownership). Decision-making authority was taken from nonstate actors and monopolized by the state. Ownership of the means of violence, at least the labor component, was shifted from the nonstate to the state realm. Market allocation was replaced by the state's authoritative allocation of violence.

In this process, a picture of the state and of state-building emerges that is rather different from those scenarios presented in the existing state-building literature. For one thing it is surprising to find how reluctant the state was to exert authority and control over nonstate violence. This is especially evident in the mercantile-company case, where it took two hundred years for the state to assert formal sovereignty over company property, despite the fact that the companies' critics, almost from the start, urged the state to do so.

Also remarkable is the state's lack of fear of the growth of private power. The East India Company ruled most of India, and the Hudson's Bay Company, at least in theory, ruled the fourth largest "kingdom" in the world. On several occasions, pirates established independent quasi-states, but it was years before the European states took action to suppress them. William Walker ruled Nicaragua for eighteen months, but the United States did nothing to unseat him beyond refusing to recognize his government. Rather than a state actively attempting to organize and monopolize violence, what we see here is a more passive state that, at most, exploits individual violence and entrepreneurship.

Most importantly, there was no assault per se on the practice of nonstate violence. Each form was delegitimated and eliminated in a different way. Mercenarism was defined as a problem by Great Britain in its war with France in the 1790s. Britain basically forced the United States to stop its citizens from acting as mercenaries for France. Once the United States had institutionalized new authority over mercenarism, virtually all the states in the system followed suit.

Privateering was defined as a problem by Great Britain, which regarded the practice as the only real threat to its naval supremacy. Yet Britain did not simply coerce other states into prohibiting the practice. Rather, all the European powers negotiated an agreement by which privateering was abolished in exchange for Britain's giving up its right to interdict neutral ships in search of enemy contraband. Thus, the demise of privateering was the result of states' simultaneously adopting a prohibition stemming from international agreement.

The piracy case is more complex in many respects. The fundamental problem lay in determining who was a pirate and who was a privateer and, then, who was responsible for acts of violence on the high seas, where no state was sovereign. Piracy could not be defined, much less suppressed, until privateering was abolished. With the abolition of privateering, all acts of nonstate violence on the high seas became criminal acts, as opposed to acts of war. Thus, pirates were defined as stateless persons for whose acts on the high seas no state would be held accountable. At the same time, states would be held responsible for suppressing piracy in their own territorial waters. It was only at this point that the European states could agree that the Barbary corsairs, which the Barbary states claimed were privateers, were pirates.

Elimination of piracy globally came through both coercive and cooperative efforts. In Algiers and Malta corsairing was eliminated with the establishment of French sovereignty. Confronted with those examples, Tripoli and Tunis ceased authorizing the practice. China cooperated with Great Britain in eliminating piracy from its jurisdiction.

The mercantile companies that persisted into the nineteenth century were defined as a problem not because they exercised violence but when their exercise of sovereignty entered into European balance-of-power calculations. Thus, the East India Company was eliminated when the British state was compelled to assert its sovereignty in order to validate the division of Eastern territory among the European powers. The Hudson's Bay Company was deprived of its sovereign powers once Britain determined that the establishment of effective sovereignty in Canada was required to stem U.S. expansionism.

Filibustering was eliminated through still another process. Here the issue was not delegitimation; the United States had unilaterally proscribed the practice with its neutrality law of 1794. Rather, the problem was enforcing the state's ban on individuals' using violence against other states for their own purposes. While weak neighboring states provided the opportunity for U.S. expansionism, both domestic and international politics shaped the state's policy on filibustering. Domestic reforms removed some of the incentives to filibuster, while interstate balance-of-power politics reduced the U.S. central state's ability to secure its interests by expanding its control of territory. The restructuring of the U.S. political system following the Civil War, however, reduced the power of the individual states and produced a central state with a much greater capacity to exert control over officials and citizens. After 1860, nonstate filibustering ceased, though the persistent state practice of covert action might be regarded as neofilibustering.

In a narrow sense, nonstate violence was eliminated through a sequence of largely unrelated actions directed at the individual actors. One could argue that the state's monopoly on external violence is an unintended consequence of a series of ad hoc actions taken against the various forms of nonstate violence. This would be consistent with the results of the Tilly team's investigation of the rise of the state in Western Europe. Tilly concluded that "small groups of power-hungry men fought off numerous rivals and great popular resistance in the pursuit of their own ends, and *inadvertently* promoted the formation of national states."[1]

More broadly, however, the process can be seen as a series of stages in the evolution of state authority and control. Of course the ever-expanding compass of state authority was related to the growth in the state's capacity to exert control. With the development of its own military and bureaucratic capabilities, the state was better able to effectively control the projection of violence from its own territory. This entailed not only the state's increased ability to exercise organized violence to suppress nonstate violence beyond its borders but the augmentation of its capacity to control the activities of individuals within its borders.

Nevertheless, the development of coercive capabilities explains only the increasing level of potential state control; it does not account for the expanding range of activities over which the state chose to exert control. The theoretically interesting problem is to account for changes in authority claims; physical capabilities are a separate and secondary concern.

Early on, states exerted very little authority or control over the exercise of violence by nonstate actors beyond their borders. For example, mercantile companies and pirates had free rein to use violence, at least in peripheral areas. At best, states attempted to exploit individual violence.

This stage gave way to one in which states attempted to regulate nonstate violence. Privateering commissions represent an effort by the state to both exploit and control individual violence in the international system. Ultimately, however, regulation failed, and this stage was followed by one in which a total ban on the practices was imposed. This stage has been the focus of this book.

Arguably, the twentieth century has ushered in another stage in which these practices are not only prohibited but have become unthinkable. The institutionalized prohibitions against them are taken for granted.[2] Though this cannot be "proven," it would be difficult to imagine that some practices, which were common in the eighteenth century, could be revived today. For example, could a rich state like the United States form an army by recruiting, say, poor, unemployed Mexicans? As we saw in chapter 4, the United States rejected the idea of recruiting Gurkhas because it would serve as grist for the "communist propaganda" mill. Also during the Vietnam War, the Thai press charged that Thai troops were serving as mercenaries for the United States. While some wealthy, and not so wealthy, states continue to recruit from poorer neighbors, it seems clear that the recruitment of foreign troops has been severely circumscribed. And despite violent attacks on corporate property and personnel, is it conceivable that a company could be authorized to hire its own army as the mercantile companies were? Finally, if we compare the shock and outrage at 1980s style "terrorism" with the approbation given Raleigh and others for even more devastating terrorist attacks, we can see the evolution of the taken-for-granted over the past three hundred years. The question is why this change in the organization of global coercive resources occurred and why it occurred when it did.

EXPLAINING THE TRANSITION

The dominant trend was toward the expansion of state authority over transborder violence. Nonstate actors may have been eliminated on an individual, ad hoc basis, but the state's assumption of authority over one aspect of nonstate violence initiated an upward spiral in which the state gained control of other forms of violence beyond its borders. Once begun, the momentum of this process did not allow for the reversal of state control, only for its expansion. This seems to bear out Giddens's argument that the production and control of violence follows a logic different from the production of wealth because in the former there is no force equivalent to the proletariat.[3] Thus, the production of violence is not a dialectical process. It may well be true that the state monopoly on violence was inevitable. What if Wallenstein had succeeded in founding a mercenary state or a pirate commonwealth had survived? In the former case, violence would have remained a market commodity and in the latter, it would have been subject to direct democracy.

Still, the territorial organization of violence was not inevitable or natural. Things might have turned out differently. Organizing violence around territoriality was not the only or necessary possible outcome. Clearly, a heteronomous organization of violence was not only possible but existed for centuries. But even under sovereignty, there were alternatives. State responsibility could have been tied not to territory but to the national origin of individuals. In that case, for example, the English state would be held accountable for the actions of English subjects wherever they went, whatever they did, and whomever they did it for. At the same time, the English state would not be held accountable for military operations launched from its territory by nonsubjects. As we saw in the cases of the North African corsairs and the polyglot European ships and of the Mogul and the East India Company, this way of establishing accountability was not only a real possibility but was actually attempted. Instead, states were held responsible only for violence emanating from their own territories.

The impetus for this change in state authority claims came not from within the state or "society" but from other state leaders. Individual states initiated the assertion of greater authority over their citizens' or subjects' activities not in response to citizens' demands but to the demands of other states. Of course, meeting those demands often provided an opportunity for states to consolidate their authority and control over people. The internal structure of individual states gave rise to particular forms of nonstate violence. Britain and the Netherlands produced the "private" mercantile company, the Barbary states the corsair, and the United States the filibuster. In the course of interstate politics these actors were defined as problems to be eliminated. Their elimination, in turn, produced an institutional isomorphism across states so that, regardless of huge differences in wealth, power, and location, all states adopted the prohibition on nonstate violence. The territorial state's monopoly on violence is principally the result of interstate relations.

The final problem is to explain the timing of the demise of nonstate violence. Put differently, what explains why the state's accountability for the actions of its citizens beyond its borders became an issue and was resolved when it was? This issue did not arise before the late-eighteenth century. On the one hand, the issue of sovereignty over the high seas had not yet been resolved. If no one was sovereign, who was responsible for violent acts committed there? So the duties of the state vis-à-vis the individual were unsettled. On the other hand, the notion that individuals had rights vis-à-vis the state was not yet institutionalized. Individuals were subject to arbitrary state decision making.

The rise of republican government and the institutionalization of citizens' rights posed the question of what rights citizens had in the international system. This, in conjunction with the realization that states could not exercise effective sovereignty over the high seas, raised the question of how order would be imposed beyond the states' borders.

Several pieces of evidence support this explanation. First of all, the solutions to the problems raised by nonstate violence came not from bureaucratic states such as France, Spain, or Prussia but from more legalistic states such as the United States, Switzerland, and Great Britain. True, Britain was the predominant power, and we would expect it to play a major role in this process. Switzerland and the United States, however, were weak, peripheral states whose elimination of mercenarism and filibustering became models that were adopted by the Great Powers, including Great Britain.

Second, the elimination of these actors came through legal more than violent action. While brute force—the traditional state's solution—was used in many instances, the permanent solution came only with changes in international and municipal law. For example, when the British state decided to act against piracy, it did not simply send out the navy to physically destroy the pirates. Rather, it reformed its domestic and imperial legal system and, more importantly, offered a number of positive inducements to the pirates to rejoin society as normal citizens. The Chinese and others did the same. Mercenarism and filibustering were suppressed not by sealing the borders but by making them criminal offenses and prosecuting suspects. So it appears that the *state's* coercive solution gave way to the *national state's* legalistic solution.

This evidence suggests what I take to be the key difference between the subject and the citizen: the rights and duties of the citizen are institutionalized.[4] A subject could be authorized to privateer, lose that authority a year later and be defined as a pirate, and be granted amnesty and a new privateering commission six months later. The citizen's rights and duties in the national state system are more precisely defined, permanent, universal and not (as) subject to arbitrary changes by state rulers.

With the possible exception of the pirates, all these actors were eliminated after the French and American revolutions. This suggests that nonstate violence was consistent with state sovereignty, but not with the sovereignty of the national state in which state-society relations are institutionalized. Put differently, it was inconsistent with the view that sovereignty emanates not from God through the monarch but from man or the citizen himself.[5] With the individual citizen as the ostensible source of sovereignty, the state could no longer disclaim responsibility for his violent activities in the international system.

To summarize, then, the institution of sovereignty was transformed by nineteenth-century state practices. This transformation was evidenced by the elimination of nonstate violence. The elimination of nonstate violence was predicated on its prior delegitimation, which was sparked by European expansion and the rise of republican government.

By the turn of the eighteenth century, European expansion had revealed the limitations of sovereignty. No state could exert effective sovereignty over the high seas. The alternatives were to leave everything out-side European sovereign territory in a state of nature or to institutionalize some norms governing or regulating extraterritorial violence. As Euro-pean expansion ran up against the governing capacity of sovereignty, that extraterritorial violence became an issue of high politics. At the same time, the rise of republican government and the institutionalization of popular sovereignty in some states raised the issue of what rights and duties citizens should have in the international system. The question was whether or not the state could claim a monopoly on violence within its territory while disclaiming responsibility for violent acts that emanated from its territory against other states.

In the context of that period, it was impossible to sort out legitimate from illegitimate practices of violence on the basis of state authority. States claimed the right to authorize nonstate violence while shirking re-sponsibility for the consequences of that violence. The practically derived solution, worked out in a number of distinctive geopolitical contexts, was for the state to give up its right to authorize nonstate violence. Thus, all violence emanating from the state's territory was either its own, for which it would be held accountable, or was unauthorized, for which the state would not accept responsibility. Nonstate violence was criminalized.

THE STATE, SOVEREIGNTY, AND WORLD POLITICS

This book's message for international relations specialists is that they would do well to abandon the notion that the state is the state is the state. The national state that emerged in 1900 was a fundamentally different entity from its predecessor. It exerted authority claims that were quantita-tively and qualitatively different from those of previous state forms. The national state expanded state decision-making authority to encompass extraterritorial coercive activities, adding to its predecessor's monopoly on the authority over violence within its borders. At the same time, the national state gave up its authority to buy violence in the international market and to exploit nonstate coercive capabilities.

Qualitatively, the national state entailed a new relationship between states and people. With the traditional state, individuals were subject to the arbitrary decision making of state rulers. With the national state, citi-zens' rights and duties vis-à-vis the state and the international system are institutionalized in the state. It is with the national state that the strict inside-outside dichotomy, noted by critical theorists, is institutionalized.

The fate of nonstate violence also has implications for theories of inter-state cooperation. First, it is clear that states have always colluded, coor-dinated, or cooperated in controlling individuals. They have a common interest in suppressing nonstate threats to the authority of the state. Second, these efforts can be quite opaque. The state's implementation of new authority claims over the people within its territorial jurisdiction is often legitimated in terms of interstate relations. For example, the controls on mercenarism and filibustering were purportedly instituted to ensure U.S. neutrality, while their effect was to increase the central state's power over its citizens. Third, the result of interstate cooperation in some cases of nonstate violence was not an international agreement but the adoption of similar changes in the municipal law of the states. That is, no international regime was created. Instead, institutions regulating state-society relations were altered so that all states exerted similar authority claims over societal actors.

This last point underscores the crucial role of interstate relations in shaping state-society relations. The state's role as a world actor lends it the power to define the nature of an issue in the first place. Nonstate violence was posed as an issue of high politics, thereby allowing the state to bypass normal domestic political processes in dealing with it. This suggests that analyses inspired by second-image-reversed perspectives should be altered in at least one major respect.[6] The international system poses not simply a set of constraints and opportunities but a source of state power. States are not simply at the mercy of exogenous international forces but are positively empowered by international institutions. Institutions like neutrality and the balance of power constrained states to behave in particular ways toward other states but they also empowered them to expand their authority and control over even such powerful actors as the mercantile companies. One potentially fruitful line for future research to pursue is the role of cultural, economic, scientific, and other international institutions in empowering states against societal actors.[7] The tendency to treat institutions as constraints on unitary state behavior should be tempered with the knowledge that institutions also serve as a potential source of state autonomy from societal actors. They may enhance the power of states in their dealings with nonstate actors.

It hardly needs stating that this research has raised more questions about the state and sovereignty than it has answered. Still, it seems clear that theorizing should dispense with attributing functions to the state. Controlling nonstate violence was not a function of the traditional state. It is a function of the modern state in the national state system. Moreover, this control was not so much functional for society as it was for the state in its dealings with other states. We should conceptualize the state as simply the bureaucratic apparatus which claims ultimate administrative, policing, and military authority[8] within a specific jurisdiction and then examine the conditions under which it assumes different functions or pursues different projects.[9]

This analysis clearly demonstrates that sovereignty is not an absolute, timeless, and invariable attribute of the state. Authority over the use of violence is generally presumed to be a state monopoly and that monopoly the hallmark of the state. If, however, authority over violence has varied so enormously, it is clear that sovereignty is far from fixed. It took at least three hundred years for the state to achieve a monopoly on external violence. The realist assumption of sovereignty is unwarranted; it limits the resulting theory to the national-state system, a creature of the twentieth century. Sovereignty has not eroded either, as interdependence theorists suggest. In the realm of international violence it has clearly been consolidated.

It seems prudent to treat sovereignty as a potentially variable institution rather than as a fixed principle.[10] While sovereignty differs from heteronomy in theoretical and empirical ways, there can be much variation in authority claims within sovereignty. One question for future research is how much and what kind of change would constitute a change from sovereignty to something else as opposed to a simple change in sovereignty itself. In short, we need to theorize about what would constitute a move from sovereignty to heteronomy, neoheteronomy, or some other authority regime.

I have posed an analytical framework in which sovereignty is unpacked into two dimensions: the constitutive and the functional. The constitutive dimension distinguishes sovereignty from historical or imaginable alternatives; the functional dimension allows for variation within sovereignty. A crucial task for future research is to further illuminate the links between these two dimensions. How much and what kind of change on the functional dimension is consistent with the constitutive dimension? Can change in the functional dimension erode the constitutive dimension? In this vein, we need to know a good deal more about the relationship between the state, state practices, and changes in the institution of sovereignty. My work suggests that while the hegemonic power does not set the rules, European state leaders most active internationally were responsible for establishing and altering the norms of sovereignty.

This has both theoretical and practical implications for "developing" countries. By delegitimating nonstate violence, the European powers effectively foreclosed one major avenue to building a strong state.[11] Exploiting nonstate violence was of inestimable value to European state rulers in building the military, political, and economic power of their states. What does it mean that states which entered the system in the twentieth century cannot engage in piracy, endow corporations with sovereign powers, or build a navy with privateers? Development studies have focused most of their attention on the global conditions that stymie or facilitate developing countries' efforts to repeat the European experience of economic development. It might be worthwhile to examine ways in which new states today are shaped or misshaped by their inability to follow the European model of building coercive forces.

Finally, this account of nonstate violence has some implications for theories of international norms. For one thing, it suggests that important norms are unintended consequences of interstate interaction. As such, their initiation is not motivated by normative concerns in the strict sense. Nobody said that nonstate violence was wrong so it should be eliminated. Instead, specific forms of nonstate violence were delegitimated and eliminated one by one as they presented diplomatic problems for state rulers. Once the antinonstate violence norms were implemented, they became the new standard of state practice. An *is* became an *ought*. But these norms are not proscriptions on state behavior. Instead, they define the kind of authority a state should exercise over its citizens. In short, they define the identity of the state.[12] Developing countries are not national states like those in the North or West precisely because they hire and supply mercenaries or sponsor "terrorists."

THE FUTURE

This study has left two major questions unanswered.[13] First, it has not addressed the question of how states were able to overcome domestic opposition to the disarming of nonstate actors. Every form of nonstate violence had powerful and wealthy advocates, supporters, and investors. How did states deal with these actors? International institutions empowered states to exert authority over extraterritorial violence, as this book argues, but that is only part of the story. Though it is beyond the scope of this study, it is surely the case that "domestic" or societal constraints played a role in shaping the form and scope of that authority.

Second, this study demonstrates the development of norms of nonstate violence that were quite robust in the nineteenth century, but the book has not dealt with certain twentieth-century practices that appear to challenge those norms. Were the Nicaraguan contras mercenaries for the United States? Did the U.S. military sell itself as a mercenary army to Kuwait? What about major instances of nonstate violence such as terrorists, drug smugglers, mafiosi, and pirates in the South China Sea? Do these contemporary practices mean the nineteenth-century norms of sovereignty are obsolete?

In my view, they do not. Exploiting nonstate violence remains a powerful temptation for state rulers. While it would be too much to say that organized crime, drug cartels, and terrorists exist only because states find them useful, there are plenty of instances in which states have used these groups for political or economic gain. Unlike their nineteenth-century counterparts, however, contemporary state leaders must do this in secret. States today cannot shirk responsiblity for nonstate violence by simply claiming that the latter is a purely private undertaking. Terrorism has been given a state address. Even high-seas pirates, for which supposedly no state is accountable, are treated as the responsiblity of their home states, as in the case of Thailand. The U.S.-led war on Iraq was financed by states other than Kuwait, most notably by Germany and Japan. If the U.S. military was a mercenary force, it was employed by the collectivity of state rulers in the defense of sovereignty as the institutional basis for global order. Indeed, the aim of most UN operations in Third World countries, such as the Congo, Cambodia, Angola, and Somalia, is to build and consolidate a sovereign state.

But while each twentieth-century practice may be interpreted as being consistent with nineteenth-century norms of sovereignty, a question meriting further theorizing and more systematic empirical research is: How much can practices change and yet remain consistent with the institution of sovereignty? If this book's arguments are correct, a shift away from sovereignty to heteronomy or something else would require a fundamental change in the identity of the national state. This would entail an end to or at least significant erosion of the state's monopoly on the authority to deploy violence beyond its borders. It is not at all clear to me that this is occurring.

R. B. J. Walker has written that "the disjunction between the seriousness of international politics and the triviality of international relations theory is quite startling."[14] I agree and would argue that that triviality stems from international relations theorists' willingness to assume away the most theoretically interesting and practically significant puzzles posed by the interstate system. How did the state get to be the state? What is sovereignty, who has it, and over what? If the state is sovereign, how did it get sovereignty? Why is sovereignty exerted territorially rather than on some other basis? How do we know a sovereign state when we see it? If international relations theory is to produce a theory of change, there is no better place to begin than with sovereignty.

Notes

Introduction

1. Charles Tilly, private correspondence.

2. As Caporaso argues, "institutional arguments stress the contingent, path-dependent nature of institutional change. These arguments generally assume a narrative form in which timing and sequences matter." James A. Caporaso, "International Relations Theory and Multilateralism: The Search for Foundations," *International Organization* 46 (Summer 1992): 627. Evans, Reuschemeyer, and Skocpol recommend for their purposes what they term an "analytically inductive and comparative-historical approach." They claim that "comparisons across countries and time periods and an emphasis on historical depth, the tracing out of processes over time, are optimal strategies for research on states. . . . Historical depth is also necessary for the study of states because of another feature that they share with many of the societal structures with which they are intertwined: historical persistence and continuity." Peter B. Evans, Dietrich Rueschemeyer, and Theda Skocpol, eds., *Bringing the State Back In* (New York: Cambridge University Press, 1985), 348. Finally, Mann argues that "we must turn pragmatically to the second method, of careful historical narrative, attempting to establish 'what happened next' to see if it has the 'feel' of a pattern, a process, or a series of accidents and contingencies." In this kind of analysis there are not enough cases, and those which do exist are not independent. Michael Mann, *The Sources of Social Power*, vol. 1, *A History of Power from the Beginning to A.D. 1760* (New York: Cambridge University Press, 1986), 503.

Chapter One
The State, Violence, and Sovereignty

1. Max Weber, *The Theory of Social and Economic Organization*, trans. A. M. Henderson and Talcott Parsons (New York: Free Press, 1964), 154 (emphasis in original).

2. Charles Tilly, ed., *The Formation of National States in Western Europe* (Princeton: Princeton University Press, 1975), 638.

3. Anthony Giddens, *A Contemporary Critique of Historical Materialism*, vol. 2, *The Nation-State and Violence* (Berkeley and Los Angeles: University of California Press, 1985), 121.

4. Tilly goes on to say that "other authorities, I would add, are much more likely to confirm the decisions of a challenged authority that controls substantial force. . . . The rule underscores the importance of the authority's monopoly of force. A tendency to monopolize the means of violence makes a government's claim to provide protection, in either the comforting or the ominous sense of the word, more credible and more difficult to resist." Charles Tilly, "War Making and State Making as Organized Crime," in Peter B. Evans, Dietrich

Rueschemeyer, and Theda Skocpol, eds., *Bringing the State Back In* (New York: Cambridge University Press, 1985), 171–72.

5. For example, Strang argues that "the institutional structure of sovereignty can thus be understood as a form of *legitimation* that both gives states the right to act (external autonomy) and privileges them over individuals, ethnic groups, multinational corporations, and world federations." David Strang, "Anomaly and Commonplace in European Political Expansion: Realist and Institutional Accounts," *International Organization* 45 (Spring 1991): 148. Giddens agrees that legitimacy is determined internationally. He argues that the post–World War I peace treaties reflected the "recognition [presumably by state leaders] of the authenticity of the nation-state as the *legitimate* arbiter of its own 'internal' affairs." Giddens, *Nation-State and Violence*, 256. Emphasis in both added.

6. If the essence of ownership is the right of alienation, then modern states can be said to own their armed forces.

7. This variance in control over labor versus armaments is itself an interesting theoretical question, which Nina Halperin pointed out to me. Addressing this question is beyond the scope of this book but for a preliminary exploration of this issue, see my "Explaining the Regulation of Transnational Practices: A State-Building Approach," in James N. Rosenau and Ernst-Otto Czempiel, eds., *Governance without Government* (Cambridge: Cambridge University Press, 1992).

8. John Gooch, *Armies in Europe* (London: Routledge and Kegan Paul, 1980), 22.

9. Richard A. Preston and Sydney F. Wise, *Men in Arms: A History of Warfare and Its Interrelationships with Western Society*, 2d ed. (New York: Praeger, 1970), 139.

10. C. C. Bayley, *Mercenaries for the Crimea: The German, Swiss, and Italian Legions in British Service, 1854–1856* (Montreal: McGill-Queen's University Press, 1977), 6–7.

11. Frank Sherry, *Raiders and Rebels: The Golden Age of Piracy* (New York: Hearst Marine Books, 1986), 202.

12. Ibid., 359–60.

13. Philip C. Jessup and Francis Deàk, *The Origins*, vol. 1 of Columbia University Council for Research in the Social Sciences, *Neutrality: Its History, Economics and Law* (New York: Columbia University Press, 1935), 14.

14. Ramkrishna Mukherjee, *The Rise and Fall of the East India Company: A Sociological Appraisal* (New York: Monthly Review Press, 1974), 59.

15. Ibid., 27–88.

16. Sherry, *Raiders and Rebels*, 105.

17. Mukherjee, *Rise and Fall*, 71; Robert C. Ritchie, *Captain Kidd and the War against the Pirates* (Cambridge: Harvard University Press, 1986), 17–18.

18. Mukherjee, *Rise and Fall*, 431.

19. Pirates, privateers, mercantile companies, and filibusters were not the only nonstate actors who exercised violence across state borders. Bandits, slave traders, religious-military orders, and nomadic raiders also engaged in organized, transborder violence. (I am indebted to Charles Tilly for emphasizing this point.) But, in terms of their impact on the organization of violence, the practices analyzed here were of decisive importance.

20. While Giddens uses the term *nation-state*, I prefer and will use through-out this book the term *national state*. As Tilly argues, "throughout most of history *national* states—states governing multiple contiguous regions and their cities by means of centralized, differentiated, and autonomous structures—have appeared only rarely. . . . The term national state, regrettably, does not necessarily mean *nation* state, a state whose people share a strong linguistic, religious, and symbolic identity." Charles Tilly, *Coercion, Capital, and European States, A.D. 990–1990* (Cambridge, Mass.: Basil Blackwell, 1990), 2–3. Thus, the nation-state is a special case of the more general form—the national state. On the problems of defining the nation in terms of language, ethnicity, historical or territorial com-monality, or cultural traits, see E. J. Hobsbawm, *Nations and Nationalism since 1780: Programme, Myth, Reality* (New York: Cambridge University Press, 1990), 20.

21. There is a massive literature on sovereignty in the field of political philoso-phy. Here sovereignty is treated as a highly abstract and legalistic concept, a fact that goes a long way toward explaining the anesthetizing effect the term has on contemporary political scientists. This literature is characterized by highly arcane, though important, debates about the locus of and limitations on sovereignty and about whether sovereignty means supreme authority or supreme power. I do not review it here for an important theoretical reason: It focuses almost exclusively on state-society relations, ignoring the global context and external influences on these relations. In short, it presupposes clear, unproblematic boundaries between polities, somehow carved out of global politics, existing in a practical and theoret-ical international vacuum. A modern classic in this genre is F. H. Hinsley, *Sover-eignty* (New York: Basic Books, 1966). For good reviews of this literature, see R. B. J. Walker, *State Sovereignty, Global Civilization, and the Rearticulation of Political Space*, World Order Studies Program Occasional Paper no. 18 (Prince-ton: Princeton University Center of International Studies, 1988); Jacques Mari-tain, "The Concept of Sovereignty," *World Politics* 44 (June 1950): 343–57; and C. E. Merriam, *History of the Theory of Sovereignty since Rousseau*, Columbia University Studies in the Social Sciences, vol. 33 (New York: AMS Press, 1968). As I will argue below, the domestic-international dichotomy and the interplay between the two are at the heart of the institution of sovereignty. My view of this literature is that it provides nothing in the way of an analytically useful concep-tion of sovereignty in international relations theory.

22. See, for example, Kenneth N. Waltz, *Theory of International Politics* (Reading, Mass.: Addison-Wesley, 1979), 96.

23. Major contributions to this literature include Robert O. Keohane and Jo-seph S. Nye, eds., *Transnational Relations and World Politics* (Cambridge: Har-vard University Press, 1972); Robert O. Keohane and Joseph S. Nye, *Power and Interdependence* (Boston: Little, Brown, 1977); Richard Rosecrance, *The Rise of the Trading State* (New York: Basic Books, 1986); Edward L. Morse, *Moderniza-tion and the Transformation of International Relations* (New York: Free Press, 1976); and Richard N. Cooper, "Economic Interdependence and Foreign Policy in the Seventies," *World Politics* 24 (January 1972): 159–81.

24. Janice E. Thomson and Stephen D. Krasner, "Global Transactions and the Consolidation of Sovereignty," in Ernst-Otto Czempiel and James N. Rosenau,

eds., *Global Changes and Theoretical Challenges: Approaches to World Politics for the 1990s* (Lexington, Mass.: Lexington Books, 1989). See also Kenneth N. Waltz, "The Myth of National Interdependence," in Charles P. Kindleberger, ed., *The International Corporation* (Cambridge: MIT Press, 1970).

25. Edward Hallett Carr, *The Twenty Years' Crisis, 1919–1939: An Introduction to the Study of International Relations*, 2d ed. (New York: Harper and Row, 1939), esp. 54–62 and 114–20; Robert Gilpin, *U.S. Power and the Multinational Corporation: The Political Economy of Foreign Direct Investment* (New York: Basic Books, 1975) esp. 31–43; idem, *The Political Economy of International Relations* (Princeton: Princeton University Press, 1987) esp. chap. 2. See also Waltz, *Theory*, 141.

26. Robert W. Cox, "Social Forces, States and World Orders: Beyond International Relations Theory," in Robert O. Keohane, ed., *Neorealism and Its Critics* (New York: Columbia University Press, 1986), 208. I agree with Ruggie that it is not correct to treat neorealism as problem-solving theory. As he writes, "I have always been puzzled why some critical theorists . . . refer to the conventional structural approach as 'problem solving.' How would any policymaker solve problems with it? What would he or she do? Alter the international configuration of power? Modify anarchy? Tell the weak to get stronger, the poor richer?" John Gerard Ruggie, "International Structure and International Transformation: Space, Time, and Method," in Ernst-Otto Czempiel and James N. Rosenau, eds., *Global Changes and Theoretical Challenges: Approaches to World Politics for the 1990s* (Lexington, Mass.: Lexington Books, 1989), 34. However, I do think the label is appropriate for "modified" or liberal realists who have produced the regimes, multilateralism, and cooperation-under-anarchy literatures. Their aim is to find peaceful solutions to interstate conflicts. See Stephen D. Krasner, ed., *International Regimes* (Ithaca: Cornell University Press, 1983); Robert O. Keohane, *After Hegemony: Cooperation and Discord in the World Political Economy* (Princeton: Princeton University Press, 1984); idem, "Multilateralism: An Agenda for Research," *International Journal* 45 (Autumn 1990: 731–64); Kenneth A. Oye, ed., "Cooperation under Anarchy," *World Politics* 38 (October 1985, special issue); and Robert Axelrod, "The Emergence of Cooperation among Egoists," *American Political Science Review* 75 (June 1981): 306–18. Wendt puts his finger on precisely why game-theoretic approaches to international relations theory are unconvincing. "Without an explicit theory of the state's powers and interests in international trade, without a theory of the 'rules of the game,' it cannot be determined whether or not this game really is a Prisoner's Dilemma rather than, as some neo-Marxists might argue, a pure cooperation game." Alexander E. Wendt, "The Agent-Structure Problem in International Relations Theory," *International Organization* 41 (Summer 1987): 343–44. Indeed, this is the basic premise of theories of ultra-imperialism. Prisoner's Dilemma may well characterize many instances of interstate relations but in other cases (e.g., North-South or state-people relations) interstate cooperation may be more likely.

27. In a sense, this criticism of neorealism is unfair. It suggests that neorealism is flawed because it cannot explain change when neorealism has never claimed to explain change. Neorealism is a theory of continuity; it purports to explain why, despite changes (e.g., technological developments), states behave the same. But

this defense severely limits the power of neorealist theory. It says, in effect, that this is a theory of international relations which applies only in a world organized into a system of sovereign states. A growing body of literature largely outside the international relations discipline suggests that such a system did not exist in Europe before 1900. As Giddens argues, "'international relations' are not connections set up between pre-established states, which could maintain their sovereign power without them; they are the basis upon which the nation-state exists at all." Giddens, *Nation-State and Violence*, 263–64. The period immediately following World War I is "the first point at which a reflexively monitored system of nation-states came to exist globally." Ibid., 256. So neorealism is, at best, a theory of international politics in the twentieth century.

Furthermore, the generic term *international relations* is inherently limiting since "nations" did not exist until the turn of the twentieth century. Fred Halliday, "State and Society in International Relations: A Second Agenda," *Millennium* 16 (Summer 1987): 219. To maximize the scope of our theories, we should focus on global politics, treating both interstate and international relations as subsets of that more general category. James N. Rosenau is one who has consistently insisted on using the term *global* or *world politics*. See his "Before Cooperation: Hegemons, Regimes, and Habit-Driven Actors in World Politics," *International Organization* 40 (Autumn 1986): 849–94; idem, "Global Changes and Theoretical Challenges: Toward a Postinternational Politics for the 1990s," in Ernst-Otto Czempiel and James N. Rosenau, eds., *Global Changes and Theoretical Challenges: Approaches to World Politics for the 1990s* (Lexington, Mass.: Lexington Books, 1989); and idem, *Turbulence in World Politics: A Theory of Change and Continuity* (Princeton: Princeton University Press, 1990).

28. John Gerard Ruggie, "Continuity and Transformation in the World Polity: Toward a Neorealist Synthesis," *World Politics* 35 (January 1983): 273.

29. According to some scholars, the current North-South system is actually best characterized as one of heteronomy. "In effect, we are suggesting that the juridical authority structure of the contemporary states system . . . is overlaid by an informal authority structure that corresponds to something more like 'feudal' authority (and which is in *those* terms not 'anarchic')." They deem the states system as "a fourth, 'heteronomous', dominance structure—that stems from the principle of sovereignty." Alexander Wendt and Michael Barnett, "The International System and Third World Militarization" (photocopy, Yale University, April 1991), 25, 33 (emphasis in original). See also Robert W. Cox, "Multilateralism and World Order," *Review of International Studies* 18 (April 1992): 161–80.

30. For the most important pieces in this debate, see Richard K. Ashley, "The Poverty of Neorealism," and replies to Ashley by Robert G. Gilpin, "The Richness of the Tradition of Political Realism"; Friedrich Kratochwil, "Errors Have Their Advantages"; and Bruce Andrews, "The Domestic Content of International Desire," in *International Organization* 38 (Spring 1984); Friedrich Kratochwil and John Gerard Ruggie, "International Organization: A State of the Art on an Art of the State," *International Organization* 40 (Autumn 1986): 753–75; Cox, "Social Forces"; Robert O. Keohane, "International Institutions: Two Approaches," *International Studies Quarterly* 32 (December 1988); and Richard K.

Ashley and R. B. J. Walker, eds., "Speaking the Language of Exile: Dissidence in International Studies," *International Studies Quarterly* 34 (September 1990, special issue).

31. Ashley, "Poverty," 272–73 n. 101. This statement was in response to Ruggie's argument that sovereignty and private property are parallel institutions.

32. Walker, *State Sovereignty*, 3.

33. Giddens, *Nation-State and Violence*, 263–64.

34. See Richard K. Ashley, "Effecting Global Purpose: Notes on a Problematic of International Organization" (paper presented at the annual meeting of the American Political Science Association, Chicago, Ill., 3–6 September 1987); idem, "Living on Border Lines: Man, Poststructuralism, and War," in James Der Derian and Michael J. Shapiro, eds., *International/Intertextual Relations: The Boundaries of Knowledge and Practice in World Politics* (Lexington, Mass.: Lexington Books, 1989); idem, "The Powers of Anarchy: Theory, Sovereignty, and the Domestication of Global Life" (photocopy, Arizona State University, March 1988); idem, "Statecraft as Mancraft: Knowledge, Power, and Resistance in Modern World Politics" (paper presented at the annual meeting of the American Political Science Association, Atlanta, Ga., 31 August–3 September 1989); R. B. J. Walker, "The Territorial State and the Theme of Gulliver," *International Journal* 39 (Summer 1984): 529–52.

35. Andrew Linklater, *Men and Citizens in the Theory of International Relations* (New York: St. Martin's Press, 1982), 44.

36. R. B. J. Walker, "Genealogy, Geopolitics and Political Community: Richard K. Ashley and the Critical Social Theory of International Politics," *Alternatives* 13 (January 1988): 85. Walker's statement suggests that international relations theory is overly narrow in yet another sense. *International* relations theory, as opposed to a theory of global politics, poses only one alternative to anarchy—hierarchy in the form of world government. But once we view sovereignty as the reflection of uniquely modern and arbitrary boundaries, other alternatives—localized or deterritorialized authority—emerge.

These arguments, which rightly point to the problematic nature of the domestic-international dichotomy, also reveal a First World bias. Third World polities have always been highly internationalized, both economically and politically. It may be that the First World's boundaries have never been as clear-cut as is assumed or that they are now being eroded to a level comparable to the Third World. I am indebted to Michael Barnett for pointing this out to me.

37. Ruggie, "Continuity and Transformation," 280.

38. R. B. J. Walker, "Ethics, Modernity and the Theory of International Relations" (photocopy, Princeton University Center of International Studies, 1988–89), 26.

39. Keohane argues that until what he terms "reflectivists" present a clear, empirical research program relevant to key issues in international relations, they "will remain on the margins of the field, largely invisible to the preponderance of empirical researchers." Keohane, "International Institutions," 392. In my view, this charge is unfair to the extent that these scholars have spawned the deconstruction project in international relations. It is largely correct to the degree that some "interpretivists" have tended to fall into a normative trap. Unlike liberal

interdependence theorists, they do not assume that the state and sovereignty ever fulfilled functions for society beyond serving the interests of powerful groups or classes. However, like some liberal interdependence theorists, they tend to leap from delineating the negative attributes of sovereignty to speculation about alternative political orders, thereby implying that sovereignty is a more malleable institution than history suggests or is even just an ideational concept. For example, see R. B. J. Walker and Saul H. Mendlovitz, eds., *Contending Sovereignties: Redefining Political Community* (Boulder, Colo.: Lynne Rienner, 1990).

40. Pauline Rosenau, "International Relations Confronts the Humanities," *Millennium* 19 (January 1990): 92.

41. See the contributions to Der Derian and Shapiro, *International/Intertextual Relations*. According to the editors this book was intended as a response to those who charged that critical theory needed to move beyond critique and "get on with it." "So we got on with it: we put poststructuralism to work, to write a book that is theoretical (but not methodological), that is empirical (but not empiricist), that problematizes (but does not problem-solve) world politics" (xi). For an incisive but friendly critique of postmodernist international relations theory, see P. Rosenau, "International Relations Confronts the Humanities."

42. P. Rosenau, "International Relations Confronts the Humanities," 103.

43. Textual (intertextual, contextual) interpretation, discourse analysis, and other deconstruction methods are not the necessary or only alternative. It is not clear that these methods will generate a "productive" research program in the Keohanian sense (see note 39 above). Moreover, by adopting such unconventional methods, critical theory allows or forces mainstream scholars to dismiss postmodernism based on its research designs, methods, and data. It hardly helps matters that much of postmodernist discourse is opaque (thus, largely meaningless) to ordinary international relations scholars. See, for example, Timothy W. Luke, "The Discipline of Security Studies and the Codes of Containment: Learning from Kuwait," *Alternatives* 16 (1991): 315–44. Beyond this, the postmodernist focus on discourse poses the danger of diverting attention from the reality of state power to the discourse about it. States are now massive, physical, bureaucratic, and coercive institutions that have been developing for some six centuries. While postmodernists are surely right to claim that discourse is the deployment of power, it is implausible to argue that the exercise of power in this form is of central importance to, much less decisive in, world politics. Discourse may contribute to the construction of the state but I am not convinced that the state might be fundamentally altered if the discourse on the state changed or that it would vanish if we stopped talking about it.

44. For examples of attempts to provide, using conventional methods, empirical content to these arguments see Janice E. Thomson, "State Practices, International Norms, and the Decline of Mercenarism," *International Studies Quarterly* 34 (March 1990): 23–47; Strang, "Anomaly and Commonplace"; and Michael N. Barnett, "Sovereignty, Institutions, and Identity: From Pan-Arabism to the Arab State System," paper presented at the American Political Science Association annual meeting, Washington, D.C., 29 August–1 September 1991.

45. The now classic discussions of scientific paradigms are Thomas Kuhn, *The Structure of Scientific Revolutions* (Chicago: University of Chicago Press, 1970);

Karl Popper, *The Logic of Scientific Discovery* (New York: Basic Books, 1959); Imre Lakatos, "Falsification and the Methodology of Scientific Research Programs," in Imre Lakatos and Alan Musgrave, eds., *Criticism and the Growth of Knowledge* (Cambridge: Cambridge University Press, 1970).

46. For an excellent review of the distinctiveness of the institutionalist perspective, see Caporaso, "International Relations Theory and Multilateralism," 620–30.

47. Stephen D. Krasner, "Sovereignty: An Institutional Perspective," in James A. Caporaso, ed., *The Elusive State: International and Comparative Perspectives* (Newbury Park, Calif.: Sage, 1989), 89–90. Viewing sovereignty as an institution resolves a major problem presented by attempts to see it as an organizing principle of global politics. Treating sovereignty as a principle implies that it is static. What is needed is a conception that enables us to distinguish sovereignty from heteronomy but still allows sovereignty to vary. For a brief overview of contending definitions of an institution, see ibid., 75–76. There is an important distinction between behavioral and critical or sociological conceptions of institutions. For behavioralists, institutions are rules and norms that regulate actors' behavior, while for critical theorists, institutions also define and constitute the actors themselves. See Douglass C. North, *Institutions, Institutional Change and Economic Performance* (New York: Cambridge University Press, 1990), 3–10, for a recent example of the behavioral perspective. For reasons that will become clear, I adopt the critical perspective nicely elaborated in John W. Meyer, John Boli, and George M. Thomas, "Ontology and Rationalization in the Western Cultural Account," in George M. Thomas, John W. Meyer, Francisco O. Ramirez, and John Boli, eds., *Institutional Structure: Constituting State, Society, and the Individual* (Newbury Park, Calif.: Sage, 1987), 12–20.

48. John Gerard Ruggie, "Planetary Politics: International Transformation in the Making," paper presented at the German-American Workshop on International Relations Theory, Bad Homburg, Federal Republic of Germany, 31 May–3 June 1987, 7.

49. Ruggie, "Continuity and Transformation," 274, 275, and 280.

50. Giddens, *Nation-State and Violence*, 120.

51. For a critique on this approach see Janice E. Thomson, "Sovereignty and the Institutional Isomorphism of States" (paper presented at the annual meeting of the American Political Science Association, Washington D.C., 29 August–1 September 1991).

52. Ruggie, "Continuity and Transformation," 274–75.

53. The continuum from weak to strong states reflects the relative size of the political and nonpolitical realms or the degree to which the state apparatus has penetrated the political space within its territorial jurisdiction. For good discussions of this distinction between weak and strong states, see Stephen D. Krasner, *Defending the National Interest: Raw Materials Investments and U.S. Foreign Policy* (Princeton: Princeton University Press, 1978), 55–90; Richard Little, "Revisiting Intervention: A Survey of Recent Developments," *Review of International Studies* 13 (January 1987): 54–57.

54. A number of leading theorists have recently called for a shift of analytical attention from the systemic or structural to the micro level because, after all, it is

human beings who are the ultimate cause of change. Structures don't act; people do. See North, *Institutions*, 5; David A. Lake, "The Theory of Hegemonic Stability: An Interim Report," paper presented at the World Congress of the International Political Science Association, Buenos Aires, Argentina, 21–25 July 1991, 23; and Robert Bates, "Problems with Case Studies" (presentation to National Science Foundation–funded Conference on Democracy, Markets, and Choice, University of Washington, 20–23 September 1991). While this is indisputable, the question is which individuals should be the focus of research. In my view, the tendency is to examine relationships between the state (or state ruler) and the people within its jurisdiction. This approach has yielded fresh insights and often counterintuitive results. See, for example, Margaret Levi, *Of Rule and Revenue* (Berkeley and Los Angeles: University of California Press, 1988); and Michael Taylor, *The Possibility of Cooperation*, in Jon Elster and Gudmund Hernes, eds., *Studies in Rationality and Social Change* (New York: Cambridge University Press, 1987). However, there is another set of individuals whose role may be as critical or even more important in explaining political change—namely, extra-polity actors, including other state rulers. It may well be that treating the external arena as a system or structure precludes a viable theory of political change but, as I argue in this book, it cannot be ignored in favor of an exclusive "bottom-up" focus. For two very different behavioralist attempts to theorize or model the "domestic" and "international" influences on state behavior, see Andrew Moravcsik, "Integrating International and Domestic Explanations of World Politics: A Theoretical Introduction" (photocopy, University of Chicago, 1991); and Michael Mastanduno, David A. Lake, and G. John Ikenberry, "Toward a Realist Theory of State Action," *International Studies Quarterly* 33 (December 1989): 457–74.

55. According to Waltz, "In both systems [international-political systems and economic markets] structures are formed by the coaction of their units. Whether those units live, prosper, or die depends on their own efforts." Waltz, *Theory*, 91.

56. See John W. Meyer, "The World Polity and the Authority of the Nation-State," in Albert Bergesen, ed., *Studies of the Modern World System* (New York: Academic Press, 1980); Robert H. Jackson and Carl G. Rosberg, "Why Africa's Weak States Persist: The Empirical and the Juridical in Statehood," *World Politics* 35 (October 1982): 23. Jackson and Rosberg argue that "in Black Africa (and, by implication, in other regions of the Third World), external factors are more likely than internal factors to provide an adequate explanation of the formation and persistence of states."

57. Meyer, "World Polity," 119.

58. Ibid., 109, 131.

59. Ashley, "Poverty," 272. Ashley also accents the role of statesmen in domesticating global political space by creating the distinction between the public and private spheres domestically. Richard K. Ashley, "Social Will and International Anarchy" (photocopy, Arizona State University, 1987).

60. Giddens, *Nation-State and Violence*, 256.

61. Meyer, "World Polity," 118–20.

62. Ashley, "Poverty," 272.

63. This follows from Kratochwil and Ruggie's definition of a norm as expressing "mutual expectations about behavior." "International Organization," 767.

64. For an excellent review of the intervention literature, see Little, "Revisiting Intervention."

65. John Gerard Ruggie, "International Regimes, Transactions, and Change: Embedded Liberalism in the Postwar Economic Order," in Stephen D. Krasner, ed., *International Regimes* (Ithaca: Cornell University Press, 1983), 195–231; Karl Polanyi, *The Great Transformation: The Political and Economic Origins of Our Time* (Boston: Beacon Press, 1944). This boundary did not really exist in the Middle Ages, when "military action, and political and economic striving, are largely identical, and the urge to increase wealth in the form of land comes to the same thing as extending territorial sovereignty and increasing military power." Norbert Elias, *The Civilizing Process*, vol. 2, *Power and Civility*, trans. Edmund Jephcott (New York: Pantheon, 1982), 43.

66. Stephen D. Krasner, *Structural Conflict: The Third World against Global Liberalism* (Berkeley and Los Angeles: University of California Press, 1985).

67. John W. Meyer, Francisco O. Ramirez, Henry A. Walker, Nancy Langton, and Sorca M. O'Connor, "The State and the Institutionalization of the Relations between Women and Children," (photocopy, Stanford University, 1984).

68. Ruggie, "Continuity and Transformation," 280–81; Ashley, "Effecting Global Purpose," 45.

Chapter Two
Nonstate Violence Unleashed

1. Because I am interested in the modern state system as it evolved and developed in Europe, the following analysis focuses primarily on that region.

2. Joseph R. Strayer, *On the Medieval Origins of the Modern State* (Princeton: Princeton University Press, 1970), 106.

3. William Edward Hall, *A Treatise on International Law*, 8th ed., ed. A. Pearce Higgins (Oxford: Clarendon Press, 1924), 620–21.

4. Ibid., 314. See also Harvard Law School Research in International Law, "Draft Convention on Piracy," *American Journal of International Law* 26 (1932) Special Supplement, 739–1013; and L. Oppenheim, *International Law: A Treatise*, 8th ed., ed. H. Lauterpacht, vol. 1, *Peace* (New York: Longmans, Green, 1955), 609.

5. Hall, *Treatise*, 310, 312, and 311.

6. Sherry, *Raiders and Rebels*, 57.

7. There is some dispute about the origin of the term *marque*. It may have derived from the word *marque*, meaning a "license of marking the men and subjects of X and their goods by land and sea." Alternatively, it may have come from the German term for *frontier*, in which case the letter of marque would authorize someone to cross a frontier in order to obtain redress. At any rate, initially there was a strong distinction between private reprisals and privateering. See Francis R. Stark, "The Abolition of Privateering and the Declaration of Paris," in *Studies in*

History, Economics and Public Law, ed. the Faculty of Political Science of Columbia University, vol. 8, no. 3 (New York, 1897): 52–53.

8. Ibid., 53–54.

9. According to Lobel, "Until the 13th century, it was common for individuals or groups acting independently of any government to make war or carry out armed reprisals against foreigners. By the 13th century, in an attempt to gain control over this incessant private warfare, many governments provided that private persons could only take up arms with the sovereign's permission in the form of a letter of marque or reprisal." Jules Lobel, "The Rise and Decline of the Neutrality Act: Sovereignty and Congressional War Powers in United States Foreign Policy," *Harvard International Law Journal* 24 (Summer 1983): 7. The key phrase here is "to gain control." States were not bent on eliminating nonstate violence but in directing and exploiting it.

10. Jessup and Deàk, *Origins,* 12–13.

11. Robert C. Ritchie, *Captain Kidd and the War against the Pirates* (Cambridge: Harvard University Press, 1986), 11.

12. Stark, "Abolition," 54–55.

13. Ibid., 58.

14. Ibid., 58–59.

15. Kenneth R. Andrews, *Elizabethan Privateering: English Privateering during the Spanish War, 1585–1603* (Cambridge: Cambridge University Press, 1964), 198–99. Elizabeth's privateers' prizes amounted to "some ten to fifteen per cent of England's total imports." Ibid., 128.

16. Louis Kronenberger, "People on Spits and Other Niceties," *Atlantic Monthly,* September 1969, 106.

17. Andrews, *Elizabethan Privateering,* 77–78 and 177.

18. Stark, "Abolition," 61–64. See also James G. Lydon, *Pirates, Privateers and Profits* (Upper Saddle River, N.J.: Gregg, 1970), 27–28; and Hugh F. Rankin, *The Golden Age of Piracy* (New York: Holt, Rinehart and Winston, 1969), 3–5.

19. Stark, "Abolition," 66.

20. Ibid., 68–70.

21. Pat O'Malley, "The Discipline of Violence: State, Capital and the Regulation of Naval Warfare," *Sociology* 22 (May 1988): 258.

22. Stark, "Abolition," 82 and 86.

23. Ibid., 89–92.

24. Ibid., 90–91.

25. Ibid., 99 and 101.

26. Ibid., 99.

27. Ibid., 94 and 95.

28. Patrick Crowhurst, *The Defence of British Trade, 1689–1815* (Folkestone, Kent: Dawson, 1977), 15, 16–17.

29. Ibid., 19, 21–22.

30. Sherry, *Raiders and Rebels,* 202.

31. Lydon, *Pirates,* 64.

32. Stark, "Abolition," 96–100.

33. Sherry, *Raiders and Rebels,* 359.

34. Lydon, *Pirates,* 88.

35. Stark, "Abolition," 69.

36. Lydon, *Pirates*, 154 and 128.

37. Stark, "Abolition," 70–71.

38. Lydon, *Pirates*, 132.

39. Ibid., 143. See also Carl E. Swanson, "American Privateering and Imperial Warfare, 1739–1748," *William and Mary Quarterly*, 3d ser. 42 (July 1985): 360.

40. Stark, "Abolition," 74.

41. Lydon, *Pirates*, 157–59.

42. William Laird Clowes, *The Royal Navy: A History from the Earliest Times to the Present* (Boston: Little, Brown, 1898), 3:232.

43. Stark, "Abolition," 75.

44. Lydon, *Pirates*, 268. Among U.S. notables who invested in privateering were Congressman Robert Morris of Philadelphia, the Cabots of Boston, George Washington, and Colonel Henry Knox. *Time* (special 1776 issue), May 1975, 44.

45. Edgar Stanton Maclay, *A History of American Privateers* (New York: Appleton, 1899), viii, ix, and xiii.

46. Stark, "Abolition," 123.

47. Maclay, *American Privateers*, xiv; and Stark, "Abolition," 124.

48. Stark, "Abolition," 77–78 and 126.

49. Maclay, *American Privateers*, xi.

50. Sherry, *Raiders and Rebels*, 360

51. Ibid., 360; Stark, "Abolition," 107.

52. Maclay, *American Privateers*, ix. See also Stark, "Abolition," 135.

53. Maclay, *American Privateers*, 274.

54. For attempts to define the "essence" of mercenarism, see United Nations, General Assembly, *Report of the Ad Hoc Committee on the Drafting of an International Convention Against the Recruitment, Use, Financing and Training of Mercenaries*, 1982, A/37/43; H. C. Burmester, "The Recruitment and Use of Mercenaries in Armed Conflicts," *American Journal of International Law* 72 (January 1978): 37–56; Robert E. Cesner, Jr., and John W. Brant, "Law of the Mercenary: An International Dilemma," *Capital University Law Review* 6 (1977): 339–70; Anthony Mockler, *The Mercenaries* (New York: Macmillan, 1969).

55. Tilly, *Coercion, Capital*, 82.

56. Mockler, *Mercenaries*, 21.

57. Ibid., 26; Preston and Wise, *Men in Arms*, 81.

58. Mockler, *Mercenaries*, 25; Preston and Wise, *Men In Arms*, 80.

59. Preston and Wise, *Men In Arms*, 81; Mockler, *Mercenaries*, 26.

60. Mockler, *Mercenaries*, 28.

61. See William H. McNeill, *The Pursuit of Power: Technology, Armed Force, and Society since A.D. 1000* (Chicago: University of Chicago Press, 1982); and Fritz Redlich, *The German Military Enterpriser and His Work Force: A Study in European Economic and Social History* (Wiesbaden: Franz Steiner Verlag GMBH, 1965), 2:95, who argue that with the decline of feudalism, European war making increasingly came to be dominated by market behavior.

62. V. G. Kiernan, "Foreign Mercenaries and Absolute Monarchy," in *Crisis in Europe, 1560–1660*, ed. Trevor Aston (New York: Basic Books, 1965), 121.

63. One of Machiavelli's sharpest criticisms of mercenaries was their faithlessness, which, as Mockler argues, equally applied to princes. Among eleven of the most prominent mercenary leaders, three were beheaded, four strangled, two poisoned, one murdered, and one executed—all by their princely employers. Mockler, *Mercenaries*, 48–49. Machiavelli's views on mercenaries may be found in *The Prince*, chaps. 12 and 13. Niccolò Machiavelli, *"The Prince" and "The Discourses"* (New York: Modern Library, 1950), 44–53.

64. Mockler, *Mercenaries*, 60–63.

65. Kiernan, "Foreign Mercenaries," 132.

66. Anthony Mockler, *The New Mercenaries* (London: Sidgwick and Jackson, 1985), 10.

67. Tilly, *Coercion, Capital*, 80.

68. Kiernan, "Foreign Mercenaries," 133.

69. Mockler, *New Mercenaries*, 14.

70. Redlich, *German Military Enterpriser*, 95.

71. John Childs, *Armies and Warfare in Europe, 1648–1789* (Manchester: Manchester University Press, 1982), 33.

72. Quoted in Charles W. Ingrao, *The Hessian Mercenary State: Ideas, Institutions, and Reform under Frederick II, 1760–1785* (New York: Cambridge University Press, 1987), 127. Hesse-Cassel made eighteen subsidy treaties between 1670 and 1730; thirty between 1702 and 1763; and eleven between 1751 and 1760. The thirty agreements concluded between 1702 and 1763 may have generated half the Hessian state's revenues. Ibid.

73. Childs, *Armies and Warfare*, 34 and 36.

74. Ibid., 34, 48; Bayley, *Mercenaries for the Crimea*, 1–25; Correlli Barnett, *Britain and Her Army, 1509–1970: A Military, Political and Social Survey* (New York: William Morrow, 1970), 197, 218; Redlich, *German Military Enterpriser*, 97.

75. Preston and Wise, *Men In Arms*, 139.

76. Redlich, *German Military Enterpriser*, 161.

77. Geoffrey Parker, *The Military Revolution: Military Innovation and the Rise of the West, 1500–1800* (New York: Cambridge University Press, 1988), 60.

78. Redlich, *German Military Enterpriser*, 161–62.

79. Childs, *Armies and Warfare*, 38.

80. Redlich, *German Military Enterpriser*, 201.

81. Herbert Rosinski, *The German Army* (Washington, D.C.: Infantry Journal, 1944), 21, 20, and 23.

82. Childs, *Armies and Warfare*, 37–38, 98, and 49.

83. Bayley, *Mercenaries for the Crimea*, 4.

84. Mockler, *New Mercenaries*, 3.

85. Bayley, *Mercenaries for the Crimea*, 7–10.

86. Barnett, *Britain and Her Army*, 128; Childs, *Armies and Warfare*, 98–99.

87. Childs, *Armies and Warfare*, 47.

88. Parker, *Military Revolution*, 49.

89. Henry Spenser Wilkinson, *The French Army before Napoleon* (Oxford: Clarendon Press, 1915), 85.

90. Mockler, *Mercenaries*, 74–104.

91. Mockler, *New Mercenaries*, 20.

92. Rosinski, *Germany Army*, 20–23; Barnett, *Britain and Her Army*, 128; Bayley, *Mercenaries for the Crimea*, 10.

93. Byron Farwell, *The Gurkhas* (New York: W. W. Norton, 1984), 14.

94. Childs, *Armies and Warfare*, 33 and 49.

95. Rosinski, *German Army*, 20–23; André Corvisier, *Armies and Societies in Europe, 1494–1789*, trans. Abigail T. Siddall (Bloomington: Indiana University Press, 1979), 104; Childs, *Armies and Warfare*, 47.

96. Childs, *Armies and Warfare*, 49.

97. Michael Howard, *War in European History* (New York: Oxford University Press, 1976), 58. The war with Germany demanded military manpower levels far in excess of Sweden's capacity, necessitating the large-scale use of mercenaries. See Michael Roberts, *Gustavus Adolphus and the Rise of Sweden* (London: English Universities Press, 1973), 105.

98. Parker, *Military Revolution*, 38.

99. Childs, *Armies and Warfare*, 38.

100. Christopher Duffy, *Russia's Military Way to the West: Origins and Nature of Russian Military Power, 1700–1800* (Boston: Routledge and Kegan Paul, 1981), 39.

101. Childs, *Armies and Warfare*, 41.

102. Redlich, *German Military Enterpriser*, 98.

103. Eugene L. Asher, *The Resistance to the Maritime Classes: The Survival of Feudalism in the France of Colbert*, vol. 66 of *University of California Publications in History*, ed. Theodore Saloutos, T. S. Brown, G. E. Von Grunebaum, and Andrew Lossky (Berkeley and Los Angeles: University of California Press, 1960), 1.

104. Ibid., 7. For details on the procurement of manpower for French galleys see Paul W. Bamford, *Fighting Ships and Prisons: The Mediterranean Galleys of France in the Age of Louis XIV* (Minneapolis: University of Minnesota Press, 1973), especially the chapters "The Procurement of Slaves" and "Condemnations to the Oar." The galleys were originally run by "maritime condottieri," who made a profit through successful campaigns and exploitation of the forced labor of their oarsmen in the off-season (13–14). According to Bamford, "there seems to have been striking similarities between maritime enterprisers using galleys (the Duke de Centurion and the Duke de Tursis, for example) and the military contractors described by Fritz Redlich" (329 n. 3).

105. Jonathan Israel, *The Dutch Republic and the Hispanic World, 1606–1661* (New York: Oxford University Press, 1982).

106. Stephen F. Gradish, *The Manning of the British Navy during the Seven Years' War*, vol. 21 of *Royal Historical Society Studies in History* (London: Royal Historical Society, 1980), 80.

107. Cynthia F. Behrman, *Victorian Myths of the Sea* (Athens: Ohio University Press, 1977), 72.

108. Christopher Lloyd, *The British Seaman, 1200–1860: A Social Survey* (London: Collins, 1968), 158–59.

109. John B. Moore, *A Digest of International Law* (Washington, D.C.: Government Printing Office, 1906), 2:987.

110. Edward L. Beach, *The United States Navy: 200 Years* (New York: Holt, 1986), 60.

111. Moore, *Digest*, 994.

112. Kiernan, "Foreign Mercenaries," 139–40.

113. Peter D. Karsten, *The Naval Aristocracy* (Riverside, N.J.: Free Press, 1971), 78–79.

114. This section focuses on the mercantile companies' use of violence. For more general treatments of mercantile companies' development, their role in expanding world commerce and European empires, their profitability, administrative structures, participants, etc., see William Robert Scott, *The Constitution and Finance of English, Scottish and Irish Joint-Stock Companies to 1720*, 2 vols. (Cambridge: Cambridge University Press, 1912); and Eli F. Heckscher, *Mercantilism*, trans. Mendel Shapiro, 2 vols. (London: George Allen and Unwin, 1935).

115. Later, in the nineteenth century, companies such as the British South Africa Company and the Imperial British East Africa Company were chartered for administrative purposes "to make treaties or administer territories which it (the company) had acquired." Administrative companies were concentrated in Africa, though there were several in the Americas and Oceania. See Percival Griffiths, *A License to Trade: The History of English Chartered Companies* (London: Ernest Benn, 1974), xiii.

116. Scott, *Constitution and Finance*, 241.

117. These are the most important because of their impact and their longevity. As mercantile companies, the Dutch East India Company existed for 194 years, the Hudson's Bay Company for 200 years, and the English East India Company for 258 years.

118. There were actually three English East India companies. The first, chartered in 1600, is known as the Old or London East India Company. In 1694, when Parliament declared that "it was the right of all Englishmen to trade to the East Indies, or any part of the world, unless prohibited by act of parliament," a group of "interlopers" received a parliamentary charter. This company was known as the New or English East India Company. Finally, these two companies were merged in 1702 to form the United Company of Merchants of England Trading to the East Indies. See Mukherjee, *Rise and Fall*, 66.

119. George Cawston and A. H. Keane, *The Early Chartered Companies, A.D. 1296–1858* (New York: Edward Arnold, 1896), 9–14. See also John P. Davis, *Corporations: A Study of the Origin and Development of Great Business Combinations and Their Relation to the Authority of the State* (New York: Capricorn, 1961), 66–113.

120. Holden Furber, *Rival Empires of Trade in the Orient, 1600–1800*, vol. 2 of *Europe and the World in the Age of Expansion*, ed. Boyd C. Shafer (Minneapolis: University of Minnesota Press, 1976), 186–88.

121. E. L. J. Coornaert, "European Economic Institutions and the New World: The Chartered Companies," in *The Economy of Expanding Europe in the Sixteenth and Seventeenth Centuries*, ed. E. E. Rich and C. H. Wilson, vol. 4 of *The Cambridge Economic History of Europe* (Cambridge: Cambridge University Press, 1967), 265.

122. See respectively, ibid., 242; A. R. Disney, "The First Portuguese India Company, 1628–33," *Economic History Review*, 2d ser. 30 (May 1977): 242–

58; Mukherjee, *Rise and Fall*, 112 and 125; Coornaert, "European Economic Institutions," 223, 234, 243, and 246. French East India companies were chartered in 1604, 1611, 1615, and 1642, but all were either stillborn or failed almost immediately. Colbert's La Compagnie des Indes Orientales (1664–1769) was the only French company of any major significance and is the one to which this chapter refers.

123. S. P. Sen, *The French in India, 1763–1816* (Calcutta: Firma K. L. Mukhopadhyay, 1958), 37.

124. Quoted in Mukherjee, *Rise and Fall*, 73.

125. Cawston and Keane, *Early Chartered Companies*, 66; Davis, *Corporations*, 83–84.

126. Griffiths, *License to Trade*, x–xi.

127. Bernard H. M. Vlekke, *Evolution of the Dutch Nation* (New York: Roy Publishers, 1945), 175.

128. Coornaert, "European Economic Institutions," 247.

129. K. N. Chaudhuri, "The East India Company and the Export of Treasure in the Early Seventeenth Century," *Economic History Review*, 2d ser. 16 (1963): 23–38; idem, *The English East India Company: A Study of an Early Joint-Stock Company, 1600–1640* (New York: Augustus M. Kelley, 1965), 13.

130. Furber, *Rival Empires*, 91.

131. Coornaert, "European Economic Institutions," 249.

132. C. R. Boxer, *The Dutch Seaborne Empire, 1600–1800*, vol. 2, *The History of Human Society*, ed. J. H. Plumb (New York: Knopf, 1965), 24, 25.

133. The charter is reprinted in Hudson's Bay Company, *Charters, Statutes, Orders in Council, etc. Relating to the Hudson's Bay Company* (London: Hudson's Bay Company, 1963), 3–21.

134. Peter C. Newman, *Company of Adventurers* (Ontario, Canada: Penguin Books, 1986), 1:119.

135. Griffiths, *License to Trade*, 85.

136. W. J. Van Hoboken, "The Dutch West India Company: The Political Background of Its Rise and Decline," in *Britain and the Netherlands*, ed. J. S. Bromley and E. H. Kossmann (London: Chatto and Windus, 1960), 43.

137. Vlekke, *Dutch Nation*, 177.

138. Boxer, *Seaborne Empire*, 25.

139. VOC is the abbreviation of the company's name in Dutch: Vereenigde Oost-Indische Compagnie.

140. Boxer, *Seaborne Empire*, 24.

141. Gary Anderson and Robert D. Tollison, "Apologiae for Chartered Monopolies in Foreign Trade, 1600–1800," *History of Political Economy* 15 (1983): 550–51.

142. Ibid., 550, 557.

143. Adam Smith, *An Inquiry into the Nature and Causes of the Wealth of Nations*, ed. Edwin Cannan (New York: Modern Library, 1937), 712. See also 690–91.

144. Anderson and Tollison, "Apologiae," 560.

145. Furber, *Rival Empires*, 93–94.

146. Ibid., 150.

147. Parker, *Military Revolution*, 134–35.

148. Ibid., 132, 85–87, and 143.

149. Newman, *Company of Adventurers* 1:158.

150. Ibid., 222.

151. William Foster, "The East India Company, 1600–1740," in *British India, 1497–1858*, ed. H. H. Dodwell, vol. 5 of *The Cambridge History of India* (Cambridge: Cambridge University Press, 1929), 78; Furber, *Rival Empires*, 40.

152. Furber, *Rival Empires*, 46, 47, and 63.

153. Ibid., 45.

154. The Moluccas are Indonesian islands of the Malay Archipeligo, lying between the Celebes on the west, New Guinea on the east, Timor on the south, and the Philippines on the north.

155. Furber, *Rival Empires*, 52 and 85.

156. Griffiths, *License to Trade*, 97–98.

157. Ibid., 87.

158. Furber, *Rival Empires*, 167.

159. Mukherjee, *Rise and Fall*, 266.

160. Furber, *Rival Empires*, 168.

161. Mukherjee, *Rise and Fall*, 268

162. Ibid., 270–72.

163. Ibid., 274–76.

164. Ibid., 275–77.

165. Griffiths, *License to Trade*, 101.

166. Newman, *Company of Adventurers* 1:108, 248–51, and 304–5.

Chapter Three
Unintended Consequences

1. Thomas J. Wertenbaker, "Virginia under the Stuarts, 1607–1688," in *The Shaping of Colonial Virginia* (New York: Russell and Russell, 1914), 29–30.

2. See M. J. Rodríguez-Salgado, "Mediterranean Corsairs," *History Today* 31 (April 1981): 36.

3. John B. Wolf, *The Barbary Coast: Algiers under the Turks, 1500–1830* (New York: Norton, 1979), 102. Also see Peter Earle, *Corsairs of Malta and Barbary* (London: Sidgwick and Jackson, 1970), 28–31, 35 and 50.

4. Earle, *Corsairs*, 30–31.

5. For texts of U.S. treaties with Tripoli, Algiers, and Morocco see William M. Malloy, comp., *Treaties, Conventions, International Acts, Protocols and Agreements between the United States of America and Other Powers, 1776–1909* (Washington, D.C.: Government Printing Office, 1910), 2:1786.

6. Earle, *Corsairs*, 10, 34, and 115–20.

7. Ibid., 24, 26, and 101–2.

8. Ibid., 102n.

9. The following anecdote attests to this point. "At the end of the thirteenth century Genoa did indeed establish a ministry of piracy to channel complaints from Mulsims, Jews, and Christians wrongfully attacked by Genoese ships; this

Office of Robbery soon foundered under the volume of claims." Robert I. Burns, *Muslims, Christians and Jews in the Crusader Kingdom of Valencia: Societies in Symbiosis* (Cambridge: Cambridge University Press, 1984), 110.

10. People also had good reasons for taking up piracy. The ordinary seaman had few alternatives to employment in commercial shipping. He could find another occupation, serve in the navy, or join the crew of a pirate ship. For many, the last was the most attractive, since life in the navy for the ordinary sailor was extremely harsh. See W. Alison Phillips and Arthur H. Reede, *The Napoleonic Period*, vol. 2 of Columbia University Council for Research in the Social Sciences, *Neutrality: Its History, Economics and Law* (New York: Columbia University Press, 1936), 20–21.

11. Michael R. Weisser, *Crime and Punishment in Early Modern Europe*, in *Pre-Industrial Europe: 1350–1850*, ed. Geoffrey Parker (Atlantic Highlands, N.J.: Humanities Press, 1979), 138–39.

12. Ibid., 140–41. For a detailed account of the role of prisoners in the French navy, see Paul W. Bamford, *Fighting Ships and Prisons: The Mediterranean Galleys of France in the Age of Louis XIV* (Minneapolis: University of Minnesota Press, 1973). Bamford chronicles the role of coerced convict labor in private and state ships. He also charts the galley's transformation from a military asset into a modern penal institution.

13. Rankin, *Golden Age* 7; Sherry, *Raiders and Rebels*, 59.

14. Sherry, *Raiders and Rebels*, 59; Rankin, *Golden Age*, 8. Sovereignty over the island of Tortuga was disputed. In 1631, the English residents petitioned the Company of Providence Island "to take Tortuga under its protection." So Tortuga was technically British until Spain took it over in 1636. Neville Williams, *Captains Outrageous: Seven Centuries of Piracy* (New York: Macmillan, 1962), 123. Seeing Tortuga as a potentially valuable base, a group of Frenchmen from Saint Christopher took possession of the island in 1640 and named one of their own governor. Rankin, *Golden Age*, 9. Finally in 1659 Spain recognized Tortuga as part of the French empire. Williams, *Captains Outrageous*, 123.

15. Rankin, *Golden Age*, 8–9.

16. Williams, *Captains Outrageous*, 124.

17. In this attack, "Morgan and his men destroyed forts, desecrated churches, killed nuns, raped captive women, and tortured children as well as adults of both sexes in an attempt to force their victims to disclose hidden gold." Sherry, *Raiders and Rebels*, 60. Panama City was burned to the ground. For more on Morgan's activities, see Kronenberger, "People on Spits," 106–9.

18. Sherry, *Raiders and Rebels*, 60.

19. Morgan's success weakened Spain so it was forced to deal with Britain. See Rankin, *Golden Age*, 15. Morgan's men stormed and sacked the city of Portobelo in 1668. In August of 1670, he, with thirty-six ships and about two thousand buccaneers, set upon Panamá City, which burned to the ground while his men were looting it. Afterward, Morgan deserted his followers and absconded with most of the booty. *New Encyclopedia Britannica*, 15th ed., s.v. "Morgan, Sir Henry." See also Kronenberger, "People on Spits," 108. He writes that Morgan's take was "250,000 pieces of eight."

20. P. K. Kemp and Christopher Lloyd, *Brethren of the Coast: Buccaneers of the South Seas* (New York: St. Martin's, 1960), 29.

21. Rankin, *Golden Age*, 16.

22. Ibid., 16; Williams, *Captains Outrageous*, 125.

23. Sherry, *Raiders and Rebels*, 62; Rankin, *Golden Age*, 18.

24. Sherry, *Raiders and Rebels*, 29 and 91.

25. Williams, *Captains Outrageous*, 178.

26. Sherry, *Raiders and Rebels*, 93.

27. Ibid., 94–95, 94–98, and 100.

28. Ibid., 99, 136, and 130, emphasis in original.

29. Ibid., 108; Williams, *Captains Outrageous*, 181 and 183.

30. Sherry, *Raiders and Rebels*, 109, 110, and 118.

31. Ibid., 195.

32. Ibid., 199–201.

33. Ibid., 202–3.

34. Rankin, *Golden Age*, 19, 43, 54–58; Sherry, *Raiders and Rebels*, 23–24, 116–18; Ritchie, *Captain Kidd*, 18–19, 36–39; Philip Gosse, *The History of Piracy* (New York: Tudor, 1946), 206–12.

35. Rankin, *Golden Age*, 76–77.

36. Ibid., 63.

37. Williams, *Captains Outrageous*, 141; Ritchie, *Captain Kidd*, 144.

38. Gosse, *History of Piracy*, 207–8, 321–22.

39. Rankin, *Golden Age*, 64. Also see Ritchie, *Captain Kidd*, 233.

40. For a reprint of the report, see Gosse, *History of Piracy*, 320–23.

41. Williams, *Captains Outrageous*, 141.

42. Ibid., 142.

43. Rankin, *Golden Age*, 57. Fletcher was actually removed from office for political corruption, not for collaboration with pirates. See Williams, *Captains Outrageous*, 136; and Ritchie, *Captain Kidd*, 50.

44. Williams, *Captains Outrageous*, 136–37.

45. Sherry, *Raiders and Rebels*, 147.

46. Williams, *Captains Outrageous*, 137.

47. Sherry, *Raiders and Rebels*, 147.

48. Ritchie, *Captain Kidd*, 170–71.

49. Sherry, *Raiders and Rebels*, 197.

50. The real test of Bellomont's intentions came with Captain Kidd's return to North America in 1699. Before leaving England for his new post, Bellomont had arranged the financial backing for a privateering mission against pirates in the Indian Ocean, the captain of which was William Kidd. The question was whether Bellomont's anti-piracy policies would apply to Kidd, who was now charged with committing piracy on the anti-piracy mission originally organized by Bellomont (Ritchie, *Captain Kidd*, 176). Bellomont persuaded Kidd to come to Boston and, after allowing Kidd to defend himself before the Massachusetts Council, had him arrested on the orders from England that he had not acted on previously (178–82). Kidd's booty, other evidence, and Kidd were shipped to England for trial (Sherry, *Raiders and Rebels*, 185).

51. Sherry, *Raiders and Rebels*, 197–98.

52. Williams, *Captains Outrageous*, 149–50 and 157.

53. Ibid., 158.

54. Sherry, *Raiders and Rebels*, 216–17; Rankin, *Golden Age*, 20.

55. Sherry, *Raiders and Rebels*, 225.

56. Ibid., 226–27.

57. Rankin, *Golden Age*, 91.

58. Sherry, *Raiders and Rebels*, 225–26 and 231–32.

59. Ibid., 232–34.

60. Ibid., 253.

61. Ibid., 256; Rankin, *Golden Age*, 21.

62. Sherry, *Raiders and Rebels*, 264 and 275.

63. Ibid., 280–84 and 293.

64. Ibid., 296–97.

65. Marcus Rediker, *Between the Devil and the Deep Blue Sea: Merchant Seamen, Pirates, and the Anglo-American Maritime World, 1700–1750* (Cambridge: Cambridge University Press, 1987), 282; Ritchie, *Captain Kidd*, 236; Sherry, *Raiders and Rebels*, 358.

66. A similar process occurred on land, where large numbers of former soldiers turned to banditry until the outbreak of new hostilities led the army to recruit them once again.

67. Mockler, *Mercenaries*, 96–97.

68. Mockler, *New Mercenaries*, 5. According to Ingrao, only 12 percent of the native Hessians deserted from the Hesse-Cassel army; the vast majority of the three thousand deserters were foreigners recruited to supplement or replace native Hessians. Ingrao, *The Hessian Mercenary State*, 153–59.

69. Mockler, *New Mercenaries*, 8.

70. William Edward Hall, *The Rights and Duties of Neutrals* (London: Longmans, Green, 1874), 20–21.

71. Ibid., 21.

72. Charles G. Fenwick, *The Neutrality Laws of the United States* (Washington, D.C.: Carnegie Endowment for International Peace, 1913), 14.

73. Hall, *Rights and Duties*, 66 n. 1.

74. Ibid., 27.

75. Jessup and Deàk, *Origins*, 20.

76. Hall, *Rights and Duties*, 30.

77. Fenwick, *Neutrality Laws*, 4–5.

78. Hall, *Rights and Duties*, 31–32 and 38.

79. Ibid., 39–40.

80. Ibid., 47.

81. U. K., *Hansard Parliamentary Debates*, 2d ser., vol 40 (1819), col. 1379.

82. Wilfred Burchett and Derek Roebuck, *The Whores of War: Mercenaries Today* (New York: Penguin Books, 1977), 181.

83. Speech by Earl Bathurst to House of Lords. U.K., *Hansard* (1819), col. 1379.

84. Ibid., col. 1384.

85. Text of the act is reprinted in Fenwick, *Neutrality Laws*, 184–91.

86. Furber, *Rival Empires*, 43–44.

87. Ibid., 44–47.

88. Ibid., 48–49.

89. Ibid., 94. See also William Seymour, "The Company That Founded an Empire: The First Hundred Years in the Rise to Power of the East India Company," *History Today* 19 (September 1969): 649.

90. E. E. Rich, *The History of the Hudson's Bay Company, 1670–1870*, vol. 2 of *Publications of the Hudson's Bay Record Society*, ed. idem (London: Hudson's Bay Record Society, 1959), 119.

91. Douglas MacKay, *The Honourable Company: A History of the Hudson's Bay Company*, (New York: Bobbs-Merrill, 1936), 134–35.

92. Ibid., 134–45, 158. For a detailed history of the North West Company, see Peter C. Newman, *Company of Adventurers*, vol. 2, *Caesars of the Wilderness* (Ontario, Canada: Viking, 1987).

93. Coornaert, "European Economic Institutions," 236.

94. Seymour, "Company That Founded an Empire," 644.

95. Chaudhuri, *English East India Company*, 64.

96. Cawston and Keane, *Early Chartered Companies*, 164.

97. Malabar refers to the southern part of India's west coast, from Goa on south.

98. Furber, *Rival Empires*, 84.

99. Ibid., 54.

100. Howard, *War in European History*, 43–44.

101. Pularoon (Pulurun) is one of the Banda Islands.

102. Arnold A. Sherman, "Pressure from Leadenhall: The East India Company Lobby, 1660–1678," *Business History Review* 50 (Autumn 1976): 333.

103. Boxer, *Seaborne Empire*, 46; Fernand Braudel, *Civilization and Capitalism, Fifteenth–Eighteenth Century*, vol. 3, *The Perspective of the World*, trans. Siân Reynolds (New York: Harper and Row, 1984), 205–6. Coornaert uses a slightly different translation: "The colonies of the East Indies are not acquisitions made by the state, but by private traders who may sell them if they wish, even to the king of Spain, or to any other enemy of the United Provinces" "European Economic Institutions," 249.

104. Coornaert, "European Economic Institutions," 266.

105. Ibid., 235.

106. Braudel, *Civilization and Capitalism*, 213; Furber, *Rival Empires*, 34.

107. Furber, *Rival Empires*, 34.

108. Ibid., 40–41; Mukherjee, *Rise and Fall*, 95.

109. Furber, *Rival Empires*, 46–47.

110. Ibid., 50 and 53.

111. A. R. Disney, "The First Portuguese India Company, 1628–1633," *Economic History Review*, 2d ser 30 (May 1977): 243.

112. Braudel, *Civilization and Capitalism*, 216.

113. Furber, *Rival Empires*, 55.

114. Ibid., 54, 57, and 83–84.

115. San Thomé (Mylapore, Mailapur, Meliapore) is located about three miles south of Madras.

116. Furber, *Rival Empires*, 111, 114, 120 and 122–23.

117. H. H. Dodwell, "The War of Austrian Succession," in *British India, 1497–1858*, ed. idem, vol. 5 of *The Cambridge History of India*, 6 vols. (Cambridge: Cambridge University Press, 1929), 119; Furber, *Rival Empires*, 147 and 166. Mukherjee (*Rise and Fall*, 116) disagrees that the English company really wanted neutrality in the East.

118. Furber, *Rival Empires*, 147.

119. The Carnatic is a linguistic region of the Deccan Plateau in south-central India. It generally corresponds to the former independent Hindu state of Mysore. *New Encyclopedia Britannica* 15th ed., s.v. "Carnatic."

120. Mukherjee, *Rise and Fall*, 116–17; Furber, *Rival Empires*, 148–50; Cawston and Keane, *Early Chartered Companies*, 127–29; Dodwell, "War of Austrian Succession," 119–24.

121. Furber, *Rival Empires*, 150. *Factory* was "the term used for a warehouse and trading post." Seymour, "Company That Founded an Empire," 643.

122. Mukherjee, *Rise and Fall*, 120–24.

123. Ibid., 124–26; Alfred Martineau, "Dupleix and Bussy," in *British India, 1497–1858*, ed. H. H. Dodwell, vol. 5 of *The Cambridge History of India*, 6 vols. (Cambridge: Cambridge University Press, 1929), 132.

124. Mukherjee, *Rise and Fall*, 126.

125. This account is taken from ibid., 128–32. See also Cawston and Keane, *Early Chartered Companies*, 131–34; and H. H. Dodwell, "The Seven Years War," in *British India, 1497–1858*, ed. idem, vol. 5 of *The Cambridge History of India*, 6 vols. (Cambridge: Cambridge University Press, 1929), 157–65.

126. Cawston and Keane, *Early Chartered Companies*, 135–36.

127. Newman, *Company of Adventurers* 1:152–64.

128. Ibid., 311–12.

129. This account is taken from W. J. Van Hoboken, "Dutch West India Company," 51–58. See also Vlekke, *Evolution of the Dutch Nation*, 201 and 217.

130. See Albert O. Hirshmann, *The Passions and the Interests: Political Arguments for Capitalism before Its Triumph* (Princeton: Princeton University Press, 1977), who argues that, in the seventeenth century, the pursuit of interests through trade (the doux commerce) was seen as a means of taming or overcoming the violence-prone aristocratic pursuit of honor and glory (the passions).

Chapter Four
Delegitimating State-Authorized Nonstate Violence

1. Stark, "Abolition," 66.

2. Ibid., 70.

3. Hall, *Treatise*, 521.

4. Stark, "Abolition," 74–75.

5. Julian S. Corbett, *England in the Seven Years' War* (London: Longmans, Green, 1907), 2:6.

6. Francis Piggott, *The Declaration of Paris, 1856* (London: University of London Press, 1919), 147. See Corbett, *England in the Seven Years' War*, for primary materials.

7. Stark, "Abolition," 77 and 82.

8. Reprinted in Edward Hertslet, *The Map of Europe by Treaty* (London: Butterworths, 1875), 2:1282–83. "Translation as laid before Parliament."

9. In Protocol No. 24; see H. W. Malkin, "The Inner History of the Declaration of Paris," *British Yearbook of International Law* 8 (1927): 39.

10. Stark, "Abolition," 142.

11. Piggott, *Declaration of Paris*, 121.

12. See, for example, Stark, "Abolition."

13. Ibid., 143–44; Malkin, "Inner History," 37.

14. Stark, "Abolition," 144. The other was Spain.

15. U.K., *Hansard Parliamentary Debates*, 3d ser., vol. 142 (1856), col. 539.

16. From the second Marcy note, reprinted in Piggott, *Declaration of Paris*, 395. Article 1, section 8 of the U.S. Constitution grants Congress the power "to declare war, grant letters of marque and reprisal and make rules concerning captures on land and water."

17. Piggott, *Declaration of Paris*, 397 and 241.

18. Stark, "Abolition," 70–71; Hall, *Treatise*, 770. Hall says that Britain's views of its belligerent rights seem "to have permitted the list of contraband articles to be enlarged or restricted to suit the particular circumstances of the war."

19. 5 April 1856. Quoted in Malkin, "Inner History," 30.

20. Piggott, *Declaration of Paris*, 8.

21. Malkin, "Inner History," 6.

22. Moreover, the French privateer had always been of a "more uncontrollable and piratical type" than those of other states. It may be that "several decades of spoliation claims had suggested to the French nation that perhaps it was better to save the money which they would have to pay for his depredations, and use it toward carrying on the war." See Stark, "Abolition," 144.

23. Ibid., 144.

24. The only other states that also declined to accede were Spain, Mexico, and Venezuela (only Piggott, *Declaration of Paris*, 138, reports Venezuela as a nonsignatory). Spain acceded in 1908 and Mexico in 1909. The United States and Venezuela, it is believed, never acceded. See Hall, *Treatise*, 621; and Stark, "Abolition," 147.

25. Malkin, "Inner History," 20.

26. The United States argued that there was only one logical basis for banning privateering: the protection of private commercial shipping from attacks on the high seas. According to the United States, both of the arguments that had been offered in support of the ban on privateering were fundamentally flawed. First of all, there was in principle no difference between raising a volunteer army of citizens and commissioning citizen volunteers for naval service. So "the proposition to enter into engagements to forego a resort to privateers . . . is not entitled to more favourable consideration than would be a proposition to agree not to accept the services of volunteers for operations on land" (Piggott, *Declaration of Paris*, 398). Secondly, there was no logical basis for arguments that privateering should be banned because, being based on the profit motive, it stimulated a "cupidity" that states could not control. This argument ignored the fact that sailors of regular navies also made prizes of private merchant ships and divided the prize money

among themselves. Also see Thomas Gibson Bowles, *The Declaration of Paris of 1856* (London: Sampson Low, Marston, 1900), 98–100, for this argument.

The United States acknowledged that privateering was the weapon of weak naval powers, and as a weak naval power itself, defended the practice. Abolishing privateering would simply allow the dominant naval powers to continue business as usual, though vessels of their regular navies would be making prize of weaker states' private commerce. But if the real intent of the proposed ban were to reduce depredations on commerce, the United States argued, the appropriate strategy was not to ban privateering but to prohibit all attacks on private property—including that belonging to subjects of belligerent states.

27. Malkin, "Inner History," 27.

28. Ibid., 41.

29. Stark, "Abolition," 376.

30. Malkin, "Inner History," 42–43.

31. Stark, "Abolition," 156.

32. Ibid., 156.

33. Hall, *Treatise*, 622.

34. Stark, "Abolition," 159.

35. Nevertheless, according to one international law scholar, "the vessels hired could not have been privateers for quite a number of reasons: (1) they were actually, by virtue of the contract of hiring, public vessels for the time being, fitted and armed and sent forth at the public expense; (2) their crews were actually public servants, having no right to cruise anywhere except under orders, and subject to the same discipline as the regular navy; and (3) they were designed for the work of a regular navy, and forbidden in fact to prey on private property at all. Under these circumstances the abuses which the first article of the Declaration sought to prevent, would have been quite impossible" (Stark, "Abolition," 159). The problem is that the circumstances did change. In January of 1871 Prussia withdrew its ban on attacking private property at sea, raising the specter of the "volunteer navy" making prize of private vessels just as privateers had always done. Moreover, in the opinion of another legal expert, "unless a navy were brought into closer connexion with the state than seems to have been the case in the Prussian project it would be difficult to show as a mere question of theory that its establishment did not constitute an evasion of the Declaration of Paris." Hall, *Treatise*, 623.

36. Piggott, *Declaration of Paris*, 438. I have been unable to determine why the United States and Spain decided not to use privateers. There are hints in some quarters that British pressure was behind it. See, for example, Bertha Ann Reuter, *Anglo-American Relations during the Spanish-American War* (New York: Macmillan, 1924), 86–87.

37. Piggott, *Declaration of Paris*, 440.

38. Hall, *Treatise*, 621.

39. Fenwick, *Neutrality Laws*, 16.

40. Charles S. Hynemann, *The First American Neutrality: A Study of the American Understanding of Neutral Obligations during the Years 1792 to 1815*, Illinois Studies in the Social Sciences 20, nos. 1–2 (Urbana: University of Illinois, 1934), 133–40; and Charles Marion Thomas, *American Neutrality in 1793: A*

Study in Cabinet Government (New York: Columbia University Press, 1931), 177–86.

41. Lobel, "Rise and Decline," n. 1.

42. James Matthews Seavey, "Neutrality Legislation in the United States" (S.J.D. thesis, Georgetown University, 1939), 10.

43. Hall, *Rights and Duties*, 44.

44. Quoted in Fenwick, *Neutrality Laws*, 19 (emphasis added).

45. Ibid., 20–21 and 23.

46. The president's proclamation provoked a major controversy over whether or not he had exceeded his authority, since Congress alone had the power to declare war. One reason for the adoption of the Neutrality Act was to clarify these issues and provide a firm legal basis for federal prosecutions. See Hynemann, *First American Neutrality*, 155–59.

47. Hall, *Rights and Duties*, 46.

48. The exceptions are "citizens of a foreign state who are transiently within the United States" and "such persons, as within thirty days after enlistment, discover upon oath the person by whom they were enlisted." Fenwick, *Neutrality Laws*, 26.

49. Ibid., 26–27. This act was later found wanting in that it gave the United States no authority over its citizens living abroad, some of whom were fitting out privateers to attack U.S. commerce. To deal with this problem Congress passed the Neutrality Act of 1797, which forbade U.S. citizens anywhere from privateering against states with which the United States was at peace and against the citizens of the United States. See ibid., 30.

50. It also required U.S. owners of armed vessels to post a bond to assure that they would not use the vessels in violation of U.S. neutrality laws. Due to the threat of piracy and other depredations on commerce, many private merchant ships were fitted out with defensive armaments. The problem was that once they were at sea, the U.S. state had no control over whether the armaments were indeed used only for self-defense or in activities that violated U.S. neutrality.

51. Lobel, "Rise and Decline," 1.

52. The law encompasses states, princes, colonies, districts and peoples. For purposes of brevity, I will hereafter refer simply to states. The current statute provides for a fine of up to $3,000 and/or a prison term of up to three years. Ibid., 2.

53. Fenwick, *Neutrality Laws*, 127.

54. Lobel, "Rise and Decline," 12.

55. Neither domestic nor international law forbids individuals from leaving the country to fight, but "groups of individuals are prohibited from even planning foreign military expeditions." This "group activity is unlawful because the group is in effect organizing a separate state entity within the United States." Ibid., 25–26.

56. Fenwick, *Neutrality Laws*, 14; Hall, *Rights and Duties*, 44; Thomas, *American Neutrality*, 6.

57. Seavey, "Neutrality Legislation," 2–3.

58. Hall, *Rights and Duties*, 46.

59. See Syngman Rhee, *Neutrality as Influenced by the United States* (Prince-

ton: Princeton University Press, 1912), 90–102 for a discussion of the *Alabama* case.

60. Fenwick, *Neutrality Laws*, 192.

61. Ibid., 191–92.

62. Australia (1874), India (1874), Ashanti (1906), Bahamas (1924), Bermuda (1874), British Honduras (1874), Ceylon (1874), Cyprus (1881), Federated Malay States (1914), Gibraltar (1877), Gold Coast (1888), Grenada (1875), Hong Kong (1874), Jamaica (1875), Lagos (1886), Natal (1875), Newfoundland (1875), Orange River Colony (1906), Saint Helena (1876), Straits Settlements (1875), Tanganyika (1920), Tasmania (1875), Transjordan (1928), and Transvaal (1906).

63. Britain's restrictions, however, were aimed at preventing its citizens from serving in the armies of particular monarchs, perhaps most especially those which threatened the British Crown. The legislation of 1735–36 prohibited British subjects from serving the king of Prussia, and that of 1755–56 prevented enlistment in the service of the French king. A later act (1769) required officers of the Scottish brigades serving with the Dutch to take "the oaths of allegiance and abjuration." Though the language in these acts was of a universal nature, prohibiting subjects from serving foreign powers per se, it is clear that the laws were aimed at specific targets. UK, *Hansard* (1819), col. 1378.

64. Hall, *Rights and Duties*, 41.

65. Of the sixty-six states existing in 1938 (see Arthur S. Banks, *Cross-National Time-Series Data Archive User's Manual* [Binghamton: State University of New York, 1975], 47–52), forty-five had enacted such statutes.

66. Lobel, "Rise and Decline," 5.

67. Focusing on these states, with their geographic proximity and common cultural and historical experiences, minimizes the number of extraneous variables that might account for their adoption of the legislation.

68. "The prohibitions contained in the Neutrality Act go beyond those required of a neutral state and encompass obligations mandated by the broad principle of non-intervention." Lobel, "Rise and Decline," 6 n. 21.

69. There is evidence that U.S. leaders were concerned that the mercenaries' guns might be turned against them. John Adams wrote, twenty years later, that he had feared that Genet's supporters would "drag Washington out of his house and effect a revolution in the government." Cited in Thomas, *American Neutrality*, 88. See ibid., 234, for further evidence of these concerns.

70. Lobel, "Rise and Decline," 24–25.

71. Francis Wharton, *State Trials of the United States during the Administrations of Washington and Adams* (Philadelphia: Carey and Hart, 1849), 84.

72. *National Gazette*, 3 August 1793, cited in Hynemann, *First American Neutrality*, 131.

73. Wharton, *State Trials*, 89.

74. Lobel, "Rise and Decline," 43.

75. Article 21 of the Code provided that "a Frenchman who, without the permission of the French Government, enters into the military or naval service of a foreign power, loses his *status* as a Frenchman, and cannot return to France without the permission of the French Government, nor resume his status of a

Frenchman, except by going through the same formalities as an alien; without prejudice to the penalties prescribed by the criminal law against Frenchmen for bearing arms against their own country." David M. Aird, *The Civil Laws of France to the Present Time* (London: Longmans, Green, 1875), 24 (emphasis in original). The problem is determining what the term *status* denotes. The French term is *la qualité de Francais*. After much research into French parliamentary archives and the writings of French legal scholars, my research assistant (a native of France) concluded that, in the case of this section of the Code, having the status of Frenchman merely makes one eligible for the civil rights included in the Code. The status of Citizen conferred both civil and political rights whereas the status of Frenchman conferred only civil rights. See Jacques de Maleville, *Analyse Raisonneé de la Discussion du Code Civil au Conseil d'Etat*, 3d ed., 4 vols. (Paris: N'eve, 1822).

76. This was by virtue of the extension of the French Civil Code of 1804. Francis Deàk and Philip C. Jessup, eds., *A Collection of Neutrality Laws, Regulations and Treaties of Various Countries*, vols. 1 and 2 (Washington, D.C.: Carnegie Endowment for International Peace, 1939), 49.

77. Ibid., passim.

78. Lobel writes that "during the 19th and 20th centuries, Latin American governments, plagued by frequent revolutions, furthered international law in this area [hostile expeditions] by concluding numerous treaties designed to prevent the territory of neighboring states from becoming a basis for hostile expeditions or hostile acts against them." "Rise and Decline," 23.

79. Bayley, *Mercenaries for the Crimea*, 111.

80. Ibid., 145–48.

81. S. J. G. Clarke, *The Congo Mercenary* (Johannesburg: South African Institute of International Affairs at the University of the Witwatersrand, 1968), 10.

82. Bayley, *Mercenaries for the Crimea*, 68.

83. Richard J. Smith, *Mercenaries and Mandarins: The Ever-Victorious Army in Nineteenth-Century China* (Millwood, N.Y.: KTO Press, 1978), passim.

84. Alvin J. Cottrell and Frank Bray, *Military Forces in the Persian Gulf*, Center for Strategic and International Studies, the Washington Papers 6, no. 60 (Beverly Hills, Calif.: Sage, 1978), 54; John Keegan, *World Armies* (New York: Facts on File, 1979), 751.

85. Cottrell and Bray, *Military Forces*, 49.

86. Keegan, *World Armies*, 524–26.

87. Dilip Hiro, *Inside the Middle East* (London: Routledge and Kegan Paul, 1982), 348 and 439.

88. To second is "to remove (an officer) temporarily from his regiment or corps for employment on the staff, or in some other extra-regimental appointment." *Oxford English Dictionary*, 1978 ed.

89. Cottrell and Bray, *Military Forces*, 52.

90. Keegan, *World Armies* (1979), 586.

91. Cottrell and Bray, *Military Forces*, 59.

92. John Keegan, *World Armies*, 2d ed. (London: Macmillan, 1983), 35.

93. Devlet Khalid, "Pakistan's Relations with Iran and the Arab States," *Journal of South Asian and Middle Eastern Studies* 5 (Spring 1982): 20.

94. Nadav Safran, *Saudi Arabia: The Ceaseless Quest for Security* (Cambridge: Harvard University Press, Belknap Press, 1985), 362.

95. Hiro, *Inside the Middle East*, 88.

96. William B. Quandt, *Saudi Arabia in the 1980s: Foreign Policy, Security, and Oil* (Washington, D.C.: Brookings Institution, 1981), 41.

97. Safran, *Saudi Arabia*, 372.

98. Hiro, *Inside the Middle East*, 395.

99. Ted Morello, "Gurkhas under Fire," *Far Eastern Economic Review* 116 (4 June 1982): 40.

100. "Domiciled" Gurkhas also serve in the Burmese army (Keegan, *World Armies* [1979], 105), but since they are Burmese residents, they are not considered true foreigners. See also ibid., 96, 308–10, 758–59; Morello, "Gurkhas," 40–41.

101. Byron Farwell, *The Gurkhas* (New York: W. W. Norton, 1984), 31–32.

102. A. L. Venkateswaran, *Defense Organization in India* (Delhi: Government Ministry of Information and Broadcasting, 1967), 45.

103. Morello, "Gurkhas," 41.

104. Farwell, *Gurkhas*, 262.

105. Morello, "Gurkhas," 42; Keegan, *World Armies* (1979), 489–90.

106. Keegan, *World Armies* (1983), 80; Bandar Seri Bagawan, "Brunei: Floating Free," *Economist* 24 (December 1983): 40.

107. Bagawan, "Brunei: Floating Free"; D. E. Brown, "Brunei on the Morrow of Independence," *Asian Survey* 24 (February 1984): 207.

108. Brown, "Brunei," 205.

109. Keegan, *World Armies* (1983), 217.

110. Ibid., 320, 139.

111. Mockler, *Mercenaries*, 133.

112. Ibid., 138. In his new book, Porch argues that one reason for the Foreign Legion's formation was to control foreigners who had flooded into France following the revolution. "Absorbing them into the army and sending them overseas would contain and tame them." The Legion emphasized loyalty to the military as an institutionalized way of life so "its traditions might outweigh any lack of sympathy with the values and policies of France." Phillip Knightley, "Unlucky in Love, Lucky in War," review of *The French Foreign Legion*, by Douglas Porch, *New York Times Book Review*, 14 July 1991, 7.

113. As of 1983, the composition of the Foreign Legion was as follows: 59 percent French speakers; 12 percent German; 11 percent Italian, Spanish, and Portuguese; 5 percent "Slavonic"; 3 percent English; 2 percent African and Asian, 1 percent Norse; and 7 percent other. French speakers include French citizens, who were originally forbidden from joining, and French-speaking Swiss, Monegasques, and Belgians. John Robert Young, *The French Foreign Legion: The Inside Story of the World-Famous Fighting Force* (London: Thames and Hudson, 1984), 208.

114. Ibid.

115. International Institute for Strategic Studies, *The Military Balance, 1986–1987* (London: International Institute for Strategic Studies, 1986), 64.

116. Keegan, *World Armies* (1979), 647–48.

117. It is not entirely clear whether this case should be included in the category

of ad hoc forces or standing armies. On the one hand, it was apparently used only in Lebanon, while on the other, Khalid implies that it was designed to be a permanent Islamic military force.

118. Khalid, "Pakistan's Relations," 20. Mockler, *New Mercenaries*, 358, also mentions "Gaddafy's Islamic Legion in Libya and Chad."

119. United Nations, Security Council, July 1950, S/1627.

120. David Rees, *Korea: The Limited War* (New York: St. Martin's Press, 1964), 38–39, 435.

121. The UAE, Oman, Qatar, Kuwait, Britain, India, Brunei, Ivory Coast, Cameroon, Solomon Islands, France, and Cyprus.

122. Cottrell and Bray, *Military Forces*, 7.

123. U.S. control of the Korean armed forces was formally declared on 7 September 1945 (General Douglas MacArthur, "General Order No. 1," reprinted in U.S. Congress, Senate, Committee on Foreign Relations, *The United States and the Korean Problem*, 83d Cong., 1st sess., 1953, 3) and ended in August of 1948, when the Republic of Korea government took control (U.S. Department of the Army, *Military Advisors in Korea: KMAG in Peace and War* [Washington, D.C.: Office of the Chief of Military History, 1962], 34). Two years later, with the Taejon Agreement, South Korea placed its forces under the command of the U.S.-led UN forces (U.S. Congress, *The United States and the Korean Problem*, 38).

124. This overview of twentieth-century ad hoc mercenary forces does not include the World Anti-Communist League (WACL), which supports what it defines as "anticommunist" causes around the world. It is neither a purely private nor purely state organization. The Korean and Taiwanese governments were cofounders, along with the head of the Unification Church and several private individuals and groups. I do not include it here because it is unclear whether WACL actually raises armies or simply provides financial, material, and other support for already existing anticommunist groups. For the best treatment of WACL, see Scott Anderson and Jon Lee Anderson, *Inside the League: The Shocking Expose of How Terrorists, Nazis, and Latin American Death Squads Have Infiltrated the World Anti-Communist League* (New York: Dodd, Mead and Co., 1986).

125. Hugh Thomas, *The Spanish Civil War*, rev. ed. (New York: Harper and Row, 1977), 469, 768, 975, and 454–55.

126. Clarke, *Congo Mercenary*, 4, 75.

127. Mockler, *Mercenaries*, 194.

128. Clarke, *Congo Mercenary*, 27–28.

129. Ibid., 87–89; Mockler, *Mercenaries*, 255.

130. Burmester, "Recruitment and Use," 48.

131. John De St. Jorre, *The Nigerian Civil War* (London: Hodder and Stoughton, 1972), 315–16.

132. Ibid., 322–26; Mockler, *Mercenaries*, 257–75.

133. Clarke, *Congo Mercenary*, 89.

134. Keegan, *World Armies* (1983), 124–25.

135. Burchett and Roebuck, *Whores of War*, 212.

136. Ibid., 135; U.S. Congress, Senate, Committee on Foreign Relations, Sub-

committee on African Affairs, *Angola*, 94th Cong., 2d sess., 3 February 1976, 108.

137. Burchett and Roebuck, *Whores of War*, 138–40.

138. For an exhaustive list and detailed description of soldier-of-fortune activities since 1960, see Mockler, *New Mercenaries*.

139. Lt. Gen. Stanley Robert Larsen and Brig. Gen. James Lawton Collins, *Allied Participation in Vietnam* (Washington, D.C.: Department of the Army, 1975), 48.

140. Ibid., 22–23.

141. Norman J. Padelford, *International Law and Diplomacy in the Spanish Civil Strife* (New York: Macmillan, 1939), 116; Thomas, *Spanish Civil War*, 983–84.

142. I am indebted to John Meyer for suggesting that these cases can be viewed in this way.

143. In international law this limitation is reflected in the doctrine of "no responsibility without fault," which holds that the state is liable only if it fails to take all reasonable measures to prevent and punish actions of private persons. M. Garcia-Mora, *International Responsibility for Hostile Acts of Private Persons against Foreign States* (The Hague: Martinus Nijhoff, 1962), 16–22. See also Hall, *Rights and Duties*, 17–18.

144. Lobel, "Rise and Decline," 32.

145. Mockler, *New Mercenaries*, 356.

146. United Nations, General Assembly, *Report*, A37/43.

147. Burmester, "Recruitment and Use." For a discussion of how Third World states have sought to legitimate greater state control in a broad range of issue areas, see Krasner, *Structural Conflict*.

148. Griffiths, *License to Trade*, 71.

149. *Country trade* is the term used to refer to trade within the non-European areas; for example, trade between the Indonesian islands and the Indian mainland.

150. Vlekke, *Dutch Nation*, 277, 280, and 283; Braudel, *Civilization and Capitalism*, 228. There is disagreement on this date. Coornaert says this occurred in 1798 ("European Economic Institutions," 273). P. Geyl, "The Dutch in India," in *British India, 1497–1858*, ed. H. H. Dodwell, vol. 5 of *The Cambridge History of India*, 6 vols. (Cambridge: Cambridge University Press, 1929), 60, says 1795.

151. Newman, *Company of Adventurers* 1:376.

152. Griffiths, *License to Trade*, 127.

153. Mukherjee, *Rise and Fall*, 85 and 87.

154. Ibid., 86–87; Griffiths, *License to Trade*, 92, 126–27; Furber, *Rival Empires*, 89 and 101.

155. Furber, *Rival Empires*, 44; Chaudhuri, *English East India Company*, 49–50.

156. Mukherjee, *Rise and Fall*, 106–7.

157. Vlekke, *Dutch Nation*, 218.

158. Braudel, *Civilization and Capitalism*, 232–35; Van Hoboken, "Dutch West India Company," 60–61.

159. Vlekke, *Dutch Nation*, 218.

160. Griffiths, *License to Trade*, 141 and 32–33.

161. Ibid., 34–35, 54–55, 59.

162. Newman, *Company of Adventurers* 1:118, 188, 120, and 175.

163. Mukherjee, *Rise and Fall*, 73.

164. Furber, *Rival Empires*, 98.

165. Newman, *Company of Adventurers* 1:122.

166. Mukherjee, *Rise and Fall*, 71, 75, 78–79; Griffiths, *License to Trade*, 96.

167. James Mill, cited in Mukherjee, *Rise and Fall*, 84. See also Newman (*Company of Adventurers* 1:172–73) who cites a 1695 parliamentary report which said that the "East India Company had been doling out £90,000 a year, £10,000 of which had been going annually into the Royal Household."

168. For a detailed examination of the company's many means of influencing the Crown and Parliament, see Sherman, "Pressure from Leadenhall," 329–53.

169. Newman, *Company of Adventurers* 1:111.

170. Maurice Dobb, *Studies in the Development of Capitalism* (New York: International Publishers, 1947), 168.

171. Boxer, *Seaborne Empire*, 23–24.

172. It was national in the sense that it was open to all interested Netherlanders. But it was actually international in that anyone, without restriction to nationality, could become a shareholder. See Furber, *Rival Empires*, 189.

173. Boxer, *Seaborne Empire*, 45.

174. Davis, *Corporations*, 137.

175. Cawston and Keane, *Early Chartered Companies*, 140.

176. James Mill, *The History of British India*, abridged ed., in *Classics of British Historical Literature*, ed. John Clive (Chicago: University of Chicago Press, 1975), 375, 376, and 381.

177. Davis, *Corporations*, 138.

178. Roberts, "East India Company," 187.

179. Mill, *History of British India*, 391.

180. Davis, *Corporations*, 139.

181. Mill, *History of British India*, 454–55.

182. Griffiths, *License to Trade*, 99.

183. Ibid., 102.

184. H. H. Dodwell, "The Development of Sovereignty in British India," in *British India, 1497–1858*, ed. idem, vol. 5 of *The Cambridge History of India*, 6 vols. (Cambridge: Cambridge University Press, 1929), 595.

185. Ibid., 595–96.

186. Ibid., 589–92,

187. Ibid., 596, 592, and 596.

188. Griffiths, *License to Trade*, 102.

189. Davis, *Corporations*, 140–42.

190. Newman, *Company of Adventurers* 1:3, 119 and 2.

191. Hudson's Bay Company, *Charters, Statutes, Orders*, 18–19.

192. Newman, *Company of Adventurers* 1:117 and 281.

193. Rich, *History of the Hudson's Bay Company*, 794–95.

194. Ibid., 797.

195. Ibid., 787, 804, and 850.

196. Douglas MacKay, *The Honourable Company: A History of the Hudson's Bay Company* (New York: Bobbs-Merrill, 1936), 171 and 180.

197. Rich, *History of the Hudson's Bay Company*, 773, 796, 798, and 851.

198. Ibid., 850.

199. R.G. Trotter, "The Coming of Confederation," in *Canada and Newfoundland*, vol. 6 of *The Cambridge History of the British Empire*, ed. J. Holland Rose, A. P. Newton, and E. A. Benians (Cambridge: Cambridge University Press, 1930), 447, 459, and 460. For a more detailed account of the Fenians' activities, see Hereward Senior, *The Fenians and Canada* (Toronto: Macmillan of Canada, 1978).

200. Griffiths, *License to Trade*, 133.

201. Hudson's Bay Company, *Charters, Statutes, Orders*, 192.

202. Trotter, "Coming of Confederation," 470.

203. Original document reprinted in Hudson's Bay Company, *Charters, Statutes, Orders*, 193–204.

204. Hudson's Bay Company, *Hudson's Bay Company: A Brief History* (London: Hudson's Bay House, 1934), 37.

205. Ibid., 38.

206. Ibid., 44–45.

207. I. Maurice Wormser, *Frankenstein Incorporated* (New York: McGraw-Hill, 1931), 26.

208. Hudson's Bay Company, *Hudson's Bay Company*, 45.

Chapter Five
Suppressing Unauthorized Nonstate Violence

1. Lydon, *Pirates, Privateers and Profits*, 28.

2. H. W. Malkin, "The Inner History of the Declaration of Paris," *British Yearbook of International Law* 8 (1927): 30.

3. Gosse, *History of Piracy*, 104.

4. Hall, *Treatise*, 312.

5. Williams, *Captains Outrageous*, 90 and 129; Ritchie, *Captain Kidd*, 21.

6. Some scholars argue that piracy is an "international crime" (Oppenheim, *International Law*, 609) or a crime against the human race (Hall, *Treatise*, 312) so that "the pirate is considered the enemy of every State and can be brought to justice anywhere" (Oppenheim, *International Law*, 609). A dictionary of international law has this to say about piracy: "Piracy has for centuries been a crime under customary law of nations, and a pirate has always been considered an outlaw and 'enemy of mankind' (*hostis humani generis*). Piracy is the first 'international crime,' which means that a piratical act is a crime directly under international law and any state may bring a pirate to justice." See Robert L. Bledsoe and Boleslaw A. Boczek, *The International Law Dictionary* (Santa Barbara, Calif.: ABC-Clio, 1987), 231. Those who deny that piracy is a crime under international law argue that the issue is how far state jurisdiction can be extended. The question is, What is the special basis of "state jurisdiction over offences committed by foreigners against foreign interests outside the territorial and other ordinary jurisdiction of the prosecuting state"? Harvard Law School Research in International

Law, "Draft Convention on Piracy," *American Journal of International Law* 26 (1932, special supplement): 760. Piracy is sui generis. It is "by the law of nations a special, common basis of jurisdiction beyond the familiar grounds of personal allegiance, territorial dominion, dominion over ships, and injuries to interests under the state's protection." Ibid., 757.

7. "According to it [the modern orthodox theory of the nature and scope of the law of nations], the law of nations is a law between states only, and limits their respective jurisdictions. Private individuals are not legal persons under the law of nations." Harvard, "Draft Convention," 754.

8. Some argue that states do have a duty to suppress piracy. Bledsoe and Boczek, for example, argue that cooperation in the repression of piracy is not just a right but a duty of all states. Bledsoe and Boczek, *Law Dictionary*, 231.

9. Harvard, "Draft Convention," 760. It is not a duty because this "would imply international liability if the duty were not fulfilled in a particular case." The fact that not all states define piracy as a criminal act in their municipal law represents a tacit refusal to acknowledge a duty to prosecute pirates. Ibid., 756.

10. Hall, *Treatise*, 189, 180–87.
11. Ibid., 300.
12. Gosse, *History of Piracy*, 58–59 and 63.
13. Wolf, *Barbary Coast*, 311, 313, and 316–17.
14. Gosse, *History of Piracy*, 58. Also see Earle, *Corsairs*, 15.
15. Gosse, *History of Piracy*, 58–59; Earle, *Corsairs*, 15 and 266.
16. Earle, *Corsairs*, 16.
17. Gosse, *History of Piracy*, 59–62.
18. This was justified on the grounds that the Congress had banned black slavery, but that the corsairs continued to take Christian slaves. See Earle, *Corsairs*, 267.
19. Wolf, *Barbary Coast*, 331.
20. Gosse, *History of Piracy*, 66–67. See also Earle, *Corsairs*, 267.
21. Williams, *Captains Outrageous*, 195.
22. Wolf, *Barbary Coast*, 320.
23. Gosse, *History of Piracy*, 69.
24. Wolf, *Barbary Coast*, 335.
25. Earle, *Corsairs*, 267.
26. Ibid., 101–4.
27. Ibid., 109, 119.
28. Ibid., 109–20, 268.
29. Ibid., 268–70.
30. This is the area between Bombay and Cochin, on the west coast of India.
31. Williams, *Captains Outrageous*, 190–93; Gosse, *History of Piracy*, 244–52.
32. Gosse, *History of Piracy*, 254–64. See also Charles Belgrave, *The Pirate Coast* (New York: Roy, 1966), 135. Belgrave and others have been charged with uncritically accepting the British characterization of the Joasmees as pirates when a strong case can be made that the East India Company legitimated its attacks on those who would resist its expansionary designs by labeling them pirates. See

Sultan Muhammad Al-Qasimi, *The Myth of Arab Piracy in the Gulf* (London: Croom Helm, 1986).

33. Williams, *Captains Outrageous*, 207–10; Gosse, *History of Piracy*, 271–77.

34. Gosse, *History of Piracy*, 285–86; Williams, *Captains Outrageous*, 219–20.

35. Williams, *Captains Outrageous*, 221–22.

36. Ibid., 222. See also Nicholas Tarling, *Piracy and Politics in the Malay World* (Melbourne: F. W. Cheshire, 1963), 128.

37. Williams, *Captains Outrageous*, 222–23.

38. Gosse, *History of Piracy*, 292.

39. This operation proved problematic for the commander for two reasons. First, he employed "hundreds of native boats," whose sailors were motivated by the prospect of plunder. Questioning whether this expedition was directed against only pirates or against peaceful traders as well, the British government formed a commission to investigate. The second problem was that according to an 1825 act of Parliament, the government was to pay twenty-five pounds for each captured or killed pirate. This Borneo expedition laid claim to a reward of nearly twenty-one thousand pounds. Parliament was outraged that this amount of money should be paid "to those who destroyed primitive tribes, armed with spears and swords," when "men who captured vessels in actions against a national enemy" received one-fourth that amount. This outrage led to the repeal of the act of 1825. Williams, *Captains Outrageous*, 224–25.

40. Ibid., 195–97.

41. Ibid., 199–202; Gosse, *History of Piracy*, 296–97.

42. Williams, *Captains Outrageous*, 206.

43. Ibid., 215, 218.

44. Ibid., 91.

45. Ibid., 117.

46. The term *filibuster* is derived from the Spanish *filibustero*, which referred to pirates, buccaneers, or freebooters "who pillaged the Spanish colonies in the West Indies during the 17th century." Later it was applied to "a member of any of those bands of adventurers who between 1850 and 1860 organized expeditions from the United States, in violation of international law, for the purpose of revolutionizing certain states in Central America and the Spanish West Indies." *Oxford English Dictionary*, 1978 ed. Though the term was not used until the 1850s, the first filibustering expeditions were launched in the first decade of the nineteenth century.

47. John A. Booth, *The End and the Beginning: The Nicaraguan Revolution* (Boulder, Colo.: Westview Press, 1982), 31–32.

48. Lobel, "Rise and Decline," 37–38.

49. Ibid., 27–37. See also Harold Hongju Koh, *The National Security Constitution: Sharing Power after the Iran-Contra Affair* (New Haven: Yale University Press, 1990).

50. Miranda wrote that "in the year 1784, in the city of New York, I formed a project for the liberty and independence of the entire Spanish-American Continent with the cooperation of England. That nation was naturally much interested

in the design, for Spain had furnished a precedent by forcing her to acknowledge the independence of her colonies in America." Joseph F. Thorning, *Miranda: World Citizen* (Gainesville: University of Florida Press, 1952), 33. Also see William Spence Robertson, *The Life of Miranda* (Chapel Hill: University of North Carolina Press, 1929), 1:43–44.

51. Robertson, *Life of Miranda* 1:43 and 53–55.

52. Robert J. Reinstein, "An Early View of Executive Powers and Privilege: The Trial of Smith and Ogden," *Hastings Constitutional Law Quarterly* 2 (Spring 1975): 310.

53. Thorning, *Miranda*, 101–2, 105–6, 136, and 170.

54. Ibid., 174. This interpretation of U.S. federal officials' attitude toward the Miranda expedition is disputed by Robertson, who argues that Miranda "stretched the truth when he asserted that the United States Government had given its 'tacit consent' to his revolutionary enterprise" (*Life of Miranda*, 296). In this he relies on Madison's account of the meetings, which, naturally, emphasizes Madison's commitment to defend international and domestic law. It is hardly likely, however, that the secretary would admit to any complicity in Miranda's project. That, of course, is the essence of plausible deniability. At any rate, Robertson is in the minority in making a strong case against U.S. officials' involvement in the expedition. Reinstein concludes that "all that is certain from this evidence is that Miranda did inform Jefferson and Madison of his general plans, and that they knew at least that he was going to buy war-related goods in this country" ("An Early View," 343). See also Charles H. Brown, *Agents of Manifest Destiny: The Lives and Times of the Filibusters* (Chapel Hill: University of North Carolina Press, 1980), 5; Samuel H. Wandell and Meade Minnigerode, *Aaron Burr*, 2 vols. (New York: G. P. Putnam's Sons, 1925), 2:61. See also Nathan Schachner, *Aaron Burr: A Biography* (New York: Frederick A. Stokes, 1937), who says that "Miranda's expedition, in spite of later official disavowals, had at least been openly winked at by the Administration" (352).

55. Thorning, *Miranda*, 177; Robertson, *Life of Miranda*, 300–301.

56. Thorning, *Miranda*, 179; Robertson, *Life of Miranda*, 297.

57. Reinstein, "An Early View," 312.

58. Thorning, *Miranda*, 180.

59. Robertson, *Life of Miranda*, 299. Smith was also John Adams's son-in-law. Reinstein, "An Early View," 311.

60. Thorning, *Miranda*, 180; Robertson, *Life of Miranda*, 299.

61. Robertson, *Life of Miranda*, 301.

62. Wandell and Minnigerode, *Aaron Burr*, 65–66.

63. Thorning, *Miranda*, 178–79.

64. Robertson, *Life of Miranda*, 301.

65. Reinstein, "An Early View," 339.

66. Thorning, *Miranda*, 179.

67. Robertson, *Life of Miranda*, 306–7. These survivors later petitioned the House of Representatives to obtain their release, arguing that Miranda had entrapped them by claiming he was acting under the authority of the federal government. Their petition was denied on the basis that since the prisoners had voluntarily expatriated themselves, they were not eligible for U.S. government assistance.

Miranda fled to Barbados, where he made an agreement with a British admiral which specified that Miranda would receive British naval protection and permission to recruit in the West Indies in exchange for his promise to grant the English economic privileges in South America. Miranda recruited another two hundred men and sailed back to Venezuela. Here the filibusters took a port town and raised the flag of "Free Venezuela." Instead of sparking the expected revolution, the event was witnessed by only "a handful of old people, the sick, who could not flee, and some little boys and girls." Again the Spanish drove Miranda out, though his flight this time was made under cover of the British navy. The British admiral did no more than escort Miranda to safety, since the Cabinet had instructed him "to limit his assistance to naval cooperation." Thorning, *Miranda*, 185–86; Robertson, *Life of Miranda*, 314–15. Britain was more interested in securing territory in the Spanish empire than in revolutionizing it and did not feel it could spare the naval forces necessary to the success of Miranda's scheme. See Robertson, *Life of Miranda*, 315.

68. Letter from Jefferson to Don Valentine de Foronda, 4 October 1809 cited in Brown, *Agents of Manifest Destiny*, 6; and Reinstein, "An Early View," 342.

69. Robert Granville Caldwell, *The López Expeditions to Cuba, 1848–1851* (Princeton: Princeton University Press, 1915), 45–46.

70. Chester Stanley Urban, "New Orleans and the Cuban Question During the López Expeditions of 1849–1851: A Local Study in 'Manifest Destiny,'" *Louisiana Historical Quarterly* 22 (1939): 1115.

71. Ibid., 1115–16.

72. Basil Rauch, *American Interest in Cuba, 1848–1855* (New York: Columbia University Press, 1948), 118.

73. Caldwell, *López Expeditions*, 55.

74. Urban, "Cuban Question," 1117–18.

75. Rauch, *American Interest in Cuba*, 120.

76. Ibid., 121, 125–26.

77. Urban, "Cuban Question," 1124–25.

78. Rauch, *American Interest in Cuba*, 128.

79. As to the number of deserters, Caldwell, *López Expeditions*, 65, says 39; Urban, "Cuban Question," 1126, says 100; Rauch, *American Interest in Cuba*, 128, says 50; and Brown, *Agents of Manifest Destiny*, 67, says 54.

80. Rauch, *American Interest in Cuba*, 128.

81. Urban, "Cuban Question," 1126.

82. Rauch, *American Interest in Cuba*, 129.

83. Brown, *Agents of Manifest Destiny*, 68–69.

84. Rauch, *American Interest in Cuba*, 135–36 and 141.

85. Caldwell, *López Expeditions*, 80–81.

86. Rauch, *American Interest in Cuba*, 134.

87. Brown, *Agents of Manifest Destiny*, 69.

88. Caldwell, *López Expeditions*, 81. Of course the issue of Cuba was of interest to other European powers, especially Britain. In an 8 June editorial, the London *Times* "voiced much European opinion which severely criticized the [U.S.] government: 'The civilized nations of the world are beginning to ask themselves

the meaning of this extraordinary state system which unites many provinces for defence of one, if attacked, but leaves that one perfectly free to attack any friendly power in defiance of the wishes of the other members of the corporate government. Had Spanish ships blockaded the port of New Orleans, Spain would have been at war with the United States collectively. An armament is fitted out at New Orleans to invade Spanish territory and the government which represents the United States is powerless to prevent its progress or departure.'" Ibid., 77. Fearing that the disagreement would lead to war with the United States, Spain had attempted to build a coalition of European states against the U.S. position. By October, however, it was clear that Britain was not willing to assure Spain of forthcoming aid, and the prisoners were released. See Rauch, *American Interest in Cuba*, 144–46. Spain made prize of the filibusters' two ships, but the United States did not press the matter. In 1858 "the Senate passed a resolution that characterized the action of Spain as 'in derogation of the sovereignty of the United States,' and there the matter rested." Ibid., 146–47.

89. Urban, "Cuban Question," 1135–37.

90. Brown, *Agents of Manifest Destiny*, 70.

91. Rauch, *American Interest in Cuba*, 151.

92. Brown, *Agents of Manifest Destiny*, 73–76.

93. Urban, "Cuban Question," 1146–47; Rauch, *American Interest in Cuba*, 159.

94. Brown, *Agents of Manifest Destiny*, 86–88.

95. Walter Flavius McCaleb, "A New Light on Aaron Burr," in idem, *"The Aaron Burr Conspiracy" and "A New Light on Aaron Burr,"* expanded ed. (New York: Argosy-Antiquarian, 1966), 12. See also Schachner, *Aaron Burr*, 282–83.

96. Brown, *Agents of Manifest Destiny*, 8.

97. Walter Flavius McCaleb, "Burr Conspiracy," in idem, *"The Aaron Burr Conspiracy" and "A New Light on Aaron Burr,"* expanded ed. (New York: Argosy-Antiquarian, 1966), 25–27; Wandell and Minnigerode, *Aaron Burr*, 33–34; Schachner, *Aaron Burr*, 285–86.

98. Brown, *Agents of Manifest Destiny*, 7; Wandell and Minnigerode, *Aaron Burr*, 38; McCaleb, "A New Light," 13; Schachner, *Aaron Burr*, 287.

99. Wandell and Minnigerode, *Aaron Burr*, 340.

100. Ibid., 55. See also McCaleb, "Burr Conspiracy," 56–57; and Brown, *Agents of Manifest Destiny*, 9.

101. Wandell and Minnigerode, *Aaron Burr*, 70.

102. Brown, *Agents of Manifest Destiny*, 11. Schachner contends that Burr pursued the colonization scheme only after Jefferson told him that there was to be no war with Spain. According to this plan, Burr "would settle a large community of young, militarily disposed adventurers on the tract, which was now in the newly carved Territory of Orleans, and close to the Spanish border. There he would establish himself as a landed gentleman, surrounded by friends and congenial associates, and bide his time. Sooner or later, he felt certain, the United States must clash with Spain. . . . At the first sign of hostilities, his settlers would march on the Spanish possessions. . . . The country would rise and hail him as a deliverer, and the original dream of Mexico and a government of his own would be fulfilled." *Aaron Burr*, 311 and 317.

103. "For over a year the newspapers had been bristling with accusations." The U.S. district attorney in Kentucky "had written him innumerable letters." Colonel George Morgan of Pittsburgh "had charged specific intention of treason." And "Judge Rufus Easton had written from St. Louis that Wilkinson was fomenting a conspiracy." At least two other people had relayed their suspicions to either the president or the secretary of state. Schachner, *Aaron Burr*, 352.

104. Wandell and Minnigerode, *Aaron Burr*, 59.

105. Brown, *Agents of Manifest Destiny*, 10. See also Schachner, *Aaron Burr*, 354.

106. Wandell and Minnigerode, *Aaron Burr*, 60.

107. Ibid., 103.

108. McCaleb, "A New Light," 21.

109. Brown, *Agents of Manifest Destiny*, 7.

110. See Schachner, *Aaron Burr*, 337–38, for a list of possible reasons. Wilkinson apparently saw the project unraveling and decided to make the best of a bad situation. By the spring of 1806 it was clear that British assistance would not be forthcoming, another American spy for Spain "knew too much" about the plan, and Burr's efforts to raise an expeditionary force had not met with brilliant success. Wandell and Minnigerode, *Aaron Burr*, 48, 77, 104.

111. In a postscript to his report, Wilkinson suggested that, in the event of war with Spain, Jefferson might consider turning this expedition to his advantage by "appeal[ing] to their patriotism to engage them in the service of their country." Presumably, had Jefferson accepted this suggestion, Wilkinson would have rejoined the conspiracy. General Wilkinson was certainly a man who knew how to keep all his options open.

112. Brown, *Agents of Manifest Destiny*, 11; Wandell and Minnigerode, *Aaron Burr*, 86–87.

113. Wandell and Minnigerode, *Aaron Burr*, 91.

114. Ibid., 91–92; McCaleb, "A New Light," 66–67.

115. McCaleb, "A New Light," 67.

116. Wandell and Minnigerode, *Aaron Burr*, 93–95.

117. Brown, *Agents of Manifest Destiny*, 11.

118. Ibid., 10. See also Wandell and Minnigerode, *Aaron Burr*, 114–15.

119. McCaleb, "A New Light," 72.

120. Wandell and Minnigerode, *Aaron Burr*, 115.

121. Wandell and Minnigerode argue that Jefferson seized the opportunity to act on "General Wilkinson's most unconvincing reports" for two reasons. First, he did not want to suffer the embarrassment of another Miranda Affair. Second, he did not want to provoke hostilities with Spain now, fearing what the French reaction might be. Ibid., 115–16. Other historians imply that Jefferson had wanted to move against Burr all along and that Wilkinson's reports were just what he needed. Brown, *Agents of Manifest Destiny*, 10; McCaleb, "A New Light," 72. Still another thesis is that Jefferson had not acted earlier because "deep down in his heart Jefferson had believed that Wilkinson was allied with Burr." It was only with Wilkinson's betrayal of Burr that Jefferson could be sure of the general's loyalty. Until then Jefferson feared that a move against Burr "might precipitate Wilkinson either into the arms of Spain, or, joined with Burr,

into a war of their own," possibly directed "against himself and the Government of the United States." Schachner, *Aaron Burr*, 354.

122. Wandell and Minnigerode, *Aaron Burr*, 129–33 and 146.

123. Ibid., 139–40.

124. Burr's decision to surrender was undoubtedly influenced by the proximity to his camp of several hundred Mississippi militiamen dispatched to intercept him. See Schachner, *Aaron Burr*, 374; Wandell and Minnigerode, *Aaron Burr*, 161.

125. Brown, *Agents of Manifest Destiny*, 12. In fact, the grand jury took this opportunity to blast General Wilkinson, President Jefferson and the governors of Mississippi and Louisiana. In their verdict, they declared, "The grand jurors present, as a grievance, the late military expedition, unnecessarily, as they conceive, fitted out against the person and property of the said Aaron Burr, when no resistance had been made to the civil authorities. The grand jurors also present, as a grievance, destructive of personal liberty the late military arrest [at New Orleans], made without warrant, and, as they conceive, without other lawful authority; and they do sincerely regret that so much cause has been given to the enemies of our glorious Constitution, to rejoice at such measures being adopted, in a neighboring Territory, as, if sanctioned by the Executive of our country, must sap the vitals of our political existence, and crumble this glorious fabric in the dust." See Schachner, *Aaron Burr*, 379–80.

126. Schachner, *Aaron Burr*, 380.

127. Ibid., 380; Wandell and Minnigerode, *Aaron Burr*, 165–66.

128. Wandell and Minnigerode, *Aaron Burr*, 177–78.

129. Schachner, *Aaron Burr*, 405.

130. Wandell and Minnigerode, *Aaron Burr*, 178.

131. Schachner, *Aaron Burr*, 423.

132. Ibid., 438–43.

133. McCaleb, "A New Light," 125–29. Mexico continued to be a filibustering target. In 1812, a former lieutenant in the U.S. Army named Magee organized in Tennessee an expedition to assist a Mexican revolutionary, Gutierrez. Defying a proclamation by the governor, their expedition invaded Texas, with Magee as colonel and Gutierrez as nominal commander-in-chief. Though there were charges that the federal government was involved, "there seems no basis for assuming . . . any complicity on the part of the government, which no doubt trusted to Governor [of Tennessee] Claiborne to enforce the law." The governor, however, later complained that "I have never understood how far the Executive Government of the U. States felt an Interest in the Revolutionary Movement in Texas." The filibusters enjoyed considerable success, so that by August of 1813, their army included about 850 Americans. Later that month, however, the army was ambushed and only ninety-three escaped, fleeing back to the United States. Among these was Toledo, who had replaced Gutierrez as leader of the revolutionary effort.

In November of 1813, a Frenchman in New Orleans attempted to organize a force of fifteen hundred filibusters to secure Texas's independence. This force was to be supplemented by three thousand Americans recruited by John Robinson. Robinson had recently been sent to Mexico by the State Department to assure

Spanish officials that the United States had no hostile intentions toward Mexico, despite the troubles in the Floridas. Upon his return, Robinson set out to form his own force to secure the independence of Mexico. His plan was to take Texas and, from there, to launch an invasion of Mexico. On 14 February "Monroe warned Robinson that his measures were contrary to law and were the more reprehensible inasmuch as his recent employment under the government might create the impression that his new designs had government support." Monroe promised to take decisive steps against him if he did not desist, and urged the governors of the Louisiana and Mississippi territories to block Robinson's expedition. Monroe believed that Robinson, the Frenchman, and Toledo were all involved in the plot.

In fact, Toledo feared the French project and distrusted Robinson. Robinson's "junta," he declared, "cared for nothing but plunder and had already apportioned among themselves the best offices in the government they intended to set up." Fearing that these two expeditions would combine, Toledo decided to form his own expedition. Nothing came of any of these plans except that the president issued a proclamation against them and Toledo and Robinson were indicted for neutrality law violations. This account is taken from Julius W Pratt, *Expansionists of 1812* (Gloucester, Mass.: Peter Smith, 1957), 249–59.

Yucatán declared its independence from Mexico in 1842. With the outbreak of war between the United States and Mexico, however, Mexican President Santa Anna made important concessions to the Yucatecans, who voted to rejoin the Mexican federation in 1846. Opponents of reunification then raised an army of Mayans in defense of their cause. By late 1847, however, it was clear to white Yucatecans that this large force of armed Indians, who had many grievances against their white rulers, was a much greater threat than the Mexicans.

To defend against the expected Indian revolt, the Yucatecans sent Justo Sierra O'Reilly to the United States to ask for military assistance. For nearly five months, Sierra waited for a decision from U.S. officials. In March of 1848 Sierra received word that the Indian revolt was underway and that foreign aid was vital. At the same time, the governor of Yucatán wrote identical letters to the United States, Spain, and Britain offering sovereignty over Yucatán in exchange for their aid. Sierra transmitted the letter to the State Department, but the president turned the question of occupying Yucatán over to Congress for resolution. The Senate Foreign Relations Committee approved the idea, but election-year politics immediately entered into the floor debate on the bill.

In May, Sierra, afraid that the bill might not pass, concocted a colonization scheme. For some time he had been receiving inquiries from individuals interested in going to Yucatán.

> Though the plan bore no immediate fruit, it was adopted later. Some time after Sierra's return to Yucatán [in June], Barbachano [president of Yucatán] sent agents to the United States to form a volunteer regiment. Inducements included a wage of eight dollars a month, a new suit of clothes every three months, and the gift of 320 acres of land to each soldier! In October, eighty North Americans were already in Yucatán, while another 150 were on their way there. The total reached some 250 men, but in March of 1849, this

small army of mercenaries returned to the United States when the Yucatán government proved able to pay them only ten dollars each for several months' fighting.

Nevertheless, Sierra's plan "may have been among the first manifestations of the spirit that was to lead to the Central American filibusters of the next decade." His colonization scheme resulted from his belief that the salvation of Yucatán depended on an influx of permanent white settlers.

Sierra did not put the plan into action because on 16 May he learned that his government and the Indians had signed a treaty. With this news, the Senate bill died. Within days, however, Sierra received word that the Indians had broken the treaty and was given instructions to renew his quest for U.S. aid. By this time, there was no hope that the United States would agree, and Sierra's efforts failed completely.

In September of 1849 the Yucatán government heard that Colonel White, the leader of the recently departed U.S. mercenaries, was organizing an expedition to go to Yucatán to obtain his regiment's pay and recover the costs of collecting it. Secretary of State Clayton assured the Yucatecans that the U.S. government would "frustrate" the expedition by enforcing its neutrality laws. This account was taken from Louis De Armond, "Justo Sierra O'Reilly and Yucatecan-United States Relations, 1847–1848," *Hispanic American Historical Review* 31 (August 1951): 420–36. As it turned out, the Yucatecans need not have worried, since the White who was organizing the expedition was a different Colonel White and his target was not the Yucatán but Cuba. This White later joined Narciso López's abortive filibuster expedition of 1849. On White, see also Brown, *Agents of Manifest Destiny*, 37–38, 48, and 50.

134. The following account is taken from Brown, *Agents of Manifest Destiny*, 194–455.

135. This 1850 treaty provided for joint U.S.-British operation of a canal across the Central American isthmus. It was replaced by the Hay-Pauncefote Treaty of 1901, which gave the United States exclusive right to the canal.

136. Helen Broughall Metcalf, "The California French Filibusters in Sonora," *California Historical Society Quarterly* 18 (March 1939): 4. French prospects in California were dealt three serious blows in 1850, with two major fires in their San Francisco communities (ibid., 4–5; Rufus Kay Wyllys, "The French of California and Sonora," *Pacific Historical Review* 1 [1932]: 343) and the passage of the Foreign Miners' Tax Law of 1850, which required foreigners to obtain prohibitively expensive licenses before they could engage in mining. Moreover, the French suffered discrimination on the grounds that their political sympathies lay more with Spanish Americans than with Anglo-Saxon and Irish Americans. Ibid., 340–42.

137. Wyllys, "French of California," 346.

138. Ibid., 345–49.

139. Metcalf, "California French," 6.

140. Some historians believe that the Frenchman, who died under mysterious circumstances, was killed by the Mexicans, who feared he would make war on them.

141. Wyllys, "French of California," 350–52.

142. Metcalf, "California French," 6.

143. Ibid., 7; Wyllys, "French of California," 352.

144. Wyllys, "French of California," 354.

145. The governor may also have been acting at the behest of a rival mining company in which he had an interest.

146. Wyllys, "French of California," 355.

147. Metcalf, "California French," 14–15.

148. Wyllys, "French of California," 355–56.

149. Metcalf, "California French," 16; Rufus Kay Wyllys, *The French in Sonora, 1850–1854: The Story of French Adventurers from California into Mexico*, vol. 21 of *University of California Publications in History*, ed. Herbert E. Bolton, William A. Morris, and Paul B. Schaeffer (Berkeley and Los Angeles: University of California Press, 1932), 160.

150. Wyllys, *French in Sonora*, 170.

151. Metcalf, "California French," 16–17. He was tried and convicted but his sentence was suspended. Shortly thereafter he was recalled by his government. Wyllys, *French in Sonora*, 179.

152. Wyllys, *French in Sonora*, 177.

153. Metcalf, "California French," 16. What was the role of the French government in these expeditions? Though Raousset actually spoke of taking the Sonora for France, historians do not believe that France was involved. Raousset probably did have an agent in Paris who lobbied for his projects, but it is unlikely that the latter met with any success. French scholars also doubt the existence of any connection between the filibusters and the French government.

154. Wyllys, "French of California," 358.

155. Wyllys, *French in Sonora*, 172, 181–82, 225, and 228.

156. The following account is taken from Pratt, *Expansionists*, 73–116, 194–98, 229–34, and 245–46.

157. Ibid., 83–84, 86.

158. Ibid., 97.

159. While Laval was justified in denying that his troops were involved, the naval commander, since his gunboats were on the scene, had to fashion a more creative denial. He replied that his forces were "not intended to act in the name of the United States," but simply to support the Spanish subjects who had decided to declare their independence (ibid.).

160. Ibid., 99.

161. Ibid., 101.

162. In his accompanying letter, Mathews indicated that because Laval had refused to supply him with troops, the amount of land to be given as bounties was much larger than expected. "Large bounties were given to adventurers that came to the support of the people—but still there will remain a large and valuable country at the disposal of the United States" (ibid., 107).

163. Ibid., 112. In a private correspondence, Monroe suggested that Mathews had violated the neutrality law. This was perhaps an implied threat to Mathews to keep quiet.

164. Ibid., 194.

165. Ibid., 246.

166. Except where noted, the following account is taken from Louis B. Wright and Julia H. Macleod, *The First Americans in North Africa: William Eaton's Struggle for a Vigorous Policy against the Barbary Pirates, 1799–1805* (Princeton: Princeton University Press, 1945). There are a number of accounts of Eaton's activities, including Samuel Edwards, *Barbary General: The Life of William H. Eaton* (Englewood Cliffs, N.J.: Prentice-Hall, 1968); Meade Minnigerode, *Lives and Times: Four Informal American Biographies* (New York: G. P. Putnam's Sons, 1925); and E. Alexander Powell, *Gentlemen Rovers* (New York: Charles Scribner's Sons, 1913). Since these differ in their interpretations of key events and actions, I have relied most heavily on Wright and Macleod because they are historians whose work is based on primary source materials, was published by an academic press, and is much less celebratory of Eaton than some of the other biographers.

167. Wright and Macleod, *First Americans*, 86.

168. Edwards argues that "it is unlikely that the President or anyone else guessed that William intended to recruit a corps of his own and march across the desert with it. . . . Jefferson personally initialed the memorandum authorizing the State Department to advance to William the sum of forty thousand dollars 'for use in restoring peaceful relations between the United States and Tripoli.' . . . It must be assumed that James Madison, who secured the funds from the Treasury Department and gave them to William, also had a fairly good idea the money would be spent to remove Yusuf from his throne. Madison was also the agent for obtaining one thousand rifles from the War Department and handing them over to William." Edwards, *Barbary General*, 33–34.

169. Edwards claims that Eaton was "the only man in the history of his country ever to hold such a title." Ibid., 134.

170. According to Edwards, after a lengthy cabinet debate, the president decided to neither accept nor reject Eaton's proposal. Rather, he apparently took the attitude that "if he [Eaton] succeeded the United States would reap the benefits of his plan. If it failed, however, the Government could claim that his idea had never won the approval of his superiors." Ibid., 113.

171. These were assigned to him by the navy, which knew it would be held responsible for Eaton's safety.

172. The army included "a company of thirty-eight Greeks, . . . about four hundred [Arabs] . . . a few British subjects, two or three Germans, Italians, Spaniards, and various kinds of [Christian] Levantines." Ten Americans were also involved: Eaton, a U.S. Navy midshipman, and eight marines, including a lieutenant and a sergeant. Wright and Macleod, *First Americans*, 158.

173. The money would come from "tribute exacted of the Swedes, Danes, and Dutch." Eaton estimated these costs at $20,000. Ibid., 156.

174. Ibid., 193. Eaton spent about $30,000 on the campaign. Of this $11,000 was provided by the navy, $17,000 was in the form of private loans and $2,000 was Eaton's own money. Ibid., 177. It is not clear whether the private loans were repaid out of Eaton's congressional allocation or out of a separate allocation, or simply were not repaid at all.

175. Ibid., 184.

176. Eaton's expedition against the Barbary state of Tripoli is an apparent exception. However, as we saw in chapter 3, what made the Barbary states exceptional was not that they lay beyond the European state system, but that the basis upon which they exercised sovereignty was problematic.

177. James Jeffrey Roche, *The Story of the Filibusters* (New York: Macmillan, 1891), 2–3.

178. Yet the expansionist tendency did not die among central state leaders. Secretary of State Seward, in 1868, predicted that "in thirty years the city of Mexico will be the capital of the United States." His purchase of Alaska was known as Seward's Folly, however. His desire to annex Hawaii, Santo Domingo, and the Danish West Indies through diplomacy were all opposed by the Congress. And his efforts to purchase Cuba, Puerto Rico, Greenland, and Iceland came to naught. During the Grant administration there was a renewed interest in "opportunities for action, glory, profit, escape from humdrum problems of peace" on the part of the president, the cabinet, and Congress. But Secretary of State Fish "opposed any adventurism and reined in Grant when he tended to get out of hand after listening to advisers urging this or that expansionist project." Brown, *Agents of Manifest Destiny*, 462–63.

179. Ibid., 462.

Chapter Six
Conclusion

1. Tilly, *Formation of National States*, 635, emphasis mine.

2. For a discussion of the taken-for-granted nature of institutions, see Ronald L. Jepperson, "Institutions, Institutional Effects, and Institutionalism," in *The New Institutionalism in Organizational Analysis*, ed. Walter W. Powell and Paul J. DiMaggio (Chicago: University of Chicago Press, 1991).

3. Giddens, 2:326.

4. As Giddens expresses it, "In many cases the mass of the population of traditional states did not know themselves to be 'citizens' of those states, nor did it matter particularly to the continuity of power within them. But the more the administrative scope of the state begins to penetrate the day-to-day activities of its subjects, the less this theorem holds. The expansion of state sovereignty means that those subject to it are in some sense—initially vague, but growing more and more definite and precise—aware of their membership in a political community and of the rights and obligations such membership confers." Ibid., 210.

5. For an elaboration of this argument, see Ashley, "Living on Border Lines."

6. See Peter Gourevitch, "The Second Image Reversed: The International Sources of Domestic Politics," *International Organization* 32 (Autumn 1978): 881–912. For exemplary empirical analyses along these lines see idem, *Politics in Hard Times: Comparative Responses to International Economic Crises* (Ithaca: Cornell University Press, 1986); Peter J. Katzenstein, ed., *Between Power and Plenty: Foreign Economic Policies of Advanced Industrial States* (Madison: University of Wisconsin Press, 1978; idem, *Small States in World Markets: Industrial Policy in Europe* (Ithaca: Cornell University Press, 1985).

7. See my "Sovereignty and the Institutional Isomorphism of States," for a preliminary outline of this type of research in the issue area of international trade.

My basic argument there is that international trade institutions, such as the GATT, bring economic issues to the realm of "high politics," thereby empowering states to make and impose rules on their societies. Thus, the expansion of world trade reflects not the eroding of the sovereignty of states, which continue to make the rules, but the decline of popular political control over economic rule making.

8. Theda Skocpol, *States and Social Revolutions: A Comparative Analysis of France, Russia, and China* (New York: Cambridge University Press, 1979), 29. See also Stephen D. Krasner, "Approaches to the State: Alternative Conceptions and Historical Dynamics," *Comparative Politics* 16 (January 1984): 223–46.

9. Especially to be avoided are empirically suspect statements such as: "A state is first of all an organization that provides public goods for its members, the citizens." Norman Frohlich and Joe A. Oppenheimer, "I Get By with a Little Help from My Friends," *World Politics* 23 (October 1970): 104. The conventional view of the state in international relations theory is, in my view, far too benevolent. Halliday, "State and Society," 226. This is because, I think, U.S. theorists at least implicitly accept the social-contractarian view of the state.

10. This perspective can accommodate such major changes as the transition from the laissez-faire liberal state to the embedded liberal state while allowing that both types of state are sovereign. On this transition see Ruggie, "International Regimes, Transactions, and Change."

11. For other instances of this see Thomson, "Explaining the Regulation of Transnational Practices."

12. This view of norms is consistent with that of Foucault, who argues that "with this new economy of power, the carceral system, which is its basic instrument, permitted the emergence of a new form of 'law'; a mixture of legality and nature, prescription and constitution, the norm." Michel Foucault, *Discipline and Punish: The Birth of the Prison*, trans. Alan Sheridan (New York: Vintage Books, 1977), 304. See also Francesca M. Cancian, *What Are Norms? A Study of Beliefs and Action in a Maya Community* (New York: Cambridge University Press, 1975), chaps. 1, 2 , and 9. For a review of different conceptions of norms, see my "Norms in International Relations: A Conceptual Analysis," *International Journal of Group Tensions* 23 [Spring 1993]: 67–83).

13. Actually there is a third question to which the book speaks, at best, only indirectly: What is the relationship between the organization of violence and the development of a global capitalist economy? Though this book establishes no causal links between them, it does suggest that nonstate violence was consistent with a political economy of plunder and mercantilism but not with capitalist commerce. See Frederic Chapin Lane, "Economic Consequences of Organized Violence," in *Venice and History: The Collected Papers of Frederic C. Lane*, ed. a Committee of Colleagues and Former Students (Baltimore: Johns Hopkins University Press, 1966), 412–28.

14. Walker, "Genealogy, Geopolitics and Political Community," 84.

Bibliography

Aird, David M. *The Civil Laws of France to the Present Time*. London: Long-mans, Green, 1875.

Al-Qasimi, Sultan Muhammad. *The Myth of Arab Piracy in the Gulf*. London: Croom Helm, 1986.

Anderson, Gary, and Robert D. Tollison. "Apologiae for Chartered Monopolies in Foreign Trade, 1600–1800." *History of Political Economy* 15 (1983): 549–66.

Anderson, Scott, and Jon Lee Anderson. *Inside the League: The Shocking Expose of How Terrorists, Nazis, and Latin American Death Squads Have Infiltrated the World Anti-Communist League*. New York: Dodd, Mead and Co., 1986.

Andrews, Bruce. "The Domestic Content of International Desire." *International Organization* 38 (Spring 1984): 321–27.

Andrews, Kenneth R. *Elizabethan Privateering: English Privateering during the Spanish War, 1585–1603*. Cambridge: Cambridge University Press, 1964.

Asher, Eugene L. *The Resistance to the Maritime Classes: The Survival of Feudalism in the France of Colbert*. Vol. 66 of *University of California Publications in History*, ed. Theodore Saloutos, T. S. Brown, G. E. Von Grunebaum, and Andrew Lossky. Berkeley and Los Angeles: University of California Press, 1960.

Ashley, Richard K. "The Poverty of Neorealism." *International Organization* 38 (Spring 1984): 225–86.

———. "Effecting Global Purpose: Notes on a Problematic of International Organization." Paper presented at the annual meeting of the American Political Science Association, Chicago, Ill., 3–6 September 1987.

———. "Social Will and International Anarchy." Photocopy. Arizona State University, 1987.

———. "The Powers of Anarchy: Theory, Sovereignty, and the Domestication of Global Life." Photocopy. Arizona State University, 1988.

———. "Living on Border Lines: Man, Poststructuralism and War." In *International/Intertextual Relations: The Boundaries of Knowledge and Practice in World Politics*, edited by James Der Derian and Michael J. Shapiro. Lexington, Mass.: Lexington Books, 1989.

———. "Statecraft as Mancraft: Knowledge, Power, and Resistance in Modern World Politics." Paper presented at the annual meeting of the American Political Science Association, Atlanta, Ga., 31 August–3 September 1989.

Ashley, Richard K., and R. B. J. Walker. "Speaking the Language of Exile: Dissidence in International Studies." *International Studies Quarterly* 34 (September 1990, special issue): 259–68 and 367–416.

Axelrod, Robert. "The Emergence of Cooperation among Egoists." *American Political Science Review* 75 (June 1981): 306–81.

Bagawan, Bandar Seri. "Brunei: Floating Free." *Economist* 24 (December 1983): 40.

Bamford, Paul W. *Fighting Ships and Prisons: The Mediterranean Galleys of France in the Age of Louis XIV.* Minneapolis: University of Minnesota Press, 1973.

Banks, Arthur S. *Cross-National Time-Series Data Archive User's Manual.* Binghamton: State University of New York, 1975.

Barnett, Correlli. *Britain and Her Army, 1509–1970: A Military, Political and Social Survey.* New York: William Morrow, 1970.

Barnett, Michael N. "Sovereignty, Institutions, and Identity: From Pan-Arabism to the Arab State System." Paper presented at the annual meeting of the American Political Science Association, Washington, D.C., 29 August–1 September, 1991.

Bates, Robert. "Problems with Case Studies." Presentation to National Science Foundation-funded Conference on Democracy, Markets, and Choice, University of Washington, 20–23 September 1991.

Bayley, C. C. *Mercenaries for the Crimea: The German, Swiss, and Italian Legions in British Service, 1854–1856.* Montreal: McGill-Queen's University Press, 1977.

Beach, Edward L. *The United States Navy: 200 Years.* New York: Holt, 1986.

Behrman, Cynthia F. *Victorian Myths of the Sea.* Athens: Ohio University Press, 1977.

Belgrave, Charles. *The Pirate Coast.* New York: Roy, 1966.

Bledsoe, Robert L., and Boleslaw A. Boczek. *The International Law Dictionary.* Santa Barbara, Calif.: ABC-Clio, 1987.

Booth, John A. *The End and the Beginning: The Nicaraguan Revolution.* Boulder, Colo.: Westview Press, 1982.

Bowles, Thomas Gibson. *The Declaration of Paris of 1856.* London: Sampson Low, Marston, 1900.

Boxer, C. R. *The Dutch Seaborne Empire, 1600–1800.* Vol. 2 of *The History of Human Society,* edited by J. H. Plumb. New York: Knopf, 1965.

Braudel, Fernand. *Civilization and Capitalism, Fifteenth–Eighteenth Century.* Vol. 3, *The Perspective of the World,* translated by Siân Reynolds. New York: Harper and Row, 1984.

Brown, Charles H. *Agents of Manifest Destiny: The Lives and Times of the Filibusters.* Chapel Hill: University of North Carolina Press, 1980.

Brown, D. E. "Brunei on the Morrow of Independence." *Asian Survey* 24 (February 1984): 201–8.

Burchett, Wilfred, and Derek Roebuck. *The Whores of War: Mercenaries Today.* New York: Penguin Books, 1977.

Burmester, H. C. "The Recruitment and Use of Mercenaries in Armed Conflicts." *American Journal of International Law* 72 (January 1978): 37–56.

Burns, Robert I. *Muslims, Christians and Jews in the Crusader Kingdom of Valencia: Societies in Symbiosis.* Cambridge: Cambridge University Press, 1984.

Caldwell, Robert Granville. *The López Expeditions to Cuba, 1848–1851.* Princeton: Princeton University Press, 1915.

Cancian, Francesca. *What Are Norms? A Study of Beliefs and Action in a Maya Community.* New York: Cambridge University Press, 1975.

Caporaso, James A. "International Relations Theory and Multilateralism: The

Search for Foundations" *International Organization* 46 (Summer 1992): 599–632.

Carr, Edward Hallett. *The Twenty Years' Crisis, 1919–1939: An Introduction to the Study of International Relations*. 2d ed. New York: Harper and Row, 1939.

Cawston, George, and A. H. Keane. *The Early Chartered Companies, A.D. 1296–1858*. New York: Edward Arnold, 1896.

Cesner, Robert E., Jr., and John W. Brant. "Law of the Mercenary: An International Dilemma." *Capital University Law Review* 6 (1977): 339–70.

Chaudhuri, K. N. "The East India Company and the Export of Treasure in the Early Seventeenth Century." *Economic History Review*, 2d ser. 16 (1963): 23–38.

———. *The English East India Company: A Study of an Early Joint-Stock Company, 1600–1640*. New York: Augustus M. Kelley, 1965.

Childs, John. *Armies and Warfare in Europe, 1648–1789*. Manchester: Manchester University Press, 1982.

Clarke, S. J. G. *The Congo Mercenary*. Johannesburg: South African Institute of International Affairs at the University of the Witwatersrand, 1968.

Clowes, William Laird. *The Royal Navy: A History from the Earliest Times to the Present*. Vol. 3. Boston: Little, Brown, 1898.

Cooper, Richard N. "Economic Interdependence and Foreign Policy in the Seventies." *World Politics* 24 (January 1972): 159–81.

Coornaert, E. L. J. "European Economic Institutions and the New World: The Chartered Companies." In *The Economy of Expanding Europe in the Sixteenth and Seventeenth Centuries*, edited by E. E. Rich and C. H. Wilson. Vol. 4 of *The Cambridge Economic History of Europe*. Cambridge: Cambridge University Press, 1967.

Corbett, Julian S. *England in the Seven Years' War*. Vol. 2. London: Longmans, Green, 1907.

Corvisier, André. *Armies and Societies in Europe, 1494–1789*. Translated by Abigail T. Siddall. Bloomington: Indiana University Press, 1979.

Cottrell, Alvin J., and Frank Bray. *Military Forces in the Persian Gulf*. Center for Strategic and International Studies. The Washington Papers, vol. 6, no. 60. Beverly Hills, Calif.: Sage, 1978.

Cox, Isaac Joslin. "Monroe and the Early Mexican Revolutionary Agents." *Annual Report of the American Historical Association for the Year 1911* 1 (1913): 199–215.

Cox, Robert W. "Social Forces, States and World Orders: Beyond International Relations Theory." In *Neorealism and Its Critics*, edited by Robert O. Keohane. New York: Columbia University Press, 1986.

———. "Multilateralism and World Order." *Review of International Studies* 18 (April 1992): 161–80.

Crowhurst, Patrick. *The Defence of British Trade, 1689–1815*. Folkestone, Kent: Dawson, 1977.

Davis, John P. *Corporations: A Study of the Origin and Development of Great Business Combinations and Their Relation to the Authority of the State*. New York: Capricorn, 1961.

Deàk, Francis, and Philip C. Jessup, eds. *A Collection of Neutrality Laws, Regu-*

lations and Treaties of Various Countries. 2 vols. Washington, D.C.: Carnegie Endowment for International Peace, 1939.

De Armond, Louis. "Justo Sierra O'Reilly and Yucatecan–United States Relations, 1847–1848." *Hispanic American Historical Review* 31 (August 1951): 420–36.

de Maleville, Jacques. *Analyse Raisonneé de la Discussion du Code Civil au Conseil d'Etat.* 3d ed. 4 vols. Paris: N'eve, 1822.

Der Derian, James, and Michael J. Shapiro, eds. *International/ Intertextual Relations: Boundaries of Knowledge and Practice in World Politics.* Lexington, Mass.: Lexington Books, 1989.

De St. Jorre, John. *The Nigerian Civil War.* London: Hodder and Stoughton, 1972.

Disney, A. R. "The First Portuguese India Company, 1628–33." *Economic History Review*, 2d ser. 30 (May 1977): 242–58.

Dobb, Maurice. *Studies in the Development of Capitalism.* New York: International Publishers, 1947.

Dodwell, H. H. "The Development of Sovereignty in British India." In *British India, 1497–1858*, edited by idem. Vol. 5 of *The Cambridge History of India.* Cambridge: Cambridge University Press, 1929.

————. "The Seven Years War." In *British India, 1497–1858*, edited by idem. Vol. 5 of *The Cambridge History of India.* Cambridge: Cambridge University Press, 1929.

————. "The War of Austrian Succession." In *British India, 1497–1858*, edited by idem. Vol. 5 of *The Cambridge History of India.* Cambridge: Cambridge University Press, 1929.

Duffy, Christopher. *Russia's Military Way to the West: Origins and Nature of Russian Military Power, 1700–1800.* Boston: Routledge and Kegan Paul, 1981.

Earle, Peter. *Corsairs of Malta and Barbary.* London: Sidgwick and Jackson, 1970.

Edwards, Samuel. *Barbary General: The Life of William H. Eaton.* Englewood Cliffs, N.J.: Prentice-Hall, 1968.

Elias, Norbert. *The Civilizing Process.* Vol. 2, *Power and Civility.* Translated by Edmund Jephcott. New York: Pantheon, 1982.

Evans, Peter B., Dietrich Rueschemeyer, and Theda Skocpol, eds. *Bringing the State Back In.* New York: Cambridge University Press, 1985.

Farwell, Byron. *The Gurkhas.* New York: W. W. Norton, 1984.

Fenwick, Charles G. *The Neutrality Laws of the United States.* Washington, D.C.: Carnegie Endowment for International Peace, 1913.

Foster, William. "The East India Company, 1600–1740." In *British India, 1497–1858*, edited by H. H. Dodwell. Vol. 5 of *The Cambridge History of India.* Cambridge: Cambridge University Press, 1929.

Foucault, Michel. *Discipline and Punish: The Birth of the Prison.* Translated by Alan Sheridan. New York: Vintage Books, 1977.

Frohlich, Norman, and Joe A. Oppenheimer. "I Get By with a Little Help from My Friends." *World Politics* 23 (October 1970): 104–20.

Furber, Holden. *Rival Empires of Trade in the Orient, 1600–1800.* Vol. 2 of

Europe and the World in the Age of Expansion, edited by Boyd C. Shafer. Minneapolis: University of Minnesota Press, 1976.

Garcia-Mora, M. *International Responsibility for Hostile Acts of Private Persons against Foreign States*. The Hague: Martinus Nijhoff, 1962.

Geyl, P. "The Dutch in India." In *British India, 1497–1858*, edited by H. H. Dodwell. Vol. 5 of *The Cambridge History of India*. Cambridge: Cambridge University Press, 1929.

Giddens, Anthony. *A Contemporary Critique of Historical Materialism*. Vol. 2, *The Nation-State and Violence*. Berkeley and Los Angeles: University of California Press, 1985.

Gilpin, Robert G. *U.S. Power and the Multinational Corporation: The Political Economy of Foreign Direct Investment*. New York: Basic Books, 1975.

————. "The Richness of the Tradition of Political Realism." *International Organization* 38 (Sring 1984): 287–304.

————. *The Political Economy of International Relations*. Princeton: Princeton University Press, 1987.

Gooch, John. *Armies in Europe*. London: Routledge and Kegan Paul, 1980.

Gosse, Philip. *The History of Piracy*. New York: Tudor, 1946.

Gourevitch, Peter. "The Second Image Reversed: The International Sources of Domestic Politics." *International Organization* 32 (Autumn 1978): 881–912.

————. *Politics in Hard Times: Comparative Responses to International Economic Crises*. Ithaca: Cornell University Press, 1986.

Gradish, Stephen F. *The Manning of the British Navy during the Seven Years' War*. Vol. 21 of *Royal Historical Society Studies in History*. London: Royal Historical Society, 1980.

Griffiths, Percival. *A License to Trade: The History of English Chartered Companies*. London: Ernest Benn, 1974.

Guillet, Edwin C. *The Lives and Times of the Patriots: An Account of the Rebellion in Upper Canada, 1837–1838, and of the Patriot Agitation in the United States, 1837–1842*. Toronto: University of Toronto Press, 1968.

Hall, William Edward. *The Rights and Duties of Neutrals*. London: Longmans, Green, 1874.

————. *A Treatise on International Law*. 8th ed. Edited by A. Pearce Higgins. Oxford: Clarendon Press, 1924.

Halliday, Fred. "State and Society in International Relations: A Second Agenda." *Millennium* 16 (Summer 1987): 215–29.

Harvard Law School Research in International Law. "Draft Convention on Piracy." *American Journal of International Law* 26 (1932, special supplement): 739–1013.

Heckscher, Eli F. *Mercantilism*. Translated by Mendel Shapiro. 2 vols. London: George Allen and Unwin, 1935.

Hertslet, Edward. *The Map of Europe by Treaty*. Vol. 2. London: Butterworths, 1875.

Hinsley, F. H. *Sovereignty*. New York: Basic Books, 1966.

Hiro, Dilip. *Inside the Middle East*. London: Routledge and Kegan Paul, 1982.

Hirshmann, Albert O. *The Passions and the Interests: Political Arguments for Capitalism before Its Triumph*. Princeton: Princeton University Press, 1977.

Hobsbawm, E. J. *Nations and Nationalism since 1780: Programme, Myth, Reality*. New York: Cambridge University Press, 1990.

Howard, Michael. *War in European History*. New York: Oxford University Press, 1976.

Hudson's Bay Company. *Hudson's Bay Company: A Brief History*. London: Hudson's Bay House, 1934.

―――. *Charters, Statutes, Orders in Council, etc. Relating to the Hudson's Bay Company*. London: Hudson's Bay Company, 1963.

Hynemann, Charles S. *The First American Neutrality: A Study of the American Understanding of Neutral Obligations during the Years 1792 to 1815*. Illinois Studies in the Social Sciences, vol. 20, nos. 1–2. Urbana: University of Illinois, 1934.

Ingrao, Charles W. *The Hessian Mercenary State: Ideas, Institutions, and Reform under Frederick II, 1760–1785*. New York: Cambridge University Press, 1987.

International Institute for Strategic Studies. *The Military Balance, 1986–1987*. London: International Institute for Strategic Studies, 1986.

Israel, Jonathan. *The Dutch Republic and the Hispanic World, 1606–1661*. New York: Oxford University Press, 1982.

Jackson, Robert H., and Carl G. Rosberg. "Why Africa's Weak States Persist: The Empirical and the Juridical in Statehood." *World Politics* 35 (October 1982): 1–24.

Jepperson, Ronald L. "Institutions, Institutional Effects, and Institutionalism." In *The New Institutionalism in Organizational Analysis*, edited by Walter W. Powell and Paul J. DiMaggio. Chicago: University of Chicago Press, 1991.

Jessup, Philip C., and Francis Deàk. *The Origins*. Vol. 1 of Columbia University Council for Research in the Social Sciences, *Neutrality: Its History, Economics and Law*. 4 vols. New York: Columbia University Press, 1935.

Karsten, Peter D. *The Naval Aristocracy*. Riverside, N.J.: Free Press, 1971.

Katzenstein, Peter J., ed. *Between Power and Plenty: Foreign Economic Policies of Advanced Industrial States*. Madison: University of Wisconsin Press, 1978.

―――. *Small States in World Markets: Industrial Policy in Europe*. Ithaca: Cornell University Press, 1985.

Keegan, John. *World Armies*. New York: Facts on File, 1979.

―――. *World Armies*. 2d ed. London: Macmillan, 1983.

Kemp, P. K., and Christopher Lloyd. *Brethren of the Coast: Buccaneers of the South Seas*. New York: St. Martin's, 1960.

Keohane, Robert O. *After Hegemony: Cooperation and Discord in the World Political Economy*. Princeton: Princeton University Press, 1984.

―――. "International Institutions: Two Approaches." *International Studies Quarterly* 32 (December 1988): 379–96.

―――. "Multilateralism: An Agenda for Research." *International Journal* 45 (Autumn 1990): 731–64.

Keohane, Robert O., and Joseph S. Nye. *Power and Interdependence*. Boston: Little, Brown, 1977.

Keohane, Robert O., and Joseph S. Nye, eds. *Transnational Relations and World Politics*. Cambridge: Harvard University Press, 1972.

Khalid, Devlet. "Pakistan's Relations with Iran and the Arab States." *Journal of South Asian and Middle Eastern Studies* 5 (Spring 1982): 16–22.

Kiernan, V. G. "Foreign Mercenaries and Absolute Monarchy." In *Crisis in Europe, 1560–1660*, edited by Trevor Aston. New York: Basic Books, 1965.

Knightley, Phillip. "Unlucky in Love, Lucky in War." Review of *The French Foreign Legion*, by Douglas Porch. *New York Times Book Review*, 14 July 1991, 7.

Koh, Harold Hongju. *The National Security Constitution: Sharing Power after the Iran-Contra Affair*. New Haven: Yale University Press, 1990.

Krasner, Stephen D. *Defending the National Interest: Raw Materials Investments and U.S. Foreign Policy*. Princeton: Princeton University Press, 1978.

———. "Approaches to the State: Alternative Conceptions and Historical Dynamics." *Comparative Politics* 16 (January 1984): 223–46.

———. *Structural Conflict: The Third World against Global Liberalism*. Berkeley and Los Angeles: University of California Press, 1985.

———. "Sovereignty: An Institutional Perspective." In *The Elusive State: International and Comparative Perspectives*, edited by James A. Caporaso. Newbury Park, Calif.: Sage, 1989.

———, ed. *International Regimes*. Ithaca: Cornell University Press, 1983.

Kratochwil, Friedrich. "Errors Have Their Advantage." *International Organization* 38 (Spring 1984): 305–20.

Kratochwil, Friedrich, and John Gerard Ruggie. "International Organization: A State of the Art on an Art of the State." *International Organization* 40 (Autumn 1986): 753–75.

Kronenberger, Louis. "People on Spits and Other Niceties." *Atlantic Monthly*, September 1969, 106–9.

Kuhn, Thomas. *The Structure of Scientific Revolutions*. Chicago: University of Chicago Press, 1970.

Lakatos, Imre. "Falsification and the Methodology of Scientific Research Programs." In *Criticism and the Growth of Knowledge*, edited by Imre Lakatos and Alan Musgrave. Cambridge: Cambridge University Press, 1970.

Lake, David A. "The Theory of Hegemonic Stability: An Interim Report." Paper presented at the World Congress of the International Political Science Association, Buenos Aires, Argentina, 21–25 July 1991.

Lane, Frederic Chapin. "Economic Consequences of Organized Violence." In *Venice and History: The Collected Papers of Frederic C. Lane*, edited by a Committee of Colleagues and Former Students. Baltimore: Johns Hopkins University Press, 1966.

Larsen, Lt. Gen. Stanley Robert, and Brig. Gen. James Lawton Collins. *Allied Participation in Vietnam*. Washington, D.C.: Department of the Army, 1975.

Levi, Margaret. *Of Rule and Revenue*. Berkeley and Los Angeles: University of California Press, 1988.

Linklater, Andrew. *Men and Citizens in the Theory of International Relations*. New York: St. Martin's Press, 1982.

Little, Richard. "Revisiting Intervention: A Survey of Recent Developments." *Review of International Studies* 13 (January 1987): 49–60.

Lloyd, Christopher. *The British Seaman, 1200–1860: A Social Survey*. London: Collins, 1968.

Lobel, Jules. "The Rise and Decline of the Neutrality Act: Sovereignty and Congressional War Powers in United States Foreign Policy." *Harvard International Law Journal* 24 (Summer 1983): 1–71.

Luke, Timothy W. "The Discipline of Security Studies and the Codes of Containment: Learning from Kuwait." *Alternatives* 16 (1991): 315–44.

Lydon, James G. *Pirates, Privateers and Profits*. Upper Saddle River, N.J.: Gregg, 1970.

McCaleb, Walter Flavius. *"The Aaron Burr Conspiracy" and "A New Light on Aaron Burr."* Expanded ed. New York: Argosy–Antiquarian, 1966.

Machiavelli, Niccolò. *"The Prince" and "The Discourses."* New York: Modern Library, 1950.

Mackay, Douglas. *The Honourable Company: A History of the Hudson's Bay Company*. New York: Bobbs-Merrill, 1936.

Maclay, Edgar Stanton. *A History of American Privateers*. New York: Appleton, 1899.

McNeill, William H. *The Pursuit of Power: Technology, Armed Force, and Society since A.D. 1000*. Chicago: University of Chicago Press, 1982.

Malkin, H. W. "The Inner History of the Declaration of Paris." *British Yearbook of International Law* 8 (1927): 1–44.

Malloy, William M., comp. *Treaties, Conventions, International Acts, Protocols and Agreements between the United States of America and Other Powers, 1776–1909*. Vol. 2. Washington, D.C.: Government Printing Office, 1910.

Mann, Michael. *The Sources of Social Power*. Vol. 1, *A History of Power from the Beginning to A.D. 1760*. New York: Cambridge University Press, 1986.

Maritain, Jacques. "The Concept of Sovereignty." *World Politics* 44 (June 1950): 343–57.

Martineau, Alfred. "Dupleix and Bussy." In *British India, 1497–1858*, ed. H. H. Dodwell. Vol. 5 of *The Cambridge History of India*. Cambridge: Cambridge University Press, 1929.

Mastanduno, Michael, David A. Lake, and G. John Ikenberry. "Toward a Realist Theory of State Action." *International Studies Quarterly* 33 (December 1989): 457–74.

Merriam, C. E. *History of the Theory of Sovereignty since Rousseau*. Columbia University Studies in the Social Sciences, vol. 33. New York: AMS Press, 1968.

Metcalf, Helen Broughall. "The California French Filibusters in Sonora." *California Historical Society Quarterly* 18 (March 1939): 3–21.

Meyer, John W. "The World Polity and the Authority of the Nation-State." In *Studies of the Modern World System*, edited by Albert Bergesen. New York: Academic Press, 1980.

Meyer, John W., John Boli, and George M. Thomas. "Ontology and Rationalization in the Western Cultural Account." In *Institutional Structure: Constituting State, Society, and the Individual*, edited by George M. Thomas, John W. Meyer, Francisco O. Ramirez, and John Boli. Newbury Park, Calif.; Sage, 1987.

Meyer, John W., Francisco O. Ramirez, Henry A. Walker, Nancy Langton, and

Sorca M. O'Connor. "The State and the Institutionalization of the Relations between Women and Children." Photocopy. Stanford University, 1984.

Mill, James. *The History of British India*. Abridged ed. In *Classics of British Historical Literature*, edited by John Clive. Chicago: University of Chicago Press, 1975.

Minnegerode, Meade. *Lives and Times: Four Informal American Biographies*. New York: G. P. Putnam's Sons, 1925.

Mockler, Anthony. *The Mercenaries*. New York: Macmillan, 1969.

———. *The New Mercenaries*. London: Sidgwick and Jackson, 1985.

Moore, John B. *A Digest of International Law*. Vol. 2. Washington, D.C.: Government Printing Office, 1906.

Moravcsik, Andrew. "Integrating International and Domestic Explanations of World Politics: A Theoretical Introduction." Photocopy. University of Chicago, 1991.

Morello, Ted. "Gurkhas under Fire." *Far Eastern Economic Review* 116 (4 June 1982): 40–42.

Morse, Edward L. *Modernization and the Transformation of International Relations*. New York: Free Press, 1976.

Mukherjee, Ramkrishna. *The Rise and Fall of the East India Company: A Sociological Appraisal*. New York: Monthly Review Press, 1974.

Newman, Peter C. *Company of Adventurers*. Vol. 1. Ontario, Canada: Penguin Books, 1986.

———. *Company of Adventurers*. Vol. 2, *Ceasars of the Wilderness*. Ontario, Canada: Viking, 1987.

North, Douglass. *Institutions, Institutional Change and Economic Performance*. New York; Cambridge University Press, 1990.

O'Malley, Pat. "The Discipline of Violence: State, Capital and the Regulation of Naval Warfare." *Sociology* 22 (May 1988): 253–70.

Oppenheim, L. *International Law: A Treatise*. 8th ed. Edited by H. Lauterpacht. Vol. 1, *Peace*. New York: Longmans, Green, 1955.

Oye, Kenneth, ed. "Cooperation under Anarchy." *World Politics* 38 (October 1985, special issue): 1–254.

Padelford, Norman J. *International Law and Diplomacy in the Spanish Civil Strife*. New York: Macmillan, 1939.

Parker, Geoffrey. *The Military Revolution: Military Innovation and the Rise of the West, 1500–1800*. New York: Cambridge University Press, 1988.

Phillips, W. Alison, and Arthur H. Reede. *The Napoleonic Period*. Vol. 2 of Columbia University Council for Research in the Social Sciences, *Neutrality: Its History, Economics and Law*. New York: Columbia University Press, 1936.

Piggott, Francis. *The Declaration of Paris, 1856*. London: University of London Press, 1919.

Polanyi, Karl. *The Great Transformation: The Political and Economic Origins of Our Time*. Boston: Beacon Press, 1944.

Popper, Karl. *The Logic of Scientific Discovery*. New York: Basic Books, 1959.

Powell, E. Alexander. *Gentlemen Rovers*. New York: Charles Scribner's Sons, 1913.

Pratt, Julius W. *Expansionists of 1812*. Gloucester, Mass.: Peter Smith, 1957.

Preston, Richard A., and Sydney F. Wise. *Men in Arms: A History of Warfare and Its Interrelationships with Western Society*. 2d ed. New York: Praeger, 1970.

Quandt, William B. *Saudi Arabia in the 1980s: Foreign Policy, Security, and Oil*. Washington, D.C.: Brookings Institution, 1981.

Rankin, Hugh F. *The Golden Age of Piracy*. New York: Holt, Rinehart and Winston, 1969.

Rauch, Basil. *American Interest in Cuba, 1848–1855*. New York: Columbia University Press, 1948.

Rediker, Marcus. *Between the Devil and the Deep Blue Sea: Merchant Seamen, Pirates, and the Anglo-American Maritime World, 1700–1750*. Cambridge: Cambridge University Press, 1987.

Redlich, Fritz. *The German Military Enterpriser and His Work Force: A Study in European Economic and Social History*. Vol. 2. Wiesbaden: Franz Steiner Verlag GMBH, 1965.

Rees, David. *Korea: The Limited War*. New York: St. Martin's Press, 1964.

Reinstein, Robert J. "An Early View of Executive Powers and Privilege: The Trial of Smith and Ogden." *Hastings Constitutional Law Quarterly* 2 (Spring 1975): 309–49.

Reuter, Bertha Ann. *Anglo-American Relations during the Spanish-American War*. New York: Macmillan, 1924.

Rhee, Syngman. *Neutrality as Influenced by the United States*. Princeton: Princeton University Press, 1912.

Rich, E. E. *The History of the Hudson's Bay Company, 1670–1870*. Vol. 2 of *Publications of the Hudson's Bay Record Society*, edited by idem. London: Hudson's Bay Record Society, 1959.

Ritchie, Robert C. *Captain Kidd and the War against the Pirates*. Cambridge: Harvard University Press, 1986.

Roberts, Michael. *Gustavus Adolphus and the Rise of Sweden*. London: English Universities Press, 1973.

Roberts, P. E. "The East India Company and the State." In *British India, 1497–1858*, edited by H. H. Dodwell. Vol. 5 of *The Cambridge History of India*. Cambridge: Cambridge University Press, 1929.

Robertson, William Spence. *The Life of Miranda*. Vol. 1. Chapel Hill: University of North Carolina Press, 1929.

Roche, James Jeffrey. *The Story of the Filibusters*. New York: Macmillan, 1891.

Rodriguez-Salgado, M. J. "Mediterranean Corsairs." *History Today* 31 (April 1981): 36–41.

Rosecrance, Richard. *The Rise of the Trading State*. New York: Basic Books, 1986.

Rosenau, James N. "Before Cooperation: Hegemons, Regimes, and Habit-Driven Actors in World Politics." *International Organization* 40 (Autumn 1986): 849–94.

———. "Global Changes and Theoretical Challenges: Toward a Postinternational Politics for the 1990s." In *Global Changes and Theoretical Challenges: Approaches to World Politics for the 1990s*, edited by Ernst-Otto Czempiel and James N. Rosenau. Lexington, Mass.: Lexington Books, 1989.

———. *Turbulence in World Politics: A Theory of Change and Continuity*. Princeton: Princeton University Press, 1990.

Rosenau, Pauline. "International Relations Confronts the Humanities." *Millennium* 19 (January 1990): 83–110.

Rosinski, Herbert. *The German Army*. Washington, D.C.: Infantry Journal, 1944.

Ruggie, John Gerard. "Continuity and Transformation in the World Polity: Toward a Neorealist Synthesis." *World Politics* 35 (Janaury 1983): 261–85.

————. "International Regimes, Transactions, and Change: Embedded Liberalism in the Postwar Economic Order." In *International Regimes*, edited by Stephen D. Krasner. Ithaca: Cornell University Press, 1983.

————. "Planetary Politics: International Transformation in the Making." Paper presented at the German-American Workshop on International Relations Theory, Bad Homburg, Federal Republic of Germany, 31 May–3 June 1987.

————. "International Structure and International Transformation: Space, Time, and Method." In *Global Changes and Theoretical Challenges: Approaches to World Politics for the 1990s*, edited by Ernst-Otto Czempiel and James N. Rosenau. Lexington, Mass.: Lexington Books, 1989.

Safran, Nadav. *Saudi Arabia: The Ceaseless Quest for Security*. Cambridge: Harvard University Press, Belknap Press, 1985.

Schachner, Nathan. *Aaron Burr: A Biography*. New York: Frederick A. Stokes, 1937.

Scott, William Robert. *The Constitution and Finance of English, Scottish and Irish Joint-Stock Companies to 1720*. 2 vols. Cambridge: Cambridge University Press, 1912.

Seavey, James Matthews. "Neutrality Legislation in the United States." S.J.D. thesis, Georgetown University, 1939.

Sen, S. P. *The French in India, 1763–1816*. Calcutta: Firma K. L. Mukhopadhyay, 1958.

Senior, Hereward. *The Fenians and Canada*. Toronto: Macmillan of Canada, 1978.

Seymour, William. "The Company That Founded an Empire: The First Hundred Years in the Rise to Power of the East India Company." *History Today* 19 (September 1969): 641–50.

Shearer, Ernest C. "The Carvajal Disturbances." *Southwestern Historical Quarterly* 55 (1951): 201–30.

Sherman, Arnold A. "Pressure from Leadenhall: The East India Company Lobby, 1660–1678." *Business History Review* 50 (Autumn 1976): 329–53.

Sherry, Frank. *Raiders and Rebels: The Golden Age of Piracy*. New York: Hearst Marine Books, 1986.

Singer, J. David, and Melvin Small. *Wages of War, 1816–1980, Augmented with Disputes and Civil War Data*. Ann Arbor, Mich: Inter-university Consortium for Political and Social Research, 1984.

Skocpol, Theda. *States and Social Revolutions: A Comparative Analysis of France, Russia, and China*. Cambridge: Cambridge University Press, 1979.

Smith, Adam. *An Inquiry into the Nature and Causes of the Wealth of Nations*. Edited by Edwin Cannan. New York: Modern Library, 1937.

Smith, Justin H. "La República de Río Grande." *American Historical Review* 25 (1920): 660–75.

Smith, Richard J. *Mercenaries and Mandarins: The Ever-Victorious Army in Nineteenth-Century China.* Millwood, N.Y.: KTO Press, 1978.

Stark, Francis R. "The Abolition of Privateering and the Declaration of Paris." In *Studies in History, Economics and Public Law,* edited by the Faculty of Political Science of Columbia University, vol. 8, no. 3. New York: 1897.

Stout, Joseph Allen, Jr. *The Liberators: Filibustering Expeditions into Mexico, 1848–1862, and the Last Thrust of Manifest Destiny.* Los Angeles: Westernlore Press, 1973.

Strang, David. "Anomaly and Commonplace in European Political Expansion: Realist and Institutional Accounts." *International Organization* 45 (Spring 1991): 143–62.

Strayer, Joseph R. *On the Medieval Origins of the Modern State.* Princeton: Princeton University Press, 1970.

Swanson, Carl E. "American Privateering and Imperial Warfare, 1739–1748." *William and Mary Quarterly,* 3d ser. 42 (July 1985): 357–82.

Tarling, Nicholas. *Piracy and Politics in the Malay World.* Melbourne: F. W. Cheshire, 1963.

Taylor, Michael. *The Possibility of Cooperation.* In *Studies in Rationality and Social Change,* edited by Jon Elster and Gudmund Hernes. New York: Cambridge University Press, 1987.

Thomas, Charles Marion. *American Neutrality in 1793: A Study in Cabinet Government.* New York: Columbia University Press, 1931.

Thomas, Hugh. *The Spanish Civil War.* Rev. ed. New York: Harper and Row, 1977.

Thomson, Janice E. "State Practices, International Norms, and the Decline of Mercenarism." *International Studies Quarterly* 34 (March 1990): 23–47.

———. "Norms in International Relations: A Conceptual Analysis." *International Journal of Group Tensions* 23 (Spring 1993): 67–83.

———. "Sovereignty and the Institutional Isomorphism of States." Paper presented at the annual meeting of the American Political Science Association, Washington, D.C., 29 August–1 September 1991.

———. "Explaining the Regulation of Transnational Practices: A State-Building Approach." In *Governance without Government,* edited by James N. Rosenau and Ernst-Otto Czempiel. Cambridge: Cambridge University Press, 1992.

Thomson, Janice E., and Stephen D. Krasner. "Global Transactions and the Consolidation of Sovereignty." In *Global Changes and Theoretical Challenges: Approaches to World Politics for the 1990s,* edited by Ernst-Otto Czempiel and James N. Rosenau. Lexington, Mass.: Lexington Books, 1989.

Thorning, Joseph F. *Miranda: World Citizen.* Gainesville: University of Florida Press, 1952.

Tilly, Charles. "War Making and State Making as Organized Crime." In *Bringing the State Back In,* edited by Peter B. Evans, Dietrich Reuschemeyer, and Theda Skocpol. New York: Cambridge University Press, 1985.

———. *Coercion, Capital and European States, A.D. 990–1990.* Cambridge: Basil Blackwell, 1990.

Tilly, Charles, ed. *The Formation of National States in Western Europe.* Princeton: Princeton University Press, 1975.

Time. (special 1776 issue). May 1975.

Trotter, R. G. "The Coming of Confederation." In *Canada and Newfoundland.* Vol. 6 of *The Cambridge History of the British Empire,* edited by J. Holland Rose, A. P. Newton, and E. A. Benians. Cambridge: Cambridge University Press, 1930.

U.K. *Hansard Parliamentary Debates,* 2d ser., vol. 40 (1819) cols. 1377–79.

————. *Hansard Parliamentary Debates.* 3d. ser., vol. 142 (1856), cols. 481–549.

United Nations General Assembly. *Report of the Ad Hoc Committee on the Drafting of an International Convention against the Recruitment, Use, Financing and Training of Mercenaries.* 1982.

United Nations Security Council. "Note Dated 25 July 1950 from the Representative of the United States of America to the Secretary-General Transmitting the Text of an Exchange of Letters between President Syngman Rhee of the Republic of Korea and General Douglas MacArthur." July 1950.

Urban, Chester Stanley. "New Orleans and the Cuban Question during the López Expeditions of 1849–1851: A Local Study in 'Manifest Destiny.'" *Louisiana Historical Quarterly* 22 (1939): 1095–1167.

U.S. Congress. Senate. Committee on Foreign Relations. *The United States and the Korean Problem.* 83d Cong., 1st sess., 1953.

————. Senate. Committee on Foreign Relations. Subcommittee on African Affairs. *Angola.* 94th Cong., 2d sess., 3 February 1976.

U.S. Department of the Army. *Military Advisors in Korea: KMAG in Peace and War.* Washington, D.C.: Office of the Chief of Military History, 1962.

Van Hoboken, W. J. "The Dutch West India Company: The Political Background of Its Rise and Decline." In *Britain and the Netherlands,* edited by J. S. Bromley and E. H. Kossmann. London: Chatto and Windus, 1960.

Venkateswaran, A. L. *Defense Organization in India.* Delhi: Government Ministry of Information and Broadcasting, 1967.

Vlekke, Bernard H. M. *Evolution of the Dutch Nation.* New York: Roy Publishers, 1945.

Walker, R. B. J. "The Territorial State and the Theme of Gulliver." *International Journal* 39 (summer 1984): 529–52.

————. *State Sovereignty, Global Civilization, and the Rearticulation of Political Space.* World Order Studies Program Occasional Paper no. 18. Princeton: Princeton University Center of International Studies, 1988.

————. "Genealogy, Geopolitics and Political Community: Richard K. Ashley and the Critical Social Theory of International Politics." *Alternatives* 13 (January 1988): 84–88.

————. "Ethics, Modernity and the Theory of International Relations." Photocopy. Princeton University Center of International Studies, 1988–89.

Walker, R. B. J., and Saul H. Mendlovitz, eds. *Contending Sovereignties: Redefining Political Community.* Boulder, Colo.: Lynne Rienner, 1990.

Waltz, Kenneth N. "The Myth of National Interdependence." In *The International Corporation,* edited by Charles P. Kindleberger. Cambridge: MIT Press, 1970.

————. *Theory of International Politics.* Reading, Mass.: Addison-Wesley, 1979.

Wandell, Samuel H., and Meade Minnigerode. *Aaron Burr*. Vol. 2. New York: G. P. Putnam's Sons, 1925.

Weber, Max. *The Theory of Social and Economic Organization*. Translated by A. M. Henderson and Talcott Parsons. New York: Free Press, 1964.

Weisser, Michael R. *Crime and Punishment in Early Modern Europe*. Atlantic Highlands, N.J.: Humanities Press, 1979.

Wendt, Alexander E. "The Agent-Structure Problem in International Relations Theory." *International Organization* 41 (Summer 1987): 335–70.

Wendt, Alexander E., and Michael N. Barnett. "The International System and Third World Militarization." Photocopy. Yale University, April 1991.

Wertenbaker, Thomas J. "Virginia under the Stuarts, 1607–1688." In *The Shaping of Colonial Virginia*. New York: Russell and Russell, 1914.

Wharton, Francis. *State Trials of the United States during the Administrations of Washington and Adams*. Philadelphia: Carey and Hart, 1849.

Wilkinson, Henry Spenser. *The French Army before Napoleon*. Oxford: Clarendon Press, 1915.

Williams, Neville. *Captains Outrageous: Seven Centuries of Piracy*. New York: Macmillan, 1962.

Wolf, John B. *The Barbary Coast: Algiers under the Turks, 1500–1830*. New York: Norton, 1979.

Wormser, I. Maurice. *Frankenstein Incorporated*. New York: McGraw-Hill, 1931.

Wright, Louis B., and Julia H. Macleod. *The First Americans in North Africa: William Eaton's Struggle for a Vigorous Policy against the Barbary Pirates, 1799–1805*. Princeton: Princeton University Press, 1945.

Wyllys, Rufus Kay. "The French of California and Sonora." *Pacific Historical Review* 1 (1932): 337–59.

———. *The French in Sonora, 1850–1854: The Story of French Adventurers from California into Mexico*. Vol. 21 of *University of California Publications in History*, edited by Herbert E. Bolton, William A. Morris, and Paul B. Schaeffer. Berkeley and Los Angeles: University of California Press, 1932.

Young, John Robert. *The French Foreign Legion: The Inside Story of the World-Famous Fighting Force*. London: Thames and Hudson, 1984.

Index

Adams, J., 88, 180n.69
Ad hoc forces, 93–97, 182n.117
Administrative companies, 32, 169n.115
Africa, 10, 25, 90, 93–94, 96, 110, 169n.115
Aix-la-Chapelle Congress, 111
Alienation, 156n.6
America, Treaty of, 47
American Civil War, 81, 87, 104, 145
American War of Independence, 24, 30
Americas: antimercenarism laws and, 85–86; Brazil and, 98; Britain and, 57–58; Dutch shipping in, 98; filibustering in, 118; foreign service and, 80–81; insurgent groups, 58; Panama Canal and, 195n.135; piracy in, 49–53; privateers and, 10, 21, 22, 69–70, 75–76; revolutions in, 57–58, 181n.78; wars in, 57–58. *See also specific states, regions*
Amines, Treaty of, 101
Amity and Commerce, Treaty of, 77
Anarchy, 158n.26
Anderson, G., 37
Anglo-Sikh Wars, 41
Antimercenarism, 83–86
Armaments, 156n.6, 7
Armed Neutralities (of 1780, 1800), 26, 70, 72–73
Ashley, R. K., 12–13, 17, 18
Austria, 30, 62, 70–71, 73, 80
Authority, 15–16, 147, 155n.4, 157n.21. *See also* State

Bahamas, 51–53, 109
Barbary coast, 44–46, 110–12
Behavioral theory, 12, 14, 20, 162n.47
Bellomont mission, 51, 173n.50
Blackbeard, 53
Bombay, 40, 101, 114. *See also* India
Borneo, 114–15, 188n.39
Braudel, F., 4
Bribery, 50
Britain. *See* England
British Foreign Act, 96
British North America Act, 105
British South Africa Company, 169n.115

Brunei, 114–15, 188n.39
Burke, E., 32
Burr, A., 124–27, 131, 191n.102, 192n.110, 193n.124

Cameroon, 90
Canada, 60, 103–4. *See also* Hudson's Bay Company
Capitalism, violence and, 199n.13
Capital punishment, 46
Caporaso, J. A., 155n.2
Carnatic Wars, 64
China, 114–15
Cinque Ports, 22, 23
Citizenship, 198n.4
Clayton-Bulwer Treaty, 128
Coerced labor, 172n.12
Cold War, 96
Communism, 146, 183n.124
Continuity, 155n.2, 158n.27
Contraband, 177n.18
Corsairs, 44–45, 110–12, 187n.18. *See also specific states, regions*
Cox, R., 12
Crimean War, 72, 73, 103, 128
Critical theory, 2, 12–14, 18, 161nn.41, 43
Cuba, 123, 190n.88, 195n.133

Davis, J., 134
Death penalty, 46
Declaration of Paris, 71–72, 74–76, 178n.35
Deconstruction, 14, 160n.39, 161n.43
de Miranda, F., 120
Denard affair, 93–94
Denmark, 70
Desertion, 54
Domestic-international dichotomy, 13, 14–17, 157n.21, 160n.36, 163n.54
Drake, F., 23
Dutch East India Company, 10, 169n.117; dissolution of, 97–98, 100; lease of army to, 96; mercenaries and, 39; organization of, 32, 33, 34, 35, 36; Portugal and, 62–63
Dutch West India Company, 35–37, 66, 98